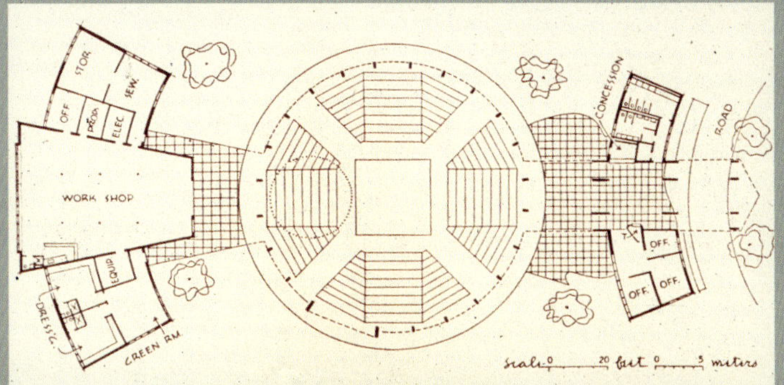

MARION MANLEY

THE UNIVERSITY OF GEORGIA PRESS | ATHENS AND LONDON

MARION MANLEY

MIAMI'S FIRST WOMAN ARCHITECT

CATHERINE LYNN AND CARIE PENABAD

Athens, Georgia 30602
www.ugapress.org

Designed by Erin Kirk New
Set in Adobe Garamond Pro and Whitney
Printed and bound by Everbest Printing Company for Four Colour Print Group
The paper in this book meets the guidelines for
permanence and durability of the Committee on
Production Guidelines for Book Longevity of the
Council on Library Resources.

Printed in China
14 13 12 11 10 P 5 4 3 2 1

Library of Congress Cataloging-in-Publication Data
Lynn, Catherine.
Marion Manley : Miami's first woman architect / Catherine Lynn and Carie Penabad.
p. cm.
Includes bibliographical references and index.
ISBN-13: 978-0-8203-3406-6 (pbk. : alk. paper)
ISBN-10: 0-8203-3406-5 (pbk. : alk. paper)
1. Manley, Marion Isadore, 1893–1984—Criticism and interpretation.
2. Architecture—Florida—Miami Metropolian Area—History—20th century. 3. International Style
(Architecture)—Florida—Miami Metropolian Area. 4. University of Miami—Buildings.
5. Architecture and society—Florida—Miami Metropolian Area—History—20th century.
I. Penabad, Carie. II. Title.
NA737.M2162L96 2010
720.92—dc22 2009022654

British Library Cataloging-in-Publication Data available

In memory of Lidia Abello

CONTENTS

ILLUSTRATIONS

FOREWORD

The University of Miami School of Architecture occupies a series of postwar graduate student housing buildings that were designed by Marion Manley and her associates in 1947. They were renovated to become academic buildings for the school in 1983 by Jan Hochstim, a university faculty member.

Sitting in the dean's office at one end of the complex and looking out over the structures that Professor Hochstim painted to allude to their early modern provenance, white with elements in primary colors—yellow window frames, red handrails, and blue doors—has given me many opportunities to think about their original designer, one of few women in the field in her time, and how her buildings serve us so well sixty years later. Large windows allow the interior to share space with the campus landscape. Their cantilevered eyebrows modulate the subtropical sunlight, minimizing need for artificial light, while allowing views into studios, offices, and the library.

Over the last decade of the school's inhabiting the buildings and adjusting them to suit our changing needs, we have come to admire them for many reasons as well as to better understand the context within which they were built. Early in my deanship I set off to renew the public spaces with furnishings from the time of the original construction. I began to realize that in the early years following World War II, the design and manufacture of office furniture was not a priority for U.S. commercial activity. Except for one very expensive prototype file cabinet purportedly designed by Ray Eames and apparently never manufactured for sale, there was little to be found among the purveyors of the 1950s furnishings that were hot at the time in New York City. I began to think that the minimalist design of our buildings was the result not only of an aesthetic decision to build a new institution in the forward-looking international style but also of the postwar economic reality.

That context of scarcity has come to light in the last decade's examination of the work of several European architects who survived the war to resume professional practice during the midcentury years of recovery. A 2001 exhibit at the Centre Pompidou on the work of Italian architect Adalberto Libera exposed a striking similarity between the cubic Italian structures that alternate flat panels of undecorated stucco and large panels of glass and the current home of the School of Architecture. Similarly, in the work of German architect Hugo Häring, reviewed in a 2001 exhibit at Berlin's Academie der Künste, expressionist prewar projects gave way to simple white forms of stuccoed masonry and glass in the postwar years. Thus with dignity and grace did architects react to the need for housing in a world recovering from the blows of war, which besides destroying economies and societies also produced amnesia of cultural experience and professional expertise.

Marion Manley's buildings have been through a period of neglect, their design, if noticed at all, considered to be banal and uninspiring. But with the perspective of advancing time, we look upon her remaining buildings with admiration for what they provided in a period of high need and low resources. I am reminded of a visit some years ago to a house designed by Manley in the Keys, which I was being asked to renovate and expand. The visit did not produce work for me, but the memory remains of walking through spaces of rational if modest disposition, whose drawings betrayed that they had been dimensioned to the block, to avoid discarding material.

Looking out my office windows at the School of Architecture buildings, one cannot help but think that their likes will not be built again. Conservative in terms of dimension and technology (they were built without air-conditioning), they nonetheless have a high proportion of perimeter wall to interior space, an old-fashioned trumping of long-term sustenance over short-term construction cost. And those simple interior spaces belie the extent to which contemporary building standards have exceeded their original design. Faced with the same program now, one would choose to sprawl less, to build taller, to reduce exterior surface—including glazing—and with a lesser relationship to the landscape.

So understanding the reduced circumstances of the provenance of these buildings, and their low-tech characteristics such as rooms with cross ventilation, large areas of shaded glass, and the almost tactile relationship to the adjacent landscape, we must admire the legacy of Marion Manley, and indeed feel privileged to inhabit her buildings.

The school's buildings call attention to a period of architecture that will be ever more difficult to remember and preserve as the demand increases for denser building in a region at once desirable and limited in land mass. The modest but rational and regionally characteristic Coconut Grove house, which she designed for herself, still stands. However, many of her other buildings have been replaced by new structures of differing ambition. The fear of the continuing loss of this legacy has inspired two of our faculty members to produce this record of the work of a remarkable woman. Pioneering, innovative, collaborative, and practical, she is a role model for successive generations of professional women. Her life has encouraged some of us already. Her buildings may still be appreciated and serve as an example for designers once again engaging ambitions of sustainability.

—ELIZABETH PLATER-ZYBERK

ACKNOWLEDGMENTS

Generous grants have supported research for this book and the production of its illustrations, and we thank each one of the donors. The University of Miami's Max Orovitz Summer Award in Arts and Humanities funded initial research. A grant from the Division of Historical Resources, Florida Department of State, supported research and photographic reproduction. The Graham Foundation for Advanced Studies in the Fine Arts underwrote further research and the production of images important to our study. The Villagers, Inc., made it possible to increase the number of illustrations in this book, underwriting costs of publication. Additional funding came from Robert C. Hector Jr., Sallye G. Jude, and two anonymous donors.

Emily Perry's generosity in turning over all the documents and tapes of interviews she and Jose Rodriguez produced for her article "Marion Isadore Manley: Pioneer Woman Architect" has been especially important to us, as was her study of Manley.

Librarians in several institutions have facilitated our work, led us to important sources, and offered encouragement. At our own University of Miami Libraries in Archives and Special Collections we are especially indebted to Rochelle Pienn, librarian; Craig Likness, former director of collections development; and Marcia V. Evanson, archives processing assistant. At the Historical Museum of Southern

Florida, Dawn Hugh, archives manager, and Patricia Barahona, assistant curator, archives, were unfailingly helpful. Farther afield, we thank Nancy Hadley, archivist and records manager, AIA Library Washington D.C., and Bryan Whiteledge, research librarian, University of Illinois.

Several owners of houses designed by Marion Manley have, with great courtesy, allowed us to study and photograph their homes, including Robert C. Hector Sr., Mr. and Mrs. Dietrich Rudin, Nora Schaffer, and Cordelia C. Wilson.

Arva Moore Parks, distinguished historian of Miami, made her unique resources, personal research, and rare knowledge available to us and read early versions of our manuscript. Others to whom we are indebted for an array of contributions include Pam Admire, Simone Chin, Christine Cordazzo, Malinda Cleary, Andrea Cole, Beth Dunlop, Kara Kautz, Dorothy McKenna, Megan McLaughlin, John Rothchild, Mary Rowley, and Ellen Ugguccione, as well as Andrea Gollin, who read the manuscript and offered critical insight.

Across the University of Miami campus we called upon many staff members for help and we are especially grateful to Janet L. Gavarrete, associate vice president, campus planning; Luis Glaser, former provost; Betty Fleming, senior planner, project management, Coral Gables Campus; Habib Haddad, architect drafter, physical plant; and Jean Yehle, archivist, Rosenstiel School of Atmospheric and Marine Science.

Colleagues within the University of Miami School of Architecture who have contributed to our research include Jan Hochstim, Jean-Francois LeJeune, Joanna Lombard, Aristides Millas, Elizabeth Plater-Zyberk, Vincent Scully, and our former faculty member Greg Castillo, all of whom vetted early versions of the text, as well as Rocco Ceo and Teofilo Victoria. Lamar Noriega, director of development, not only helped with fund-raising but also introduced us to the owners of surviving houses by Manley.

Students in the university's School of Architecture have helped with research, with the measuring and drawing of extant buildings by Manley, and with the redrawing of her plans in formats suitable for publication. They include Leticia

Acosta, Zachary Adelson, Abraham Alluicio, Hassan Bagheri, Rhea Bosland, Cynthia Bouchard, Alvaro Briganti, Marcus Chaidez, Elisa Cuaron, Amie Edmiston, Rene Habib, Aaron Heinrich, Krista Kasprzyk, Sergey Krupsky, Ivette Landestoy, Gorata Madigele, Moushumi Manda, Christina Miller, Alice Oliveira, Elena Romero, Andrew Silva, Rania Solh, Molly Teter, and Travis Wild.

We are indebted to our editor Anne Gibbons for her thoughtful review of the manuscript and to the University of Georgia Press for the design and production of the book, most especially Jon Davies, Regan Huff, Kathi Morgan, and Erin New.

CATHERINE LYNN AND CARIE PENABAD

On a more personal note, I thank my loving family for their continuous encouragement, most especially Novel and Alicia Penabad, Orestes and Cora Mena, Coralee, and Jose; special thanks to Adib Cure for his discerning eye and unwavering support; and finally to my young son, Adib Jose, for allowing me to see the world anew.

CARIE PENABAD

MARION MANLEY

INTRODUCTION

There she is, again and again, the only woman in the picture, Marion Isadore Manley: in the early 1900s, one of eleven architecture and engineering students leaning over their drafting tables at the University of Illinois (figure 1); in 1946, posed front and center, shoulder to shoulder with twenty-four colleagues at the annual convention of their Florida Association of Architects in Saint Petersburg (figure 2); or there, in a panoramic view of a grand room full of banqueting architects, her dress conspicuous in a sea of black evening jackets. In the pictures and newspaper clippings that she saved through her long life, Marion Manley, Miami's first female architect, faces the camera straight and serene, a woman proudly holding her own in a man's profession (figure 3). After her death in 1984, at age ninety, these pictures came to the Historical Museum of Southern Florida, along with three hundred sheets of her drawings, photographs of her buildings, clippings about her work, and many other materials, to form a major collection in its archive. In combination with records at the University of Miami, for which Manley did her best-known work, these collections are rare in their detailed documentation of an unusual career. They are the basis for this study of a woman who successfully maintained an independent architectural practice through most of the twentieth century.[1]

FIG. 1. University of Illinois, senior drafting room (Record Series 11/1/10). Courtesy of the University of Illinois at Urbana-Champaign Archives.

FIG. 2. Thirty-second annual convention of the Florida Association of Architects, Saint Petersburg, November 1946. Courtesy of the Historical Museum of Southern Florida, Marion Manley Collection.

Women architects were rare enough anywhere in the world before World War I. In the United States, their number in 1910 has been estimated as only "more than fifty."[2] As late as 1948, when Manley was doing some of her most widely publicized work, the editors of *Architectural Record*, one of the profession's leading journals, confessed themselves surprised to learn that there were "a thousand women in architecture," as they titled an article. They identified 1,119 women who had studied architecture in the United States, but only 47 percent of the 231 who responded to their survey were actually practicing.[3] Statistics documenting a history of women's education and participation in the field are shaky, partly because young people, both men and women, still found routes for informal entry into architectural offices well into the twentieth century via drafting courses in technical schools and on-the-job training. Among informally trained architectural designers, the women's roles are murkier because many assumed supportive or part-time and anonymous roles within offices, often those of their husbands. Writing the first substantial history of women in American architecture, Doris Cole estimated that in 1973 they made up only 2 percent of practicing architects. In 1975, a survey by the American Institute of Architects found that the percentage was smaller, only 1.2 percent among all who were registered. Nearing the century's end, Clare Lorenz could suggest in 1990 a percentage of no more than 5. But a survey of women in the profession published by the AIA in 2003 showed impressive gains: of about 108,000 licensed architects, 20 percent, or 21,600, were female. However, even after that percentage rose to 26 in 2006, it still meant that while women filled half the enrollment in architecture schools, they constituted only about a quarter of the profession.

FIG. 3. Marion Manley. Courtesy of the Historical Museum of Southern Florida, Marion Manley Collection.

The arrival of an aspiring architect in skirts was quite unexpected in the Miami of 1917. It was a small town that had begun to grow only a decade earlier, after train tracks reached the end of the nation's southernmost peninsula (figure 4). Marion Manley had come, as she later said, to "raw frontier,"[4] where "the streets were all made out of white rock" creating a terrific glare, and mosquitoes held the citizenry in a "state of siege. . . . You couldn't just open up a door. You just couldn't" (figure 5).[5]

Manley crossed half the continent to get to Florida, reversing the general direction of an earlier generation's pioneering ventures. In 1917 Miami was by all accounts still perched on a pretty rough frontier, no more settled than Junction City, Kansas, had been in 1883, when Manley's parents, Charles Haines Manley and Marion Isadore Jones Manley, arrived there as homesteaders from Buffalo, New York. The architect's mother, the youngest of eleven children, had been

FIG. 4. Downtown Miami, Flagler Street, March 1919. Courtesy of the Historical Museum of Southern Florida.

FIG. 5. Pioneer house, Miami, 1896. Courtesy of the Historical Museum of Southern Florida.

a schoolteacher in Wisconsin before her marriage. Charles Manley turned to teaching and banking in Junction City soon after settling his twenty acres. When the architect recalled her early life as the youngest of nine children on the place they named Cherrycroft (figure 6), she not only told a reporter about how she enjoyed its orchards, nature and the outdoors, riding horses, and gardening but also spoke of the many books lining the walls of her parents' home. She described not a scene of isolated hardship, but rather a cultured one "befitting an educated gentlewoman." The poetry Manley remembered quoting, the good manners her family instilled were doubtless all the more cherished so far from their sources.

The family's religious faith was that of the Universalists, a progressive, evangelical offshoot from New England's nineteenth-century Unitarianism. Membership in the denomination that had been, in 1863, the first in the country to ordain a woman minister, and would go on to ordain eighty-eight women by 1920, could well have encouraged girlish ambition beyond the domestic sphere. So too must the accomplishments of a beloved, "brilliant" maiden aunt, Amanda Jones, "an inventor" who had patented oil burners and was a published poet familiar to readers of the *Century* and *Scribner's*. Amanda Jones was one of Marion Manley's two maternal aunts who lived in the family home, along with a grandfather and "for a while" a cousin from Chicago, swelling to fifteen the number of household residents.[6] Their number however, included no architects, and when Marion Manley was asked late in life why she decided to pursue architecture, an interviewer reported, "She cannot explain. She knew no architects as a child and she never saw the inside of an architect's office until she was a senior in college." But, the architect recollected, "I wanted to work at something in which I could use my brain and my hands."[7]

FIG. 6. Marion Manley, circa 1893, being held by her father, Charles Haines Manley. Courtesy of Emily Adams Perry.

The storied West of Manley's childhood was in many ways a more likely breeding ground for an independent-minded, intellectually curious, professionally ambitious young woman than the conservative East. At the time of her birth in 1893, Kansas was in the forefront of the women's rights movement led by the resourceful and enterprising pioneer women whose lives have furnished colorful material for historians of feminism. As early as 1861 Kansas women won the right to vote in school board elections, as women could do in no other state. By 1867 women got a slot for a suffrage amendment onto a state ballot, and though it failed, as it would do again the year Manley was born, they persevered. In 1912 a woman's suffrage amendment was added to the Kansas state constitution, an important benchmark along the way to the ratification of the Nineteenth Amendment in 1920.

Two years before that amendment gave Marion Manley the right to vote in federal elections, the State of Florida registered her certification to practice architecture. Her license, dated September 6, 1918, was the second that the state issued to a woman. The number it bears, 105, is a reminder that the professionalization of architectural practice was still at an early stage, not only in Florida but also in the nation at large. Close behind the doctors and lawyers of the late nineteenth century, architects had only two decades earlier begun to set standards for professional qualification and put tests in place to certify competence. According to the AIA, there was no legal definition of "architect" before 1897 when Illinois passed the first architectural licensing law. Manley's prompt acquisition of certification signaled the purposeful way she would lay the foundations for a professional career, as did her apprenticeships with leading Miami architects before she opened her own office by 1924. Though she was forced to close that office through a few lean years following 1929, she was able to open one again in 1934, and to sustain it off and on through the mid-1970s, with notable interruptions to work full time for the University of Miami during the war years and to join briefly in partnerships for specific jobs.

During the 1920s, as Marion Manley was establishing herself within her profession, she was working against what are now recognized to have been formidable national odds: the already small proportion of women entering all the professions in America was dropping rapidly enough to alarm feminists. Winning the right to vote in national elections soon proved bitterly disappointing to their hopes, ushering in a decade of regression for the feminist cause. Manley's decision to follow her brother Lester to Miami brought her to a place of rare opportunity for bucking those national odds. During the storm of land speculation and building that swept across Florida during the early 1920s architects' and developers' interest in putting her design skills to use outweighed any concern about her gender (figure 7).

FIG. 7. Marion Manley (circa 1917). Courtesy of Emily Adams Perry.

By the 1930s, when it had become clear to discouraged feminists that women's voting power had failed to meet their expectations, Emily Newell Blair recalled: "What these feminists wanted was not merely a chance to work for some man, but a chance to rise to positions of authority so they could again be effective in determining the conditions under which they lived. What these women hoped for was a world in which men and women would work in competition with each other and the best individual win. The sex line was to be dropped and the world become the composite work of individuals of both sexes."[8] Marion Manley's career in her remote but very lively corner of America's architectural profession seems, in retrospect, exemplary of devotion to the personal attainment of just such goals. Her achievement was noted in her day—nationally within the profession, locally in the popular press—but it has been all but ignored in the major studies of women in American architecture that have been published since the early 1970s.

Her capacity for success was based on a solid education in the architecture department of the School of Engineering at the University of Illinois, to which she transferred after three years at the University of Kansas (figure 8). Illinois was one of the nine land-grant universities that had established schools of architecture before the turn of the century. These schools were required, like it or not, to admit women under specific provisions of the Morrill Act of 1862, which set up the system granting federal lands to states to subsidize the institutions. The eagerness of western states to qualify for this valuable grant outstripped that of the eastern ones, where men's colleges had been entrenching themselves since the seventeenth century. In the West, federal funding more readily overcame the era's reluctance to educate women equally, and in the same institutions, with men. The program that established land-grant colleges gave girls like Marion Manley legal grounds for admission to the architecture schools within them, even if male faculty members resented the female presence.

Although Illinois had opened admission to women in its architecture department as early as 1873, joining four other American schools in doing so by that

FIG. 8. University of Illinois, studio for elementary freehand drawing (Record Series 11/1/10). Courtesy of the University of Illinois at Urbana-Champaign Archives.

early date, Manley was, in 1917, the lone woman among the 26 graduates who earned a degree of bachelor of science in architecture.[9] In the university's graduating class of 1,223 that year, there were 264 women, and Manley's academic distinction among them had been recognized during her junior year when she was one of 14 elected to Phi Delta Psi, the women's honorary senior society (figure 9). In Manley's class, the majority of women, 152, had majored in liberal arts, and of those, 48 were "household science" majors, preparing for the normative career of wife and mother.[10] But Manley chose to compete with the boys, and her grades were high, consistently highest in design. At this early juncture she was already an exceptional woman.

Had Marion Manley's parents stayed in the East, perhaps their gifted daughter would have found her way to one of the few eastern architecture schools that were admitting women during that era. MIT, the oldest American architecture school, produced women graduates even before Manley's generation who were to become some of the most accomplished in the country. Or she might have gone to Cornell, a land-grant college with the second-oldest American architecture school and the record of being the first, in 1878, from which a woman had graduated. Still, quotas limiting the admission of women to the eastern architecture schools, even of public universities, stayed in place well into the twentieth century. As the AIA's Committee on Education put it in a report of 1906 the goal of these schools was to produce the "gentleman of general culture with special architectural ability," and that idea has died hard.[11] In 1906 Columbia's architectural program, which was founded in 1881, dropped a stated policy excluding women, while continuing in its bulletin to advise them to study elsewhere. Harvard's Graduate School of Design, founded in 1895, refused to admit women until the Second World War.

Alternatively, had Manley's parents not ventured west, she might have been attracted to one of the most important new training grounds for the few women architects of her era, the Cambridge School of Architecture and Landscape Architecture. It was founded in 1915 by a Harvard professor, Henry Frost, who

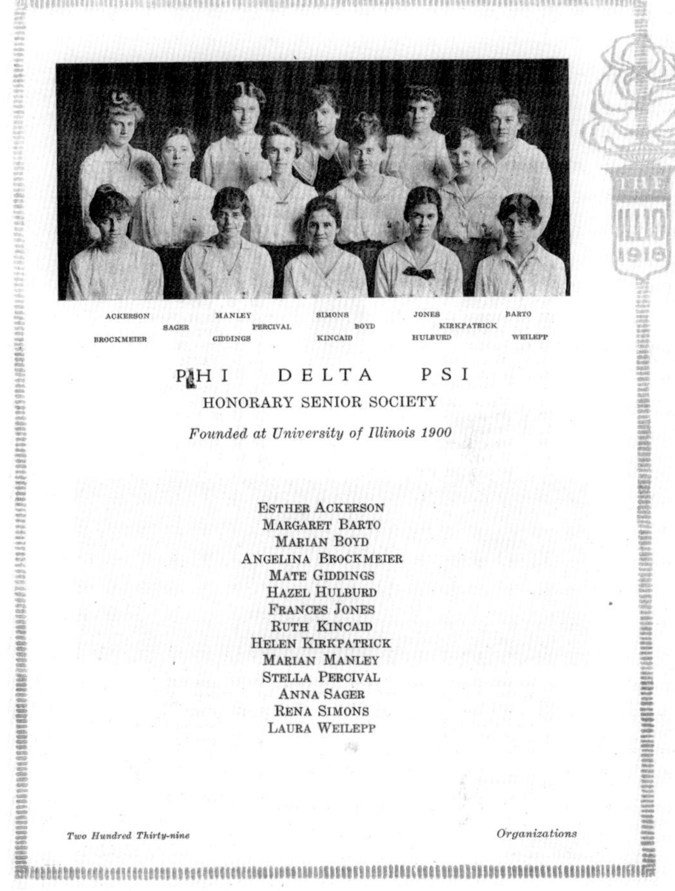
ACKERSON SAGER MANLEY PERCIVAL SIMONS BOYD JONES KIRKPATRICK BARTO
BROCKMEIER GIDDINGS KINCAID HULBURD WEILEPP

PHI DELTA PSI
HONORARY SENIOR SOCIETY
Founded at University of Illinois 1900

Esther Ackerson
Margaret Barto
Marian Boyd
Angelina Brockmeier
Mate Giddings
Hazel Hulburd
Frances Jones
Ruth Kincaid
Helen Kirkpatrick
Marian Manley
Stella Percival
Anna Sager
Rena Simons
Laura Weilepp

Two Hundred Thirty-nine *Organizations*

FIG. 9. University of Illinois, Phi Delta Psi Honor Society, 1918 *Illio* (yearbook) (Record Series 41/8/805). Courtesy of the University of Illinois at Urbana-Champaign Archives.

felt the injustice of his own institution's refusal to accept qualified female applicants. Separate but equal architectural education in his school, closely affiliated with Smith College in its later years, produced more than one hundred graduates before Harvard, eager for registrants to fill its largely deserted wartime classrooms, took it over in 1942.[12] Frost's school laid the groundwork for some of its graduates to band together and form all-female architectural firms. In contrast to that professionally sororal experience, Manley's architectural education took place in relative isolation from other women. Her schooling within male-dominated institutions seems to have set the tone for her independence as a practitioner. She often hired draftsmen, but she formed partnerships, and those with men, only for the duration of specific jobs.[13]

Capitulating to the profession's grumbling willingness to leave some house design to women, a specialty to which Catharine Beecher had staked a proprietary claim for her gender in her *American Woman's Home* of 1869, Frost's Cambridge School prepared students specifically to be designers of houses, their interiors, and their gardens. His girls' chances for success were better, Frost calculated, if they restricted their practices to the traditionally female domestic realm, dealing largely with female clients. Women's roles in the planning of houses had been dismissed by the editors of *American Architect and Building News* in 1876 as "not Architecture at all," since, they insisted, "the ability to arrange a house conveniently does not in the least make an architect."[14] Some of Frost's students who formed the most successful all-female firms of Manley's era limited their practices to house design, taking advantage of a perceived natural ability in the most "ladylike" area of architectural expertise. Manley rejected that strategy. A reporter in 1952 noted Manley's acknowledgment that "specialization of domestic places is expected of her because she is a woman."[15] But Manley went after institutional and commercial jobs when she could get them, and she did win many.

Nonetheless, the majority of her commissions were for houses, and among her surviving buildings, they seem to us to be her best designs. All her designs for houses that we have been able to identify are listed in the appendix, and some of them are treated at greater length in the text. The houses chosen for more detailed examinations are, we believe, representative of her work, in most cases of her best work, during its successive phases. In several cases they are also among the buildings for which Manley preserved the most comprehensive documentation in drawings that are now at the Historical Museum of Southern Florida.

If the supposedly feminine specialization of designing houses simply fell to her lot, within it, as well as in her larger commissions, Manley actively cultivated expertise in decidedly unfeminine areas: She excelled in on-site supervision of construction and focused on the most specific details of structure and materials. Her expertise here owes more than a little to patterns fixed during her days at the University of Illinois, where the architectural program was subordinate to a school of engineering. The architecture department's early "tendency to over-emphasize practical details of construction," was noted rather archly in *A Study of Architectural Schools* published in 1932. Its authors commented on the relative lateness of Illinois' taking up the Beaux-Arts atelier system and characterized the school as "largely a product of purely American, and especially Middle Western, conditions."[16]

Writers who interviewed Manley over the years invariably commented on the practicality of her approach to design and sometimes on the eagerness with which she greeted the introduction of new building materials, happily studying advertisements for innovations. An article about Manley published in 1953 went into some detail: "In the building world, the age-old world of men, she has earned the respect of men by requiring a very high standard of workmanship from herself and from anyone who builds a house she draws. She has a reputation for being rugged on any job she is supervising, and she won't take a job without supervision. . . . She writes a very tight specification, and says exactly what she wants. If the job doesn't come up to specifications exactly, in grade of material or in workmanship, out it goes."[17]

Other reporters of the 1950s were impressed by her physical presence, "tall, brisk, and overpowering," with an "inflexible flat blue-gray stare calculated to preclude any argument," which surely served her well on construction sites. They called her "tough on workmen," noting her local reputation for being "skilled in everything pertaining to building" and for taking "complete charge of the workmen, masons, plumbers, carpenters and bricklayers." Dorothy McKenna, with whom Manley shared office space after 1959, vividly remembered Manley's "going up on the roof and cussing out the roofer for not doing something right or the electrician for doing sloppy work or the contractor for not looking at the plans."[18] On the other hand, a woman friend told a *Herald* reporter in 1973, "She's always been a lady."[19] Yet it would seem that she was determined, single-handedly, to disprove the profession's widely held assumption that women could not supervise construction, a perceived inability architects cited again and again when refusing to add qualified women to their staffs.[20]

And she had a swagger that stayed with her into old age. An interviewer described her when she was eighty: "A perky, often witty woman who smokes Kools, drinks afternoon cocktails and throws out teasers like 'I'm a hedonist.'"[21] Manley's wit impressed reporters sent to interview her late in life; it was also recalled years later by friends in Junction City and colleagues like Trip Russell, an architect who first worked with her in the 1940s. When interviewed in 1990, Russell described her as "extremely witty," adding that she was "strong-willed and persuasive, though not aggressive."[22] Devoid of sentimental piety, she would in 1974 refer back to a time "when I was a Christian."[23] In her youth, her swagger was sometimes shocking to colleagues. One Miami architect still remembered his first impression of Marion Manley when he was a young draftsman in a local office nearly a half century earlier. He recalled being startled from his work by the loud voice of a woman giving somebody hell in terms no lady was supposed to know, and being told, "Oh, that's just Marion Manley."[24]

The manly demeanor of this woman named Manley, her determination to match if not outdo her male colleagues on their own turf, in their own terms, might well lead contemporary historians specializing in gender studies to focus on her. Manley's domestic arrangements have indeed given rise to latter-day speculation about her intimate life. For about three years during the Great Depression, financial need forced her to accept a small spare room from Marjory Stoneman Douglas (1890–1998), the celebrated crusader for the restoration and preservation of Florida's Everglades (figure 10). Douglas and Manley had met in 1918 or 1919 soon after Manley arrived in Miami.[25] Manley "later set up housekeeping," as Douglas put it, with Lillian Beaman Fly (b. 1915), a botanist who earned a PhD from the University of Miami in 1949 and taught botany there into the 1960s (figure 11). In 1948, the three women, Douglas, Manley, and Fly, made a trip west, visiting New Orleans and staying with friends and relatives in Texas. Lillian Fly, twenty-two years younger than Manley, lived with the architect right through the later years of her life and was "always with her," in the words of Trip Russell. Such mutually supportive living arrangements have a long history. Close, loving, and platonic friendships among eighteenth- and nineteenth-century women within "the bonds of womanhood" have been astutely explored by Nancy Cott in her book of that title. Such bonds could hold fast well into the twentieth century among those single women who broke the domestic bonds to brave public life. Female partnerships such as Manley's were treated with discretion in her era and class, so we do not know the precise character of Manley's partnership, nor is the matter relevant to this study.[26]

As a young woman in Miami, Manley became part of a group "centered around the houses that belonged to Arthur and Helen Gulliver on St. Gauden's Road" in Coconut Grove. Marjory Stoneman Douglas referred to the place as the center of her own social life, recalling that the Gullivers "had several little clapboard cottages built for the tropics, cool and comfortable, and they lived in one and rented out the others. . . . Marion Manley, the architect whom we called Archie, lived in one of the Gulliver houses. She became one of my best friends."[27] Another friend they met at the Gullivers', Elizabeth Virrick, was so alarmed by the unsanitary and unhealthy conditions in the crowded Coconut Grove slums that she took up the cause of righting the wrongs she saw before her. She enlisted her friends as board members to help form the Coconut Grove

FIG. 10. Marion Manley (*left*) with Marjory Stoneman Douglas and Uncle Charlie. Courtesy of State Library and Archives of Florida, Tallahassee.

FIG. 11. Lillian Fly and Marion Manley (date unknown). Courtesy of Emily Adams Perry.

Slum Clearance Committee. Virrick used Douglas's skills as a writer to publicize their programs and Manley's as an architect to design a day care nursery for the black working mothers of the area.

During the postwar period Manley and Douglas were prominent in the public life of Miami, both of them as committed social activists working with Virrick. Douglas also waged her campaign to save the Everglades, and Manley served on civic review boards and assumed leadership roles in the local chapter of the AIA. However, neither was listed in the local *Social Register*, where nearly all the women were wives. Manley and Douglas had other priorities. At the turn of the twenty-first century, Douglas "liked to say that she channeled the energy and emotion that others wasted on sex—which she said she had for the last time in 1915—into her work."[28]

Whether Manley made a positive decision not to marry, as did many feminists and professionally aspiring women of the late nineteenth and early twentieth centuries (some of whom abjured the bestial nature of subjection to men within marriage), we do not know. But clearly her status as a single woman favored her steady continuation in practice. For all women who studied architecture, marital status was a crucial factor determining whether they actually became architects. An obscure little piece of fiction from 1874, titled "Rose Fleming, Architect," tells a tale that anecdotal evidence suggests was, and at least in its outcome has remained, close to the experiences of many aspiring female architects. The story follows poor, orphaned, "sweet faced" Rose through rejection after rejection "because she is a woman" as she seeks an apprentice's place in an architectural office. She eventually finds a teacher in a receptive office and studies hard for years so she can win her livelihood. Her story comes to a happy end when she is relieved of the necessity of working for a living because her teacher proposes and they draw up "a little plan of partnership which was sealed with a sweeter seal than usual."[29] In the late 1940s, among those thousand women who had formally studied architecture and about whose large number *Architectural*

Record was surprised to learn, many were reported to be too busy "raising little architects" to keep up their practices.

Marriage to an architectural partner could ease the way to relative fame for some of the best studied of the pioneering American women architects, such as Louise Blanchard Bethune (1856–1913), who in 1881 opened an office in Buffalo, New York, a few months before marrying her partner, Robert Armour Bethune. Louise Bethune became, in 1889, the first female Fellow of the AIA. However, marriage to an architect more often subordinated the woman architect's role within her husband's office, as it did Marion Mahoney Griffin's (1871–1962) during the early twentieth century. Even before her marriage, Mahoney's importance as a designer was muffled by the fame of her employer, Frank Lloyd Wright. Her beautiful renderings are generally credited with enhancing Wright's reputation and then for clinching victory for her husband, Walter Burley Griffin, in the competition of 1912 for the (unrealized) design of a new Australian capital, Canberra. Walter Burley Griffin, a fellow employee of Wright's, married Marion Mahoney in 1911, the year before the competition. Walter's name alone appeared on the winning entry, although Marion's importance as its codesigner is now widely recognized. Like the majority of wives who were also professional partners of their husbands, Mahoney remained one of those "valuable coadjutors to architects," subordinates in the positions to which the editors of the *American Architect and Building News* had, in their very first issue, relegated women with architectural skills.[30]

Manley's status as a single woman left her free of the time-consuming duties and distractions of wives and mothers. She was able to concentrate on her practice, on public service, and on the activities of many organizations to which she belonged. As a college student she had joined two distinct groups—those dominated by men and professionally oriented, and the more social clubs of women friends—setting patterns that were to be lifelong. The University of Illinois yearbook for 1917 listed her membership in the male-dominated Architectural Club and in the social sorority Kappa Alpha Theta, and noted, significantly, that she was president of the "Women's League." As one of her classmates testified years later, "Marion held an enviable position on the campus and her leadership in student activities was indicative of what she would afterward achieve in the greater scope of her business professional career."[31] She maintained active allegiance to Kappa Alpha Theta for the rest of her days, listing herself as a "life member of the Panhellenic Association."

She was an enthusiastic joiner, an active member, and a leader of many groups. Soon after settling in Miami, she joined the Business and Professional Woman's Club, becoming its state treasurer by 1920, and throughout her life she assumed leadership roles in the local club. She had been just as quick to attend a meeting in 1918 of the newly organized Florida State Board of Architects. In 1926 she became only the fourteenth woman to join the Florida chapter of the AIA. After suspending her membership when she could not afford to pay the dues during the Depression, she resumed active membership by 1937. The only female member of the Florida South Chapter of the AIA, she was soon elected its secretary and seated on the editorial board of the association's journal, *Florida Architecture and Allied Arts*, in which her work was first published. Throughout the 1940s and 1950s she was a delegate to national AIA conventions and served on several national committees, especially those concerned with planning issues. She also attended international conventions of architects during these years, traveling to Lima, Peru; Havana, Cuba; and Mexico City.

Even before finishing her studies at Illinois, Manley enrolled in a summer seminar on planning at the University of Michigan, again setting an early direction for lifelong activism. Very soon after arriving in Miami she made known her interest in the citizenry's "spark of recognition of the need for city planning" by attending a meeting in 1917 when "several members of the town's pioneer families—the Orrs, the Jacksons, the De Garmos—met in the downtown Presbyterian church to discuss the area's future." Manley later recalled, "They knew something should be done, but they didn't know what."[32] She continued to read about planning, and she attended national conventions of planners, trying to keep abreast of the latest expertise on what that "something" should be. She was frustrated as she witnessed what she called the "unplanned disaster" of development in Miami. In the summer of 1942 she went back to school to update her training by attending a city planning course at MIT. Several overlapping years of service on the Coral Gables Board of Supervising Architects and on the City of Miami's Planning Board ended by the mid-1940s, in both cases with resignations announcing her dismay over their proceedings.[33] But this hardly marked the end of her assumption of civic roles, even during periods when she was carrying a heavy workload, as she was through this immediate postwar period, designing the new University of Miami. However, after the mid-1940s, her interest shifted from government service to a focus on service to local nonprofit groups promoting social welfare, to committees of the AIA, and to the American Planning and Civic Association. She did all this work for nonprofit and professional organizations right through the period when she was busiest with many large-scale jobs.

FIG. 12. Chi Omega Alumnae Awards Presentation. Manley received the Bertha Foster Award in 1957. Courtesy of the Historical Museum of Southern Florida, Marion Manley Collection.

Marion Manley's work was nationally recognized during her lifetime. Her induction into the AIA's College of Fellows in 1956 marked only the fourth time the national organization recognized a woman's work and service with this high honor. Locally, her contributions were celebrated on the pages of the *Miami Herald* in articles that have been important sources for this book. In 1957 Chi Omega, an honorary society at the University of Miami, awarded her its Bertha Foster Award for her "countless contributions to culture" and her "inspiration and encouragement to many" (figure 12). Her colleagues honored her with the gold medal of the Florida Architectural Association in 1973. But for a decade after her death in 1984, her work garnered little attention until Emily Adams Perry's "Marion Isadore Manley: Pioneer Florida Architect," a chapter in *Florida Pathfinders*.[34] Based on thorough research undertaken by Perry with the help of Jose Rodriguez, it was a basic starting point for the present study.

The modest size of some of Manley's best houses and of her buildings at the University of Miami has doomed too many to the wrecker's ball in an era of mega-mansions and enormous "facilities." But her work presents other problems as well, problems common to much that was designed by mid-twentieth-century American architects who were converted in midcareer to modernism, problems that render their buildings unlovable in the eyes of much of the public today. In their excited discovery of the new gospel of modernism, they all too often overburdened each project with ambition to invent, to be original—even while naively imitating iconic modernist models and sometimes choosing models ill suited to a client's needs or to a specific site. In the name of functionalism, many indulged aesthetic preferences—such as that for the flat roof—in climates unsuited for them, and experimented with untried structural systems and materials that soon failed.

Manley ignored and even scorned the richness and order of American town planning precedent and turned instead to the dictates of the most respected avant-garde planners of her young adulthood for her ideas on the subject. She joined with another architect who shared her enthusiasm for modernism, Robert Law Weed, to apply the new principles to the most important planning project of her career, the campus that the University of Miami began to build immediately after World War II. The architects gave it meandering roads, free-form green spaces, and a multitude of low buildings, buildings whose forms were nearly indistinguishable from one another, whose uses seemed interchangeable. They dispersed those buildings in irregular patterns along the curving roads and on the oddly shaped spaces between them. They succeeded in creating a non-place, one that was intended to accept an indefinite number of additional buildings. Conversely, they refused to make one of those comfortable familiar places that the orderly, usually symmetrical, siting of clearly differentiated building types had traditionally brought to the special, beloved campuses of America and to its towns. Because their design for Miami's campus, like many of Manley's architectural designs, was executed outside a built-up area, its demonstration of the preference for surfaces stripped of all ornament and much detail did not upset the character of any traditional surrounding neighborhood.

However, while breaking with most design traditions in her enthusiastic embrace of modernism, Manley continued, along with many of her Florida colleagues during the mid-twentieth century, to embrace much of the regionalism in architecture that had only a few decades earlier been a pride of the American architectural profession. Like their colleagues all over the country, Florida's first generation of formally trained architects had given prominence to the task of adapting current architectural fashions to the local climate using the region's building materials. Heat and humidity had dominated the concerns of those who built the earliest vernacular houses in Miami during the late nineteenth century, and through the first half of the twentieth century had encouraged successive generations of traditionalist architects who arrived here to adapt European precedents to a climate unique in the United States. That climate retained its priority among the concerns of Miami's first generation of modernist architects. Like modernists worldwide, they responded both to an appeal for the internationalization of a supposedly style-less new architecture and to a demand for solutions to specific local problems, which were often climate related, and in doing so, they engendered recognizable local styles. In trying to make living spaces more comfortable by opening her self-consciously modern houses to nature and its breezes, Manley contributed to the history of modernism in America some of the gentlest and most comfortable of local variants on a theme common to architecture in warm climates internationally.

As we have searched the records, examined Manley's surviving buildings, studied drawings and photographs, and closely reviewed all that is known of her work, we have come to lament her dismissal of most of her own early accomplishment. In embracing modernist ideas, she was perhaps too quick to neglect her initial creative response to local traditional architecture that was derived from classical sources. However, she did continue throughout her career to enhance other discoveries that she had made early on within the local wooden cracker vernacular. These worked better with modernism on a small scale, and she used the local wooden vernacular skillfully to create comfortable homes for clients who prized their easy melding with the semitropical landscapes that she left growing around their sites.

On the other hand, for her big architectural projects and at the larger scale of city planning, she—along with the great majority of her professional generation—too readily followed the dictates and preoccupations of the stars of the European avant-garde whose ideas were being introduced to American architects by the émigrés to Cambridge and Chicago and by their promoters at the Museum of Modern Art. She was the product of an architecture school far from the sources of avant-garde thinking, where the major European architectural publications were so venerated that the dean personally translated them and made copies of those translations available in the library.[35] And she practiced architecture in a "raw" town, equally remote. Perhaps she never shook the sense of having to make up for the distance by trying a little too slavishly to demonstrate knowledge of the latest European architectural fashions, even wearing big black round-rimmed glasses like Le Corbusier's. As a lifelong pupil, perhaps she remained a little too eager to accept supposedly expert authority, too ready to swallow whole the lessons published by a succession of new masters, the trends admired by her colleagues at the national meetings she so often attended, and by new teachers of the courses in which she enrolled. She was perhaps too eager to apply her latest lessons, not wholly digested, to the jobs at hand. Half a century later, with the wisdom of experience and hindsight, it became all too obvious to a later generation that most of the theories about city planning that were being inculcated at MIT the summer she studied there, especially the priority accorded the automobile, were disastrous.

Was her gender at fault here? It would seem not. The entire American architectural profession fell victim at midcentury to a highly successful propaganda campaign to replace traditional architectural and planning values with the radical requirements of European modernism. While advocating total originality in every building, it produced a great many pale and cheapened imitations of European prototypes. Manley's occasional ineptitude as she made the great leap into modernism was not hers alone. It typifies much that troubled building in this country for the half century following the Second World War.

Marion Manley's most lovable buildings are her simplest, the almost primitively modern ones at the University of Miami, the fast-disappearing houses blending in with the hammock-like growth that she took such care to preserve on her client's lots in suburban Dade County. But perhaps it is not primarily the quality of her design work but her role as a woman architect-citizen that merits historical attention and admiration. Her interest in what has been called "socialized architecture"—design with an emphasis on social welfare—came to the fore in the most active phase of Manley's career. Professor Frost of the Cambridge School of Architecture and Landscape Architecture had recognized early in the twentieth century that this socialized architecture was of little interest to the male competitors for lucrative commissions and was therefore particularly appropriate for his female pupils. He hoped to prepare them for effective service on local planning boards and social service organizations. Manley gave just such service, but unlike many of Frost's former pupils, she—true to early feminist ambition—also fully engaged that professional architectural "world in which men and women would work in competition with each other."[36]

As a woman who took a leading role in introducing modernism to shape the University of Miami during the postwar period, she set national precedents. As a respected architect she built upon her reputation for competence in her field and called upon the professional alliances forged within the AIA and the social ones sustained within women's groups to win "positions of authority" in local government and the nonprofit sector. In so doing, she became for her fellow citizens "effective in determining the conditions under which they lived," to borrow again the words of that feminist of the 1930s. In Manley's best houses for her fortunate clients she enhanced the conditions of privileged private life in Florida's semitropics. She worked at the same time to improve life on a broader scale with her work for slum clearance, her projects for housing, her child care center for the African Americans who were her neighbors, and with her advocacy of what she believed to be better planning for Miami.

—CL

PRACTICING FROM THE OUTPOST

In 1917, soon after graduating from the University of Illinois with a bachelor of science degree in architecture, Marion Manley moved to Miami at the urging of her brother Lester (figure 14).[1] In doing so, she joined the region's first generation of professional architects, landscape architects, and town planners who arrived in the opening years of the twentieth century and began transforming a frontier town just emerging from pine rockland and hardwood hammock into a thriving, modern metropolis (figure 13). Trained in the country's leading universities and armed with a faith in progress, these individuals shaped the image of Miami, and by extension, Florida, for decades to come.

FIG. 13. Bird's-eye view of Miami, circa 1925. Courtesy of the State Library and Archives of Florida, Fishbaugh Collection, Tallahassee.

MIAMI BOUND

The place, the times, and the growing corps of professionals made for a place on the verge of phenomenal development. In fact, Miami had grown unceasingly almost from the moment of the arrival of the first train on April 13, 1896. Henry Morrison Flagler (1830–1913)—a railway magnate and Rockefeller partner in Standard Oil—saw the vast potential of this underdeveloped state. He constructed railroad lines from Jacksonville to Key West and built grand hotels along the way. In 1885 he began construction on the Ponce de Leon Hotel in Saint Augustine and purchased the Jacksonville, St. Augustine, and Halifax Railroad, later to become the Florida East Coast Railway. By 1894 the railroad reached Palm Beach where Flagler built the Royal Poinciana Hotel and a few years later the Breakers Hotel and White Hall—his private, fifty-room winter mansion. These three structures, coupled with the extension of the railroad, established Palm Beach as the premier winter resort for the wealthy American northerner.[2]

Palm Beach was to be the terminus of Flagler's railroad, but the severe freeze of 1894–95 caused him to reconsider his original decision. It is said that Julia Tuttle (1848–98), a prominent Miami landowner, sent orange blossoms to Flagler to prove that the local groves had been unaffected by the freeze and encourage him to extend development south. To further persuade him to bring the railroad as far south as Miami, Tuttle, along with William and Mary Brickell, offered Flagler land on which to develop his transportation system. In return, Flagler was to establish a town and build a hotel. He agreed; and in 1896 the Florida East Coast Railway reached present-day Biscayne Bay. Slowly, people arrived from all over the United States, transforming this pioneer outpost into a thriving urban center.[3]

In 1913, Lester Manley (1883–?) visited Miami and acquired the commission to pave the main streets of its fledgling downtown. He fell in love with the young city and took up residence, bringing his wife, Josephine, with him. When his sister Marion arrived four years later, Lester was able to introduce her to important local architects, opening doors to the area's leading firms where she was quickly taken on as an apprentice—an opportunity that was virtually nonexistent for women within the established architectural "gentlemen's clubs" of the North and indeed in most of the country.[4]

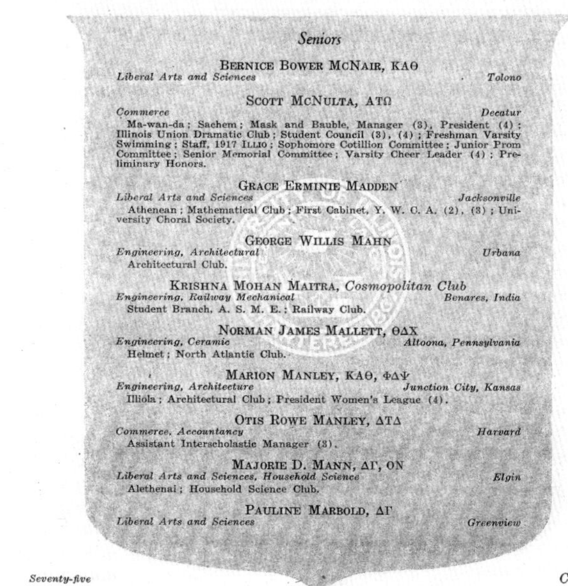

Seniors

BERNICE BOWER MCNAIR, ΚΑΘ
Liberal Arts and Sciences — *Tolono*

SCOTT MCNULTA, ΑΤΩ
Commerce — *Decatur*
Ma-wan-da; Sachem; Mask and Bauble, Manager (3), President (4); Illinois Union Dramatic Club; Student Council (3), (4); Freshman Varsity Swimming; Staff, 1917 ILLIO; Sophomore Cotillion Committee; Junior Prom Committee; Senior Memorial Committee; Varsity Cheer Leader (4); Preliminary Honors.

GRACE ERMINIE MADDEN
Liberal Arts and Sciences — *Jacksonville*
Athenean; Mathematical Club; First Cabinet, Y. W. C. A. (2), (3); University Choral Society.

GEORGE WILLIS MAHN
Engineering, Architectural — *Urbana*
Architectural Club.

KRISHNA MOHAN MAITRA, *Cosmopolitan Club*
Engineering, Railway Mechanical — *Benares, India*
Student Branch, A. S. M. E.; Railway Club.

NORMAN JAMES MALLETT, ΘΔΧ
Engineering, Ceramic — *Altoona, Pennsylvania*
Helmet; North Atlantic Club.

MARION MANLEY, ΚΑΘ, ΦΔΨ
Engineering, Architecture — *Junction City, Kansas*
Illiola; Architectural Club; President Women's League (4).

OTIS ROWE MANLEY, ΔΤΔ
Commerce, Accountancy — *Harvard*
Assistant Interscholastic Manager (3).

MAJORIE D. MANN, ΔΓ, ΟΝ
Liberal Arts and Sciences, Household Science — *Elgin*
Alethenai; Household Science Club.

PAULINE MARBOLD, ΔΓ
Liberal Arts and Sciences — *Greenview*

Seventy-five — *Classes*

FIG. 14. Marion Manley, senior photograph, 1918 *Illio* (Record Series 41/8/805). Courtesy of the University of Illinois at Urbana-Champaign Archives.

While life on the Florida frontier was spartan, Marion's early internships were invaluable experiences that emboldened her to establish an independent office as early as 1924. Manley steadily developed a formidable practice for herself in the small pioneer city by Biscayne Bay. Her career spanned six decades and produced nearly one hundred residential and commercial buildings. Against many odds, through two world wars, during national and local economic crises, this remarkable woman's accomplishments are noteworthy.

Although unusual for a female practitioner, Manley's career is emblematic of the twentieth-century regionalist architect who worked first to bring academic models derived from classical precedents to many parts of the country, then to supplant those traditional styles with the new international style, successively adapting each of them to a variety of extreme American climates, and finally to create a local vernacular inspired by the spirit of a given place and reflective of regionalist attitudes about the building of a city. Manley is best known for her institutional designs for the University of Miami during the 1940s and early 1950s, but it is her extensive portfolio of domestic architecture that best exemplifies her efforts to adapt national architectural trends to the specific conditions of a particular place. A review of the best examples of Manley's residential work demonstrates the ways these currents in architectural history were interpreted in South Florida.

THE MEDITERRANEAN— AN IMPORTED ARCHITECTURE

In the early 1920s Miami was being promoted as a tropical paradise, attracting free-spirited pioneers and wealthy northerners alike. Early visionaries such as George Merrick (1886–1942), founder of Coral Gables, and James Nunnally, developer of the residential neighborhood Morningside, constructed nearly utopian cities amid the native landscape and citrus groves. In an effort to imbue their cities with an aura of history, these early developers sought an evocative architecture that would attract northern tourists. They conceived the theme of an American Mediterranean, and Manley joined the ranks of the architects who were drawing up these dreams in seductive renderings and buildable blueprints. She, along with her colleagues, was developing an architecture that borrowed from alluring images of distant European cities, transforming precedents to reflect the realities of the local building culture (figure 15).

In the summer of 1924, H. George Fink (1891–1975), George Merrick's cousin and one of the two original architects for Coral Gables, took a two-month study tour of Spain, Italy, and France. While in Europe, he sent drawings back to Walter De Garmo (1876–1952) and Phineas Paist (1875–1937), who were working with him on the development of Coral Gables and who immediately began adapting many new elements into their designs. When Fink returned to South Florida, he described the type of architecture as Mediterranean or Rivera style. In describing the various elements of the style, Fink said: "From the Spanish and Italian we derive the cool, inviting loggias, the large and attractive patios, the terraces that are a delight in the evening and late afternoons, and the grills and ornamental stone doorways. From the Moorish and Persian we obtain the delightful effects from using colored and glazed tile for inserts, wrought iron lanterns, ornate columns and other unique treatments too numerous to enumerate. But the one feature common to all which we have retained in all the houses are the delightfully varied tile roofs and the tile floors."[5] In 1925, Fink designed Coral Gables' New York sales office in a Mediterranean language, effectively introducing Coral Gables' Mediterranean style to a national audience.[6]

A diligent and eloquent practitioner of the Mediterranean style was Rexford Newcomb (1886–1968), who arrived to teach at his alma mater, the University of Illinois, in 1916, the year before Marion Manley graduated. Newcomb, an architectural historian who wrote extensively about Spanish colonial architecture, became dean of the University of Illinois' College of Fine and Applied Arts. He

MIAMI SHORES

America's Mediterranean

IN addition to its long frontage on Biscayne Bay, various streams and lakes in and through the property will bring the total waterfrontage of Miami Shores to nine miles. The most is to be made of this unusual setting in developing the property.

The four principal highways leading into Miami from the North pass through Miami Shores, as does also the Florida East Coast railway, so that any one bound for Miami from the North must pass through Miami Shores en route. All together, Miami Shores has a total of ten miles of frontage on these main highways.

The street improvement program undertaken at Miami Shores includes not only permanent pavement and sidewalks, but also water and electric light service, and a complete system of landscaping with the profuse use of beautiful shrubs and trees.

The general development program at Miami Shores is being followed by a big building campaign of homes, stores and apartment buildings. Throughout Miami Shores the Mediterranean type of architecture is being followed, as being the type most suitable to the climate and setting of this magnificent development, "America's Mediterranean."

Miami Shores is being developed following a carefully studied plan, with ironclad restrictions setting the boundaries of the business section, the apartment house and hotel sections and the residence section. This, it is expected, will form an important protection for each type of improvement.

The officers of the Shoreland Company, which is putting Miami Shores on the market, are men well-known in Florida for their successful undertakings of similar character in the past. Hugh M. Anderson is president; Roy C. Wright, vice-president; J. B. Jeffries, treasurer and secretary; Vernon C. Seaver, vice-president; E. S. Harris, vice-president and office manager; J. A. Riach, director of publicity and assistant sales manager; J. W. Livingston, art director, and Frank K. Ashworth, general engineer.

MIAMI SHORES

125 East Flagler Street, Miami, Florida

Branch Offices—FORT LAUDERDALE, DELRAY, LAKE WORTH, ORLANDO, TAMPA, ST. PETERSBURG, JACKSONVILLE, WEST PALM BEACH AND SANFORD.

FIG. 15. Miami Shores advertisement, circa 1924. Courtesy of the Historical Museum of Southern Florida.

described contemporary American Mediterranean architecture in 1928, detailing its melding of sources: "Spanish, Italian, Moorish, Byzantine-Mediterranean types generally—instead of being archeologically segregated are under the orchestral process merged, as were those golden threads long ago, into a new, sun-loving style, which, while eminently American in its plan and utilities, is never-the-less distinctly Mediterranean in its origins and spirit."[7]

While examples of such architecture could be found throughout the United States, it was most prevalent in Florida and Southern California. This is not surprising, for the two places shared a number of striking similarities that made them ideal settings for it. In both states, early Spanish colonization had left traces of an architecture largely composed of thick stuccoed walls and clay-tiled roofs that served as inspiration for early twentieth-century architects. The geography and climate of both California and Florida, with their blazing skies and brilliant light, were ideal for the development of an architecture that encouraged the seamless flow of life from exterior to interior. Thus the extensive use of loggias, patios, verandas, and courtyards—architectural elements from countless examples in the countries surrounding the Mediterranean—were borrowed and adapted to the particular circumstances of each new setting.

The popularity of these Mediterranean models was also inspired by romantic fantasies of the early twentieth-century settlers, the Beaux-Arts-trained architects and wealthy clients alike, who indulged those dreams in sometimes extravagant creations for two states that were at the time relatively barren outposts of American culture. Along with their architectural importations they simultaneously cultivated a landscape composed of largely foreign plant varieties to complete the image of a New Eden.

In Miami, the Mediterranean arrived most spectacularly with the building of the Villa Vizcaya between 1914 and 1916 (figure 16). Vizcaya was the winter home of James Deering (1859–1925), one of two brothers who built mansions in and near Miami, spending shares of the vast fortune they had inherited and then increased by manufacturing farming machinery. James Deering commissioned an extraordinarily talented team—some of them surprisingly young men—to design his grand house, spectacular formal gardens, and extensive complex of farm buildings. The project's artistic supervisor was Paul Chalfin (1874–1958), a Harvard graduate, trained as a painter at the New York Art Student's League and the Ecole des Beaux-Arts; its architect was Francis Burrall Hoffman (1882–1980), also a Harvard graduate with a diploma from the Ecole des Beaux-Arts; and its landscape architect was Diego Suarez, a Colombian-born architect trained in Italy. Deering and Chalfin traveled to Europe in search of an appropriate model for the house and garden. They found their inspiration in the striking and sober Renaissance villas of the Veneto Region and transported this image to the shores of Biscayne Bay.[8]

FIG. 16. Bayside of Villa Vizcaya, Miami, circa 1919. Courtesy of the State Library and Archives of Florida, Tallahassee.

The result was beguiling, for the new Villa Vizcaya, with its ornamented and manicured surroundings, seemed like an apparition set against the lush backdrop of the native hardwood hammock. Once completed, Vizcaya became the most important model for subsequent building in the city. Many of the craftsmen and some of the designers who worked on the villa stayed on, providing a repository of knowledge for a young generation of Miami architects and builders rapidly constructing a new city.

Manley arrived in Miami only one year after the completion of Vizcaya. Like most American architects of the period, she was the product of a Beaux-Arts system of education. She was well trained and capable of designing in any one of the principal European historical styles, having been taught to approach design through the careful application of traditional imagery. Therefore the roots of the Mediterranean within the classical tradition made the style familiar enough to her, allowing her to seamlessly adapt to the specific characteristics of its new local applications.

Manley's first job was as an intern at the Coconut Grove office of Walter De Garmo, which soon immersed her in the language of the Mediterranean (figure 17). De Garmo had moved to Miami in 1904 and quickly established one of the most successful architectural practices in the city. He was Miami's first formidably trained architect, having received his bachelor's degree in architecture from Cornell in 1900 and trained in the office of John Russell Pope (1874–1937), a master of the Beaux-Arts style who is now best known for his design of the Jefferson Memorial in Washington. These credentials helped De Garmo acquire important civic commissions early in his career, including the first Miami city hall and the first Miami fire station, which was adjacent to it (figure 18).[9]

Working with De Garmo also taught Manley the basics of building in the materials of the local wooden vernacular, the finest surviving example of which is the Barnacle (figure 19). She was also exposed to a variety of other locally preferred architectural languages ranging from the neoclassical to the Mediterranean, the latter being extensively explored by De Garmo throughout the 1920s and 1930s.

FIG. 17. Walter De Garmo. Courtesy of the Arva Moore Parks Collection.

FIG. 18. City building and fire station, Miami, circa 1915. Courtesy of the State Library and Archives of Florida, Tallahassee.

Following her internship with De Garmo, Manley worked briefly as a junior draftsman for Martin L. Hampton. Hampton appears for the first time in Miami's *Polk City Directory* in 1916 as a draftsman in August Geiger's office. He is listed as an independent practitioner, sharing office space with another architect, Gordon E. Mayer, in 1918. In 1922, he was hired by the developer George Merrick to design a variety of buildings for the City of Coral Gables, including the country club and the Casa Loma Hotel. Later, he participated in Miami Beach's building boom, designing numerous art deco hotels and residences there.[10]

By early 1918 Manley found herself out of work, an apparent victim of the economic disruptions, including a slowdown in domestic construction that had followed the country's entry into World War I the previous April. Meanwhile, she broadened her architectural experiences by helping to redesign a convent in

FIG. 19. "The Barnacle," home of Ralph M. Munroe, Coconut Grove. Courtesy of the State Library and Archives of Florida, Tallahassee.

The State of Florida.

#105

WHEREAS **Marion I. Manley** has shown to the satisfaction of THE STATE BOARD OF ARCHITECTURE his competency and fitness to practice Architecture NOW THEREFORE by virtue of the powers vested in it by THE STATE OF FLORIDA the said Board of Architecture HEREBY ISSUES to the said **Marion I. Manley** a Certificate to practice Architecture in the State of Florida as provided in an Act to regulate the Practice of Architecture approved May 29th 1915 subject to the Powers of Revocation vested in said Board by said Act.

IN TESTIMONY WHEREOF Witness our signatures and seal of the Board this sixth day of September 1918

Murray S. King PRESIDENT

SECRETARY & TREASURER

Received in the office of the Secretary of State at Tallahassee, this seventeenth day of September A.D. 1918 and recorded in Book of The Florida State Board of Architecture on page

SECRETARY OF STATE

FIG. 20. Manley's certificate to practice architecture in the State of Florida, issued on September 6, 1918. Courtesy of the Historical Museum of Southern Florida, Marion Manley Collection.

Key West as military barracks for soldiers. Shortly afterward she accepted a temporary job in Philadelphia designing ships for the Emergency Fleet Corporation of the U.S. Shipping Board.[11] Manley's stay in Philadelphia was brief; she was back in Miami by mid-1918. In September of that year, she sat for the licensing exam and became the first woman architect licensed in the city (figure 20).[12]

With her new credentials in hand, Manley soon went to work for Gordon E. Mayer, another prominent Miami architect. Mayer was born in Brooklyn, New York, and spent much of his youth in Europe. He studied architecture in Bridgeport, Connecticut, and New York and worked on many of the grandest residences on Long Island. He later traveled to the Caribbean to execute architectural projects for the colonial government of Nassau in the Bahamas. He arrived in Miami in 1917 and began to design large-scale Mediterranean houses for prominent members of the local community, among them Charles L. Briggs, a northern industrialist.[13] Recalling this period in an interview in 1977, Manley stated that during her internship with Mayer, she produced most of the drawings for the Briggs-Morley residence (figure 21).[14] This house was a magnificent example of Miami's early Mediterranean domestic architecture. The beauty and the architectural refinement of the house were noted in a 1920 publication titled *Miami, Jewel of the South*. Among only four residences that were included, this one, captioned "C. L. Briggs' Italian Villa," was featured in the very select company of the Villa Vizcaya, Carl Fisher's Shadows on Miami Beach, and the Matheson's residence in Coconut Grove. The opportunity early in her career to work on an important local example of the Mediterranean style was invaluable training that enhanced Manley's expertise.

FIG. 21. Briggs Morley house, Miami. Demolished, year unknown. Courtesy of the Arva Moore Parks Collection.

With the conclusion of World War I, economic activity dramatically increased throughout the city; the most desirable commodity was land, and architects were much in demand to design the improvements upon it that every developer envisioned. The rumblings of the Florida real estate boom were beginning; and new subdivisions sprang up in all directions. In these circumstances, Manley's architectural abilities must have been extremely valuable to Mayer. By 1921 she was listed in the city directory as his partner in a firm newly called Mayer and Manley. For a young woman to be taken on in an architectural partnership by a successful male architect of the era seems a remarkable accomplishment. But the partnership was short lived. In 1922 Manley once again left the city, this time for a position in James J. Baldwin's office in Anderson, South Carolina.[15] Little has come to light about her experiences there, and in about 1924 she returned to Miami, where she remained for the rest of her life.

FIG. 22. George Merrick. Courtesy of Special Collections, University of Miami Libraries, Coral Gables, Florida.

Manley returned just as local real estate development was reaching a fever pitch, and she was soon designing houses for one of the most ambitious local projects of the era, Coral Gables, founded by the visionary developer George Merrick (figure 22). Merrick, who had spent much of his early youth in New York and Massachusetts, came to Miami with his parents in 1899, when they fled the harsh New England winters that had taken a toll on the health of some family members. They chose the area on the advice of H. G. G. Fink, Merrick's maternal grandfather, and purchased a 160-acre homestead, sight unseen, five miles south of Miami. In 1902, the Merricks extended their landholding to include eighty acres south of present-day Coral Way, where they planted grapefruit groves.[16]

In 1921 George Merrick began to replace the family's groves with the early coral rock houses of his new garden city, Coral Gables. He envisioned it as a place of formal wholeness, and to unify that vision he used Mediterranean-inspired architecture for the generous amenities of its public places—sun-drenched plazas, gateways to lushly landscaped streets, and a Venetian entry to a lavish public swimming pool. When selling lots, he also required the use of Mediterranean-inspired architecture for private houses, many of which looked over circulating waterways that he planned to adorn with gondolas.[17]

Merrick filled Miami's newspapers with full-page daily advertisements promoting his dream city, and his aggressive promotional campaign paid off. More than five thousand people attended the opening auction for the sale of the first lots on November 28, 1921. When the first section of the city sold out, Merrick acquired more land on which to expand his vision. His much-repeated mantra that "beauty can be made to pay" had come true; countless local developers followed in his footsteps in the hope that they could create cities that were as beautiful—and profitable—as Coral Gables.[18]

Manley seized the opportunity, taking advantage of the real estate boom by establishing a small, independent architectural practice in about 1924, and for several years thereafter she designed Mediterranean-inspired houses in new developments throughout the city. Her work of this era displays a keen understanding of the best local architectural preferences and reveals the hand of a refined and sophisticated designer. The Scott house (1924), located in Morningside, a neighborhood just north of Miami's downtown along Biscayne Bay, and the Quinn house (1925), situated in Miami Shores, a new town established a little farther north of Morningside and incorporated in 1932, are Manley's finest surviving houses from this period. They contain many features characteristic of her early residential architecture.

The development of Morningside began in 1922 when James H. Nunnally, president of the Bay Shore Investment Company, purchased a large, undeveloped tract of bayfront property near Miami's northern city limits. Originally named Bay Shore and currently known as the Morningside Historic District, three of its subdivisions were platted between 1922 and 1924, and a later one in 1936. Prior to selling the first lot, Nunnally ensured that the infrastructure was fully developed to include paved and curbed streets, underground wiring for street lighting, and lushly planted parkways. A 1924 promotional brochure described the neighborhood: "Boulevards run at graceful angles and the parkways are of varying width and differ in floral adornment. Everywhere the view is like overlooking an immense garden."[19]

Set within this tropical Eden were a series of detached, single family residences constructed largely between 1922 and 1941, the now-historic area's major "period of significance" as the National Register of Historic Places Nomination Form designates it. Duplexes, apartments, and hotels were prohibited, as were houses constructed of wood. Building setbacks and lot frontages were carefully regulated, and Nunnally required that all plans be submitted for approval prior to construction. In this way, he could control the architectural language of the place as well as each individual building's contribution to the collective. The first houses were predominantly Mediterranean and were designed by some of the leading local architects of the day; residences built in the 1930s and 1940s frequently employed the art deco style.

Manley's Scott house (1924), located on a large corner lot in Morningside's historic district, was designed for a prominent Miami lawyer, John Scott, and his family (figure 23). Today, the house is virtually intact with minor interior renovations including the enclosure of the original first-floor screened porch. The architecture is sober, restrained, and far more regularized than the typically animated, picturesque compositions of most of the local Mediterranean houses of the period. Here Manley, working with the concrete block and stucco of ordinary local builders, captured some sense of the grandeur of a distant past with relatively modest means, relying more on the overall proportions of the work than on fine architectural detailing for its elegance. The main body of the house is a compact, rectangular mass that creates a formal, planar facade along the main road, with a perpendicular wing housing the attached garage that serves as a transition between the street and the garden. The facades have large expanses of smooth stuccoed walls pierced by windows repeated in a regular rhythm. Oolitic limestone and ironwork details are used sparingly, concentrated along the entry vestibule and in the quoins detailing of the main block of the building (figures 24 and 25).

The plan is organized along a centralized hall that runs the depth of the house, dividing the main living space from the dining room and kitchen. One of the most striking features of the ground plan is the large south-facing porch, which

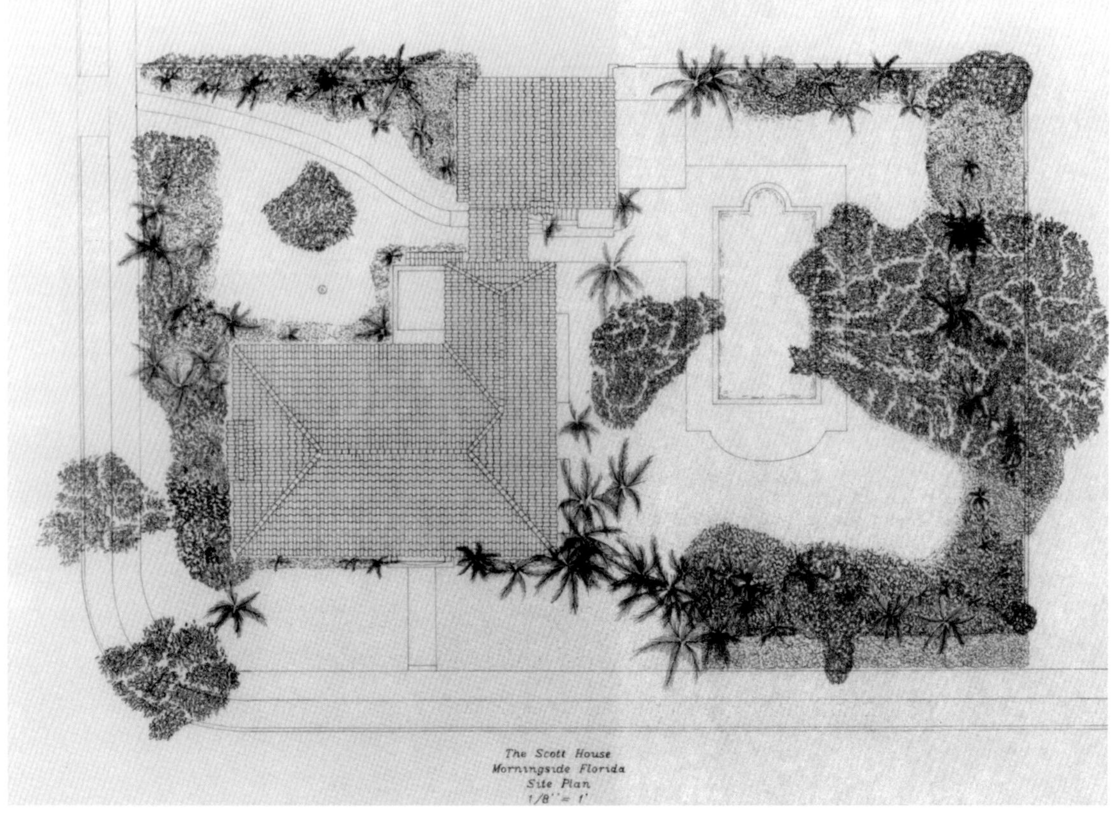

FIG. 23. Scott house, Morningside, Florida, site plan (ink on mylar, 18′ x 24′). Drawing by University of Miami School of Architecture faculty: Carie Penabad and Carmen Bigles; students: Zachary Adelson, Abraham Aluicio, Rhea Bosland, Cynthia Bouchard, Aaron Heinrich, Sergey Krupsky, Andrew Silva, Rania Solh, Molly Teter, and Travis Wild.

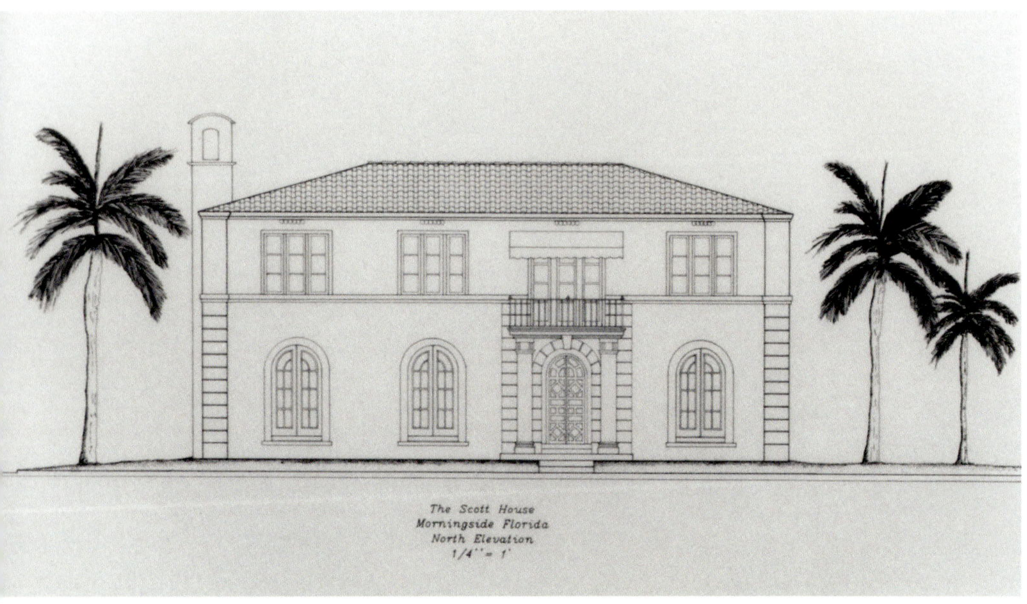

FIG. 24. Scott house, Morningside, Florida, north elevation (ink on mylar, 18′ x 24′). Drawing by University of Miami School of Architecture faculty: Carie Penabad and Carmen Bigles; students: Zachary Adelson, Abraham Aluicio, Rhea Bosland, Cynthia Bouchard, Aaron Heinrich, Sergey Krupsky, Andrew Silva, Rania Solh, Molly Teter, and Travis Wild.

FIG. 25. Scott house, Morningside, Florida. Photograph by Amie Edmiston.

extends the full length of the living room. Such outdoor rooms, including loggias, porches, and verandas, are abundant in Manley's early residences. These spaces blur the lines between indoor and outdoor living, serving as extensions of the main rooms in the house, protecting the interior from the intense tropical sun, and extending the living space out toward the garden. Upstairs the plan is compact and utilitarian. Private rooms are arranged along a double-loaded corridor, with the primary bedroom opening out onto a spacious porch overlooking the garden (figures 26 and 27).

Following the Scott house commission, Manley was hired by the Shoreland Development Company to design four houses in Miami Shores. The company was established in January 1924 by Hugh M. Anderson and Roy C. Wright—real estate developers who made their fortune on several fortuitous Miami real estate ventures including the sale of properties along Flagler Street, one of Miami's principal thoroughfares, and the development and construction of the Venetian Islands and Causeway.[20]

By late 1923 Anderson and Wright were prepared to begin a new project. They decided that this development would be similar in nature to that of the Venetian Islands—a largely residential community of Mediterranean-inspired architecture located near the water. Through the Shoreland Company, they purchased twenty-eight hundred acres alongside the northern portion of Biscayne Bay. The property extended eastward, from Arch Creek (present-day NE 135th Street) to the north, NE Eighty-seventh Street to the south, NW Fourth Avenue to the west, and Biscayne Bay to the east. The purchase also included two islands in Biscayne Bay (today's Bay Harbor Islands and Indian Creek Village).[21] The master plan was designed with approximately nine thousand building sites, nearly five and a half miles of bay frontage, four miles of inland waterways, and ten miles of main roads. The plans called for the building of a new causeway to Miami Beach and the construction of two golf courses, a forty-acre park, business districts, grand hotels, schools, and churches.

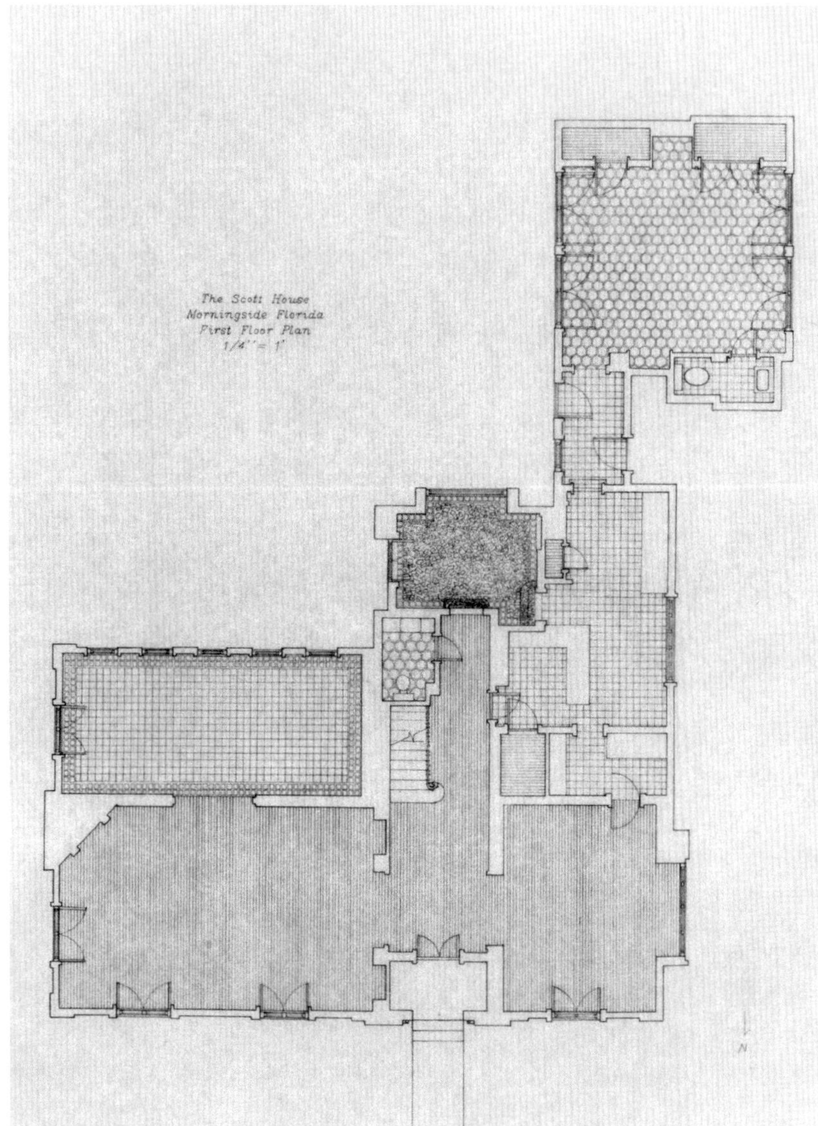

FIG. 26. Scott house, Morningside, Florida, first-story floor plan (ink on mylar, 18' x 24'). Drawing by University of Miami School of Architecture faculty: Carie Penabad and Carmen Bigles; students: Zachary Adelson, Abraham Aluicio, Rhea Bosland, Cynthia Bouchard, Aaron Heinrich, Sergey Krupsky, Andrew Silva, Rania Solh, Molly Teter, and Travis Wild.

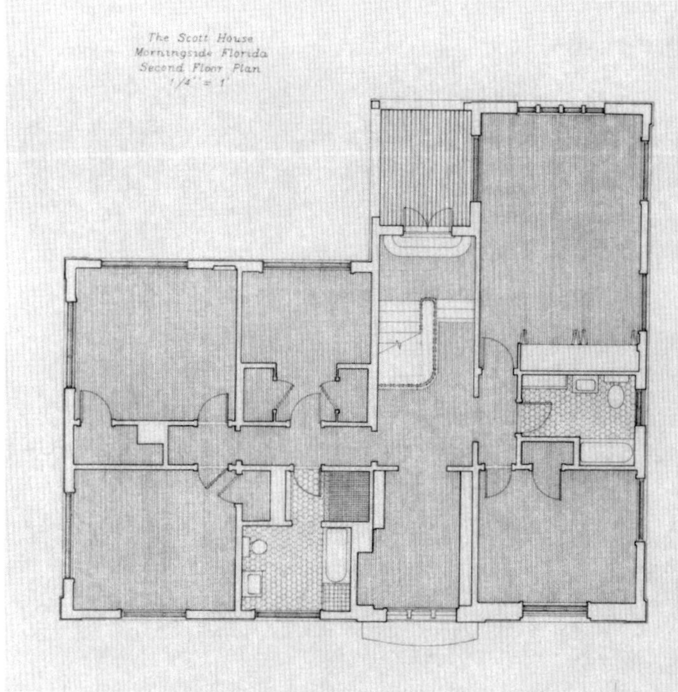

FIG. 27. Scott house, Morningside, Florida, second-story floor plan (ink on mylar, 18' x 24'). Drawing by University of Miami School of Architecture faculty: Carie Penabad and Carmen Bigles; students: Zachary Adelson, Abraham Aluicio, Rhea Bosland, Cynthia Bouchard, Aaron Heinrich, Sergey Krupsky, Andrew Silva, Rania Solh, Molly Teter, and Travis Wild.

As Nunnally had done in Morningside, Anderson and Wright required Mediterranean architecture for both residential and commercial construction. Building plans were to be approved by the company prior to construction to ensure architectural coherence, a unified language for a town they promoted as "America's Mediterranean." Their advertisements included evocative renderings of model houses and grand public buildings by some of the leading local architects.[22]

Residential construction began in early 1925. By the following year Miami Shores was well on its way to becoming a vibrant and successful residential community until the devastating hurricane of September 18, 1926, halted development plans and hastened the Shoreland Company's demise. Despite adversity, Miami Shores continued to grow, albeit at a greatly reduced scale and pace, and while virtually none of the public buildings were ever built, a substantial number of the original, Mediterranean-style houses remain. Twenty-five of these are listed in the National Register of Historic Places, including Marion Manley's Quinn house.

The house, first occupied by Miss Penny Quinn, is located at 477 NE Ninety-second Street (figure 28). It is believed that the house suffered some hurricane damage in 1926, since a building permit was issued for repair work in 1927.[23] Here, Manley employed a site strategy similar to that of the Scott house, developing a two-part composition with the primary two-story volume fronting the street and an attached one-story structure housing the garage at the rear (figure 29). However, the massing here is far more picturesque than that of the Scott house. She arranged multiple roofs to create a distinct and varied skyline in sharp contrast to the flatness of the Florida landscape.

An additive composition is also apparent in the plan where individual rooms are either set back or projected by a few feet to create an undulating building envelope. This compositional strategy imbues the house with a sense of history, making it appear as though it had grown over time through a number of additions. This approach appealed to clients who, in the spirit of the day, were

REGARDING
THIS PROPERTY
FARM & TOWN REALTY CORP

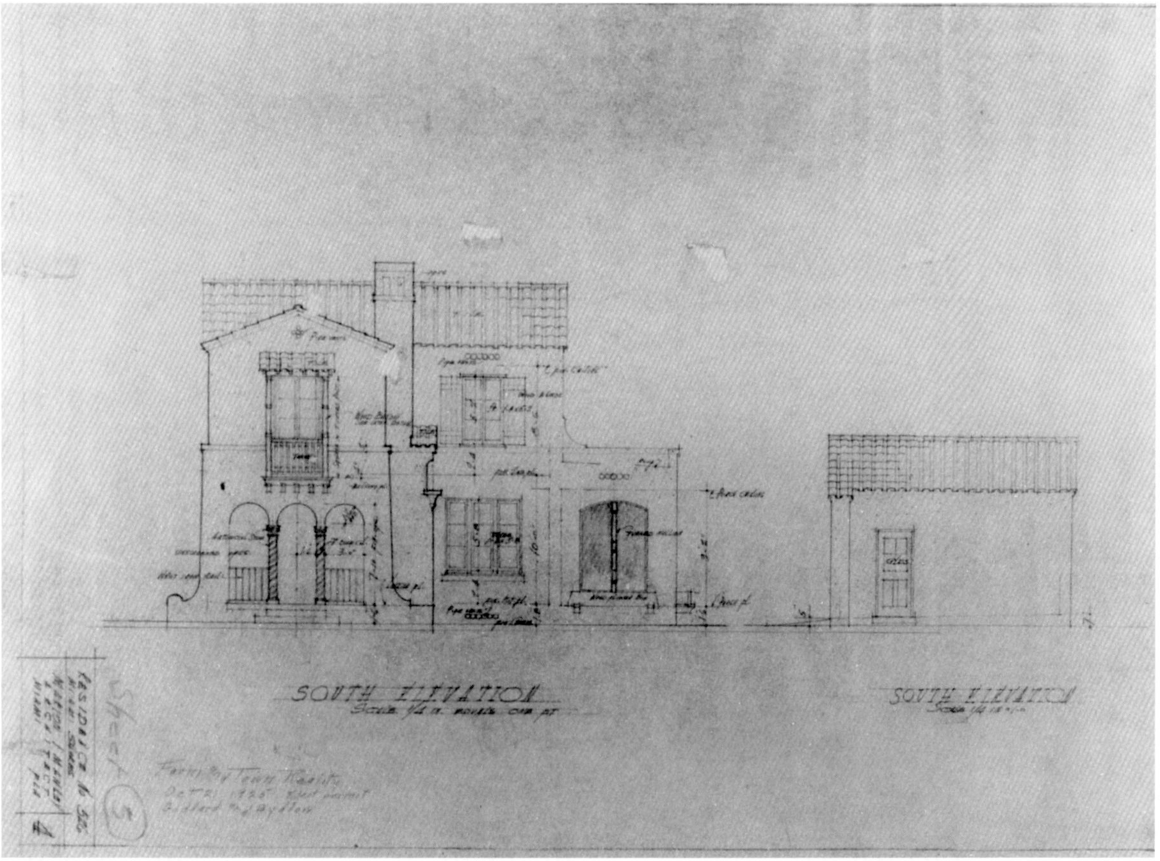

FIG. 29. Quinn house, Miami Shores, south elevation. Original Drawing, (pencil on trace, 18′ x 24′). Courtesy of Mr. and Mrs. Rudin.

FIG. 28. Quinn house, Miami Shores. Courtesy of Brockway Memorial Library Archives, Miami Shores, Florida.

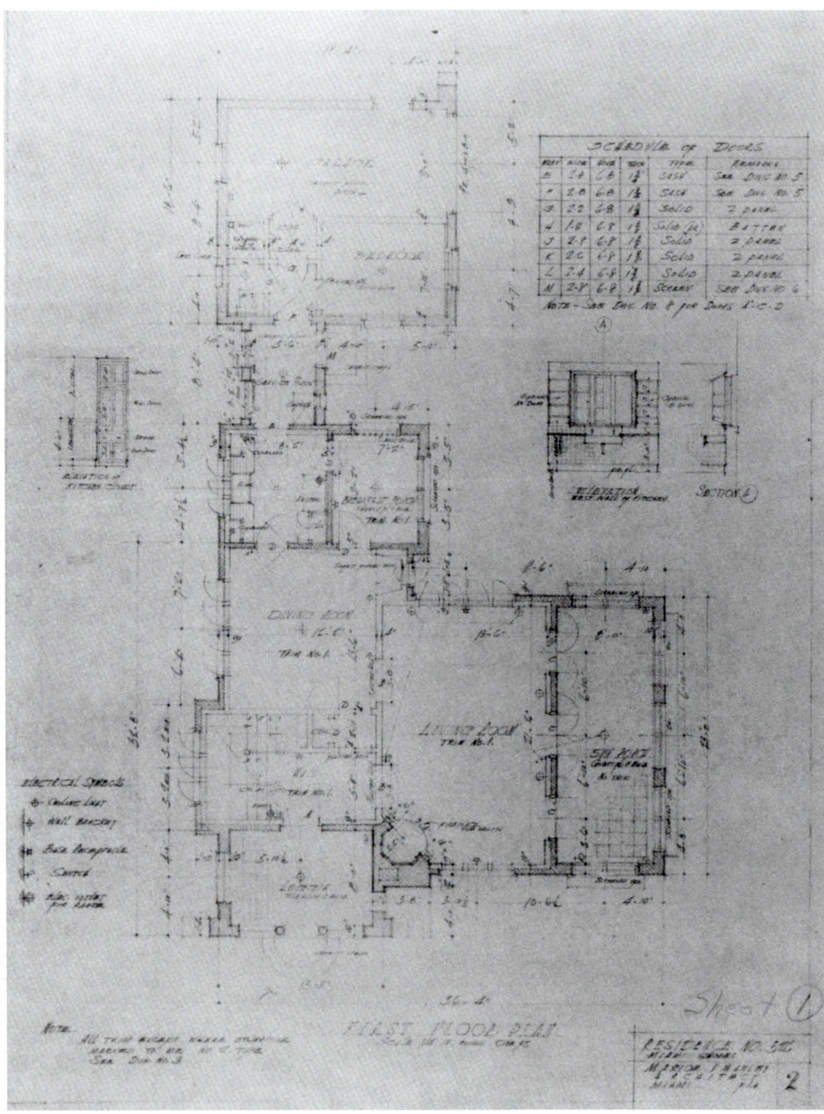

FIG. 30. Quinn house, Miami Shores, first-story floor plan (pencil on trace, 18′ x 24′). Courtesy of Mr. and Mrs. Rudin.

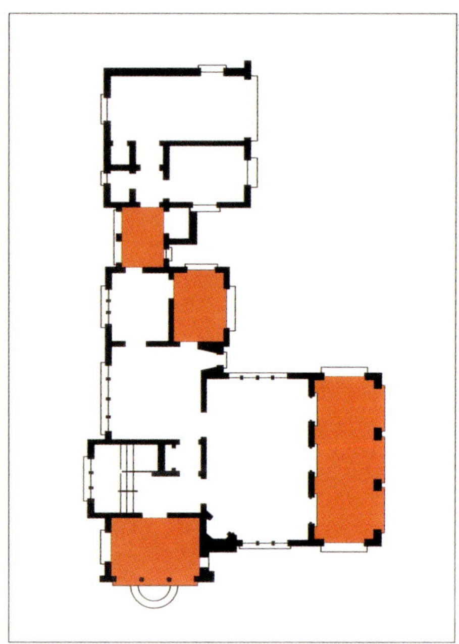

FIG. 31. Quinn house, Miami Shores, first floor, open-space diagram. Drawing by Carie Penabad.

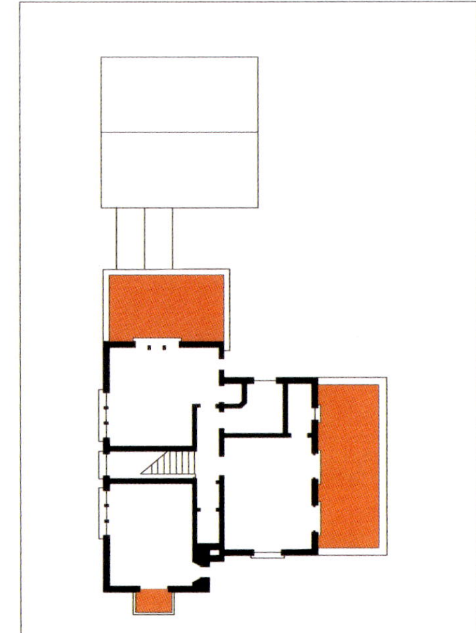

FIG. 32. Quinn house, Miami Shores, second floor, open-space diagram. Drawing by Carie Penabad.

enamored with the illusion of age in a place that was in fact very new (figure 30). Once again, in the Quinn house, Manley cleverly explored the possibilities of indoor and outdoor living by creating numerous and varied exterior spaces including an entry loggia, a large sunporch that serves as an extension of the main living room, a breakfast porch, a small service porch, two large terraces, and a balcony on the second floor. These outdoor rooms constitute nearly half of the building footprint and give each of the living spaces direct access to the exterior. The final result is a compact plan that easily cross ventilates, keeping the house cool during the long, hot summer months (figures 31 and 32).

The Quinn house remains standing today. Unfortunately, renovations have significantly altered its original appearance. A new carport, with a large sloping roof and overscaled opening, is not in keeping with the smaller, more carefully choreographed volumes of the original residence. Screened porches have been enclosed, and the second-floor terrace has been eliminated. Wood frame casement windows and shutters have largely been replaced with jalousies, and much of the original wood detailing—particularly the second-floor projected wooden balcony—has been removed and replaced with inexpensive metal railings.

Manley designed three additional Mediterranean houses in Miami Shores, at 145 NE Ninety-fourth Street (1928), 601 Concourse (1929; figure 33), and 1291 NE Ninety-sixth Street (1929). In them, she explored themes similar to those of the Scott and Quinn houses. All have survived, although in each house important character-defining architectural features have been removed and replaced with elements that are not comparable with the quality and craftsmanship that Manley designed and specified. Examples include handmade clay barrel roof tiles replaced with new clay tiles that lack the thickness, richness of color, and texture of the original. Wood casement windows have been replaced with fixed aluminum windows or jalousies of varying proportions, and the houses have been restuccoed and repainted with techniques inferior to the richly textured surfaces and subtle patinas of the original walls. These important characteristics should be restored in order to preserve these houses properly for future generations.

FIG. 33. House at 601 Concourse, Miami Shores.
Courtesy of the Brockway Memorial Library Archives,
Miami Shores, Florida.

DOUGLAS AND THE WOMEN'S CLUB

Following the plentiful early commissions of the mid-1920s, Manley's practice suffered during the Great Depression. Information about the impact of that national disaster on Manley's life comes to us from Marjory Stoneman Douglas (1890–1998), the journalist and preservationist renowned for her campaign to save Florida's Everglades. In her autobiographical book *Voice of the River*, Douglas recorded that while the Depression did not greatly impact her, it did affect many of her friends who were involved in real estate. Of Manley, Douglas recalled: "The Bust left her high and dry. I had a little extra room off my kitchen, a tiny little room not much more than a closet, where maybe you could stick a cot and a bureau. I told her if she could put up with it, she could share the house. She did."[24]

Marjory Stoneman Douglas and Manley were to become lifelong friends. Douglas was born in Minneapolis, Minnesota, in 1890 but spent most of her youth in Massachusetts, where she attended Wellesley College, graduating in 1912 with a bachelor's degree in English. In 1914 she met and was briefly married to Kenneth Douglas, a newspaper editor thirty years her senior. Soon after the marriage ended she moved to Miami to live with her father, Frank Bryant Stoneman (1857–1912), the first publisher of the *News Record*, the paper that had, in 1910, become the *Miami Herald*. Douglas was appointed society editor, and her responsibilities included writing personals and covering parties and weddings. She found her greatest source of information in the city's small but vibrant women's clubs.[25]

Manley was an active participant in these clubs, which became an important part of her life. In *Florida: The Long Frontier* Douglas describes the culture of the clubs and the important role they played within the community: "Perhaps two hundred women came and went there as audiences or taking part in programs of their frequent afternoon meetings or patronizing their little library, the only one in town." Douglas found "such small clubs, in isolated places like this in many parts of the country," to be "a kind of self-produced university." She recognized "that the training we were given, by being pushed into standing on our feet and talking about something as intelligently as we could before an audience at once sympathetic and critical, was to be invaluable. School and college had not given this kind of experience. From it I also gained a heightened interest in the whole place."[26]

Miami's first women's club was the Housekeeper's Club (currently the Coconut Grove Woman's Club), founded on February 19, 1891. Its main objective was to promote camaraderie among the mothers and housekeepers of the community and to contribute to the building of a new Sunday school.[27] Similarly, the Married Ladies' Afternoon Club (now the Miami Woman's Club), was founded in 1900 by twenty-one pioneers who gathered for "mutual improvement and pleasure" and used their weekly dues to purchase books for the group. By 1903 their membership had grown to eighty and their library to approximately one thousand volumes. As early as 1905 members were actively maintaining a public reading room. In 1912 Henry M. Flagler donated a tract of land on the corner of East Flagler Street and Second Avenue for a new clubhouse and library, which opened on June 1, 1913, as the first public library in the city.[28]

While these early groups engendered a sense of community, and undoubtedly raised the educational aspirations of their members and the community alike, they continued to foster a traditional view of women's role in society. The Housekeepers' Club of Coconut Grove's stated objectives were "FIRST: To bring together the mothers and housekeepers of our little settlement and by spending two hours a week in companionship, to learn to know each other better, and SECOND: To add to the Sunday School Building Fund."[29] It seems clear, both from accounts of the women's clubs and from our knowledge of women's roles at the time, that these individuals accepted caregiving as their primary duty in life. Douglas, a journalist and recent divorcée, and Manley, a single, working professional, did not fit comfortably into that role.

In 1916 members of the Woman's Club of Miami suggested that the business women of the group organize a new club that would better address their particular needs. After much discussion, a group gathered to establish the Business Women's League on February 10, 1916.[30] Marjory Stoneman Douglas was a founder and the first president of the organization. In 1919 it became a chapter of the newly organized National Federation of Business and Professional Women's Club; a year later Manley was appointed treasurer of the local group.[31]

Manley's friendship with Douglas and her devotion to the Business Women's League may well have played a major role in repeatedly drawing the architect back to the city. Camaraderie among female professionals would have been rare anywhere in the United States during this period. Very few women were practicing architecture, and women were also rare in other professions. The social and intellectual network the club provided helped support Manley during her lifetime.[32] The club fostered a spirit of inquiry that brought about a new awareness of ideas. It also provided an important forum for discussing one's own work.

It is interesting to trace the correlations in the work of Douglas and Manley over time. Intriguingly similar concerns are apparent in Douglas's publications and Manley's buildings throughout much of their careers. For instance, during the years that Manley was exploring a Mediterranean architecture for South Florida, Douglas was writing *Coral Gables: America's Finest Suburb*, in which she championed that architecture as appropriate for that new city: "The geography, the climate, the tropical horticulture and tropical characteristics of South Florida are matters which have nothing in common with the west or the north or the old south. The straight levels of the land, the brilliance of the light, the unique backgrounds of tropical trees and sky [demand] an architecture which is not imitative of other forms or suited to other places. To be right, it must answer local problems of living. It was determined first of all, therefore, that a modified type of Spanish architecture, thoroughly adapted to local needs, should be the style of the whole." If one were to build it should be in the manner of a modified "Spanish architecture," later referred to as the Mediterranean style. Manley's early residential architecture attests to her basic agreement with Douglas's suggestions for a style befitting Florida's climate and topography.[33]

Overspeculation, the devastating hurricane of 1926, and the advance of the Depression brought an end to the Florida real estate frenzy. Yet despite the economic downturn, all was not bleak for Manley, now in her mid-thirties. After dismantling her office in 1929 and moving in with Marjory Stoneman Douglas, she accepted a position as a senior draftsman at the office of Phineas Paist (1875–1937) and Harold Steward (1896–1987).

Paist played an important role in the development of Coral Gables, serving as the supervising architect for the city after it was created in April 1925. He had studied at Philadelphia's Drexel Institute and Pennsylvania Academy of the Fine Arts and had established a firm in that city whose work caught the eye of Paul Chalfin. Chalfin lured Paist to Miami in 1913 to work as an associate architect

FIG. 34. Phineas Paist at Vizcaya, circa 1915. Photograph by Alice Wood. Courtesy of the Arva Moore Parks Collection.

on the Villa Vizcaya (figure 34).[34] Later, Paist formed a partnership with Harold Steward, who had studied architecture at Syracuse University and moved to Miami after serving in the navy during the First World War.[35]

During the Depression, the firm of Paist and Steward was awarded several Works Progress Administration projects including the design of the U.S. post office and federal courthouse in downtown Miami. Once again, Manley was working for one of the leading local firms of the day, and this time she had the opportunity to assist in the design of one of the city's most important public commissions. The building was to house fourteen federal departments, and offices and work space were needed for approximately eight hundred employees. The first floor contained the post office; the second, the Department of Justice, federal court, and its dependencies; and the third, the remaining federal departments including customs, immigration, internal revenue, and public health. According to Assistant Postmaster General John W. Philip, Miami's large construction project would employ approximately one thousand men for one year—a much-needed source of income for the city and its many unemployed workers.[36]

The new federal building was fundamentally a neoclassical design in which characteristics of the Mediterranean are apparent in the plan and the details. It was finely crafted using local materials, primarily native stone, and built around an open central courtyard that served as public space and provided natural light and ventilation to both the post office and the federal courtrooms.[37] The courtyard typology, responsive to the local climate, was one that the architects believed was an appropriate model for a federal building in the tropics, and the openness of its plan represented a radical departure from the hermetic sealing of other federal buildings that were going up throughout the country at the time, as the nomination of this building to the National Register of Historic Places noted in 1983.

Manley appears to have been primarily responsible for the detailing of the building, inspired by Mediterranean ornamentation and executed in native

FIG. 35. Post office and federal building, circa 1934, Miami. Courtesy of the State Library and Archives of Florida, Fishbaugh Collection, Tallahassee.

stone. Unfortunately, she was given very little credit for her contributions—a situation that would occur throughout her life, particularly when she collaborated with larger architectural firms directed by men. Years later her colleague Alfred Browning Parker acknowledged her critical role in the design project, writing: "Ms. Manley worked during the two to three years the design process went on. . . . She drew full size all details of the building . . . working at a 4 × 10 board. It was her belief that the best part of the detailing can be seen in the patio, although she did all of the details for the [courtrooms]."[38]

Manley remained at Paist's office from 1930 through the building's completion in 1933. However, during the mid-1930s, the local economy began to improve, supported by the Federal Housing Administration plan established to alleviate unemployment, particularly within the construction industry. This initiative made it easier for ordinary people to get mortgages at low interest rates and launched a new building boom throughout the country.

A NEW BEGINNING

In 1934 Manley reopened her independent architectural practice. Among her most important commissions of this period was the Fink house in Coral Gables, designed in 1938 for Denman and Betsy Fink (figure 36). The drawings for the house are the most complete set of Manley's working drawings that survive from the period (figures 37 and 38).[39] Denman Fink (1881–1956), the uncle of Coral Gables' founder, George Merrick, was the visionary artist of Coral Gables. He was an accomplished muralist and illustrator whose watercolors were frequently used to promote land sales in the young city and were published in such magazines as *Harper's Weekly* and *Scribner's*. He assisted Merrick in drawing the master plan for Coral Gables and designed most of the city's civic spaces between

FIG. 36. Fink house, Coral Gables, south elevation. *Florida Architecture and the Allied Arts* (1940). Courtesy of Special Collections, University of Miami Libraries, Coral Gables, Florida.

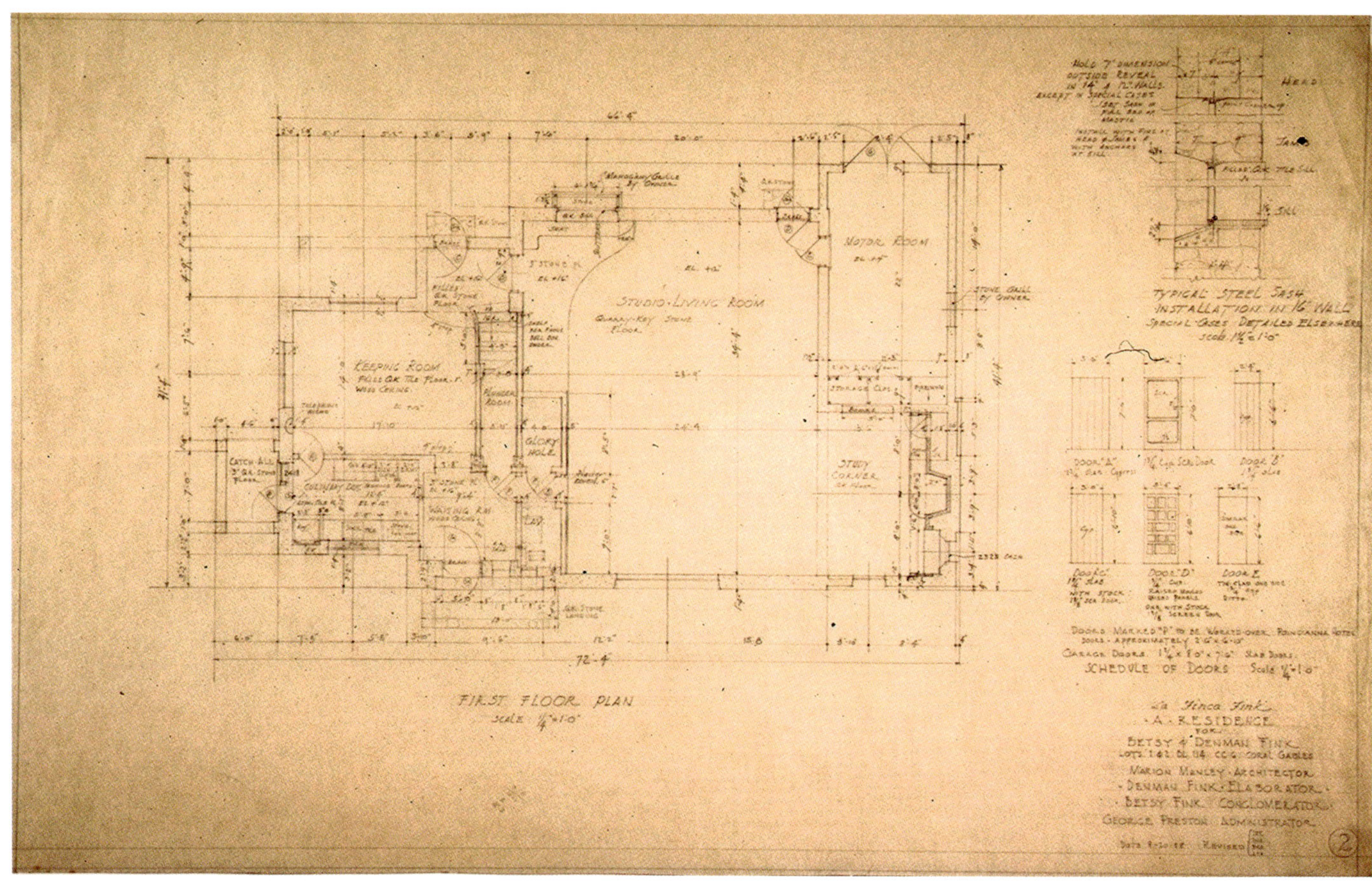

FIG. 37. Fink house, Coral Gables, floor plan (pencil on trace 18′ x 24′). Courtesy of the Historical Museum of Southern Florida, Marion Manley Collection.

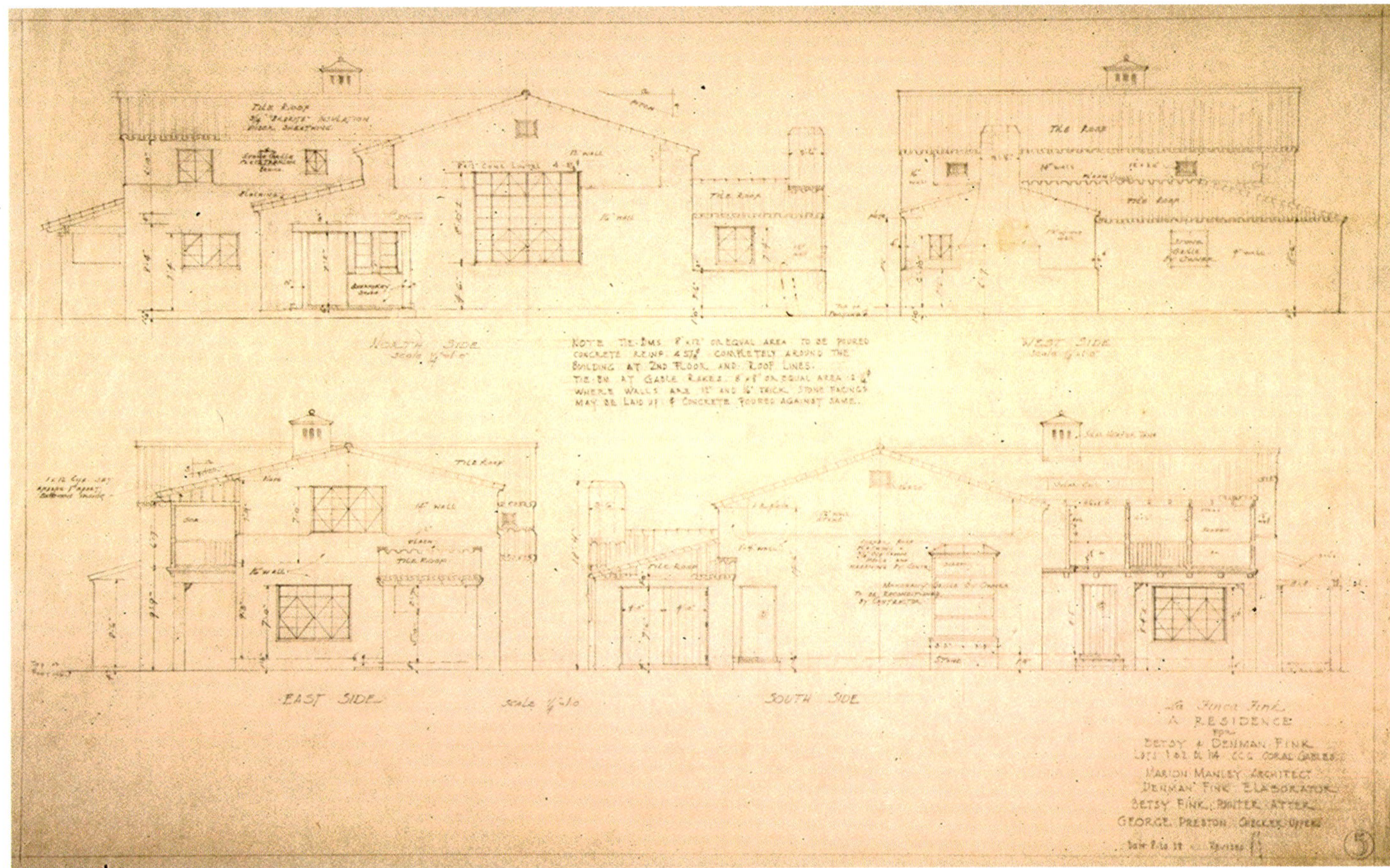

FIG. 38. Fink house, Coral Gables, elevations (pencil on trace, 18′ x 24′). Courtesy of the Historical Museum of Southern Florida, Marion Manley Collection.

1922 and 1928. Fink also served as chair of the University of Miami's Department of Art.[40]

The design for his family's house is quite modest in comparison with Manley's residences of the mid-1920s and more closely recalls the simplicity of Spanish farmhouses than the splendor of Mediterranean villas. The appeal of the Mediterranean models in the United States owed something to the adaptability of noble forms that did not depend on rich ornament but instead derived their character from picturesque simplicity. In *Spanish Influence on American Architecture* Randolph W. Sexton noted: "The peasant dwelling or farmhouse of Spain, offers, perhaps, most for adaptation to American needs. Its chief characteristic lies in a pleasing combination of simplicity and dignity."[41]

The Fink house possessed such a "pleasing combination of simplicity and dignity." Manley's title for this house, "Finca Fink," reveals quite explicitly that her choice of the farmhouse precedent was a conscious one, for *finca* is Spanish for "farm." The overall plan is informal and utilitarian, consisting primarily of a two-story studio/living room on the ground level and a small bedroom upstairs. The massing is broken down into a number of volumes to produce a varying roofscape over an otherwise relatively simple volume. The house extensively incorporates native materials such as oolitic limestone, a deeply pitted rock that is quarried throughout South Florida and, in a rough-cut state, was used in many of the earliest houses in Coral Gables, laid up to look after aging as if it might almost be coral taken straight from the sea (figure 39). Oolitic limestone is not only used structurally for the walls of the first floor but also in much of the architectural detailing.

FIG. 39. Fink house, Coral Gables, north elevation. *Florida Architecture and Allied Arts* (1940). Courtesy of Special Collections, University of Miami Libraries, Coral Gables, Florida.

In choosing native materials for his house, Fink was practicing what he had earlier described as "a fine art," making "a new house or a new bit of construction take its place quietly and restfully in its environs," even though, as Manley later recalled, "it got very expensive to build coral rock houses because of the labor and amount of mortar needed. Even in the twenties, it cost twice as much and took twice as long to build a rock house as any other kind."[42] Expensive or not, using this local rock was important to Fink, as it not only blended with the local terrain but was also timeless. He had noted that "few and far between are the places which when completed do not cry aloud of their newness. They come out at you perhaps from a lovely setting like some great new toy, fresh from its wrappings and with its price-marks still in evidence. You almost feel that were you to turn back the fresh green shutter of such a house you might find its price-tag unmolested." Fink chose to avoid the look of the brand new for Coral Gables, where, as he wrote, "you are not going to sense this blatant newness even from the start, for in very truth it will not be new. It will simply be ages-old material taking on new forms. What you see as a house today was the same time-mellowed rock a score of centuries ago. The rock that yesterday slept in the shade of the lovely lantana today is but a restful structural foreground to the grey-green of the spreading live oak."[43]

Manley's drawings for the Fink project provide us with a rare glimpse into her early working methodology and the structure of her practice. On seven sheets, working in pencil on tracing paper, she made the final drawings that served as the construction documents. Interestingly, they closely resemble the style of drawings produced by De Garmo's office during the same period. This was not unusual for the time, as most Beaux-Arts-trained architects shared similar design methodologies and drawing techniques. However, unlike De Garmo, Manley's body of work is curiously devoid of sketches and presentation drawings. She seems to have rarely produced these drawings for her clients. Rather, her working method included several meetings with clients in order to refine the program and arrive at an understanding of their requirements. Then Manley systematically produced a number of drafts or variations of the scheme that were used to compose the final drawing sets.[44] This economy of means reduced her output of architectural drawings and made it possible for her to build numerous houses steadily throughout the city despite having a very small firm.

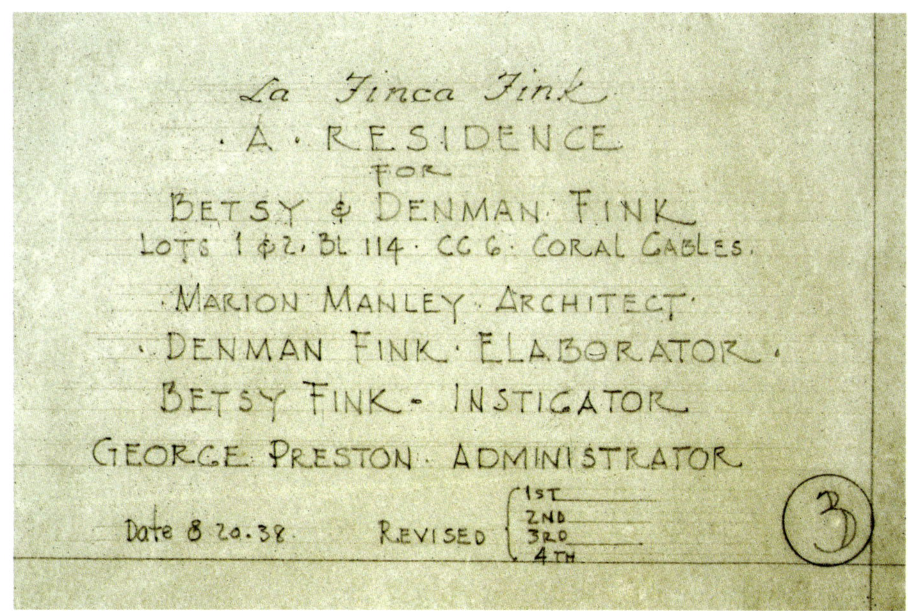

FIG. 40. Fink house, Coral Gables, title block from original set of drawings. Courtesy of the Historical Museum of Southern Florida, Marion Manley Collection.

The Fink drawings also shed light on Manley's personality. The title block for the drawing set is highly unorthodox and varies from page to page, with the names of the principal participants and their "titles" listed in descending order:

Marion Manley: Architect
Denman Fink: Elaborator
Betsy Fink: Instigator
George Preston: Administrator
and
Marion Manley: Architect
Denman Fink: Elaborator
Betsy Fink: Pointer-Atter
George Preston: Check-Upper

These titles attest to a sharp wit and, more importantly, to an ability to speak, or in this instance write, exactly what was on her mind. They also suggest that she had an extremely convivial relationship with client and contractor. She not only nurtured long-term relationships with a variety of builders, especially John B. Orr, but also developed lifelong friendships with many of her clients.[45]

Today, the Fink house is a historic landmark. It stands at the corner of Anastasia Avenue and Anderson Road. A substantial two-story addition has been made at the east end of the primary elevation, and a new masonry and wrought iron perimeter wall has been constructed along the edges of the lot. While the addition is not greatly differentiated from the original (i.e., it shares similar roof types and architectural details), it has significantly altered the modest scale and therefore the overall character of the original residence. The new perimeter wall negatively impacts the composition by obscuring the view of the house from the street.[46]

NEW DESIGN IDEALS

The late 1930s brought a period of transition for Manley. While she continued to design Mediterranean houses throughout the city, including the Jamieson house in Coral Gables (1937; figure 41) and the Davenport house in Miami Beach (1938; figure 42), she also began to seek inspiration from a variety of other sources for these domestic commissions. The Von Paulson house (1938) in Coconut Grove (figure 43) and the Marks house (1939; figure 44) in Key West are two small structures that appear to be inspired by local nineteenth-century wooden vernacular buildings such as the one-room pioneer house and the shotgun houses built throughout Coconut Grove by Bahamian immigrants.

The humble Von Paulson house was a wood-frame structure covered by a large, gently sloping, shingled roof. It was slightly raised above the ground on concrete foundations to avoid water damage. The elevations, composed of a series of repetitive casement windows, were interrupted by a small screened porch giving the

FIG. 41. Leland S. Jamieson house, Coral Gables. *Florida Architecture and Allied Arts* (1937). Courtesy of Special Collections, University of Miami Libraries, Coral Gables, Florida.

FIG. 42. Davenport house, Miami Beach. *Florida Architecture and Allied Arts* (1938). Courtesy of Special Collections, University of Miami Libraries, Coral Gables, Florida.

FIG. 43. Von Paulson house, Coconut Grove. *Florida Architecture and Allied Arts* (1938). Courtesy of Special Collections, University of Miami Libraries, Coral Gables, Florida.

FIG. 44. Marks house, Key West. *Florida Architecture and Allied Arts* (1939). Courtesy of Special Collections, University of Miami Libraries, Coral Gables, Florida.

inhabitants a little outdoor space to enjoy the surrounding landscape.[47] Sadly, the house has been demolished.

The Marks house has many of the same elements. It is built of wood, with sloping roofs and an elevated floor. However, in this instance Manley exposed the post and lintel construction and developed a system of infill panels, some with screens, some with wooden jalousies. She also explored ways of effecting a more seamless relationship between interior and exterior spaces, blurring the lines between them, especially by using wooden jalousies to enclose the primary living space (figure 45). Both the Von Paulson and Marks residences were featured in *Florida Architecture and Allied Arts*—a reputable architectural journal that presented the work of leading Florida architecture firms. Manley served on the editorial board of the journal from 1939 to 1942.[48]

About the same time Manley was working on the Von Paulson and Marks residences, she collaborated with a Chicago architect, Chester Hart, on the design of the Cloyd Head house (1938) built in Coconut Grove (figure 46). The clients, who had formerly lived in North Africa, were interested in Tunisian vernacular architecture, so for them Manley and Hart developed a design inspired by North African precedents, but modified to respond to the particular conditions of Florida's climate and geography. The result was an additive composition in which each room of the house was articulated as an independent blocklike mass with unusually large windows in order to promote greater ventilation (figure 47). Today, the overall massing of the house is virtually intact; however, many of the architectural details—including the original windows and doors—have been removed. Manley and Hart were interested in producing a "functional" house. As Manley explained in a newspaper article, no space in the house was considered superfluous, and no building material was viewed as excessive.[49] They developed a compact building footprint and explored a simple method of construction that relied on the use of exposed adobe and concrete bricks. The bricks were not only structural but also served to provide the final finish. In adopting this stripped-down functionalist aesthetic, Manley and

FIG. 45. Marks house, Key West, living room interior. *Florida Architecture and Allied Arts* (1939). Courtesy of Special Collections, University of Miami Libraries, Coral Gables, Florida.

Hart were surely influenced by architectural trends that had been surfacing in Europe since the early 1910s.

By the late 1930s the traditional Mediterranean-inspired architecture that had been so popular in Miami during the 1920s and much of the 1930s was gradually giving way to new design ideals—primarily those that the Museum of Modern Art had identified as the "international style" in an important exhibition of 1932. Architects in Miami, and all over the country, were excited by the work

FIG. 46. Cloyd Head house, Coconut Grove. *Florida Architecture and Allied Arts* (1938). Courtesy of Special Collections, University of Miami Libraries, Coral Gables, Florida.

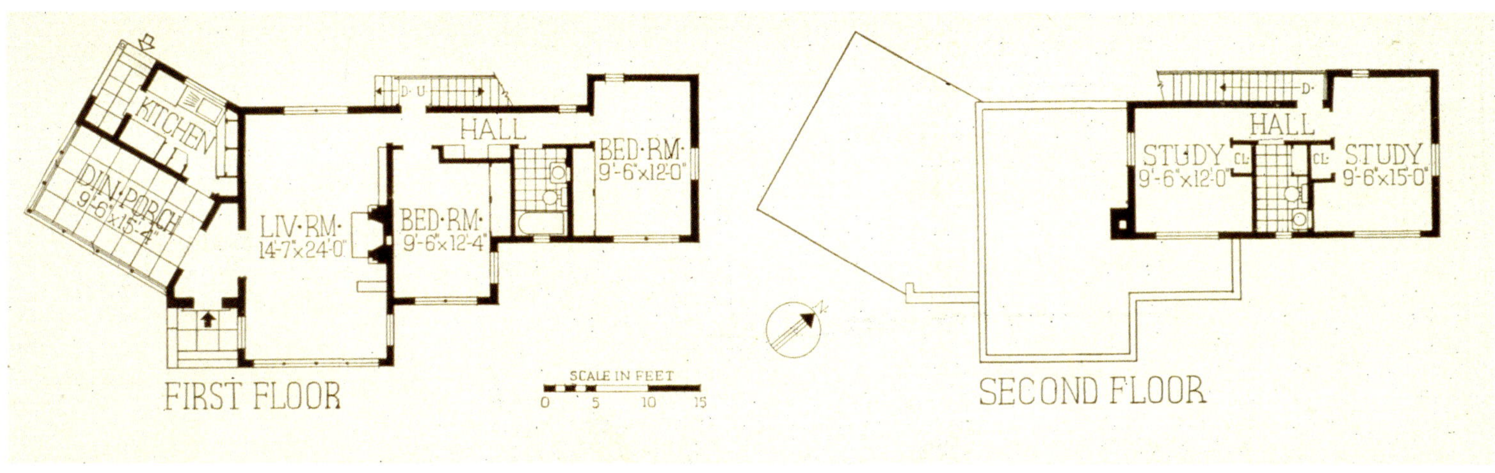

FIG. 47. Cloyd Head house, Coconut Grove, floor plans (1938). Courtesy of Emily Adams Perry.

of the prominent European modernists, most influential among whom were Le Corbusier and Walter Gropius, men whose writings encouraged the rejection of all associations with historical precedent, architects who gave priority in their own buildings to functionalism and to experimentation with new construction methods and materials.

Manley, like many other regional architects of the period, radically changed her fundamental ideas about architecture and the building of the city under the tutelage of the Europeans' publications. This once prodigious designer of Mediterranean houses in Miami experienced a modernist epiphany sometime before 1940, the year she produced bold sketches of experimental forms that had their basis in engineering calculations (see figure 55). In 1942, she enrolled in city planning courses during a summer term at MIT, an experience that had a profound impact on her development both as an architect and a planner.

Soon after she had returned to Miami from Cambridge, she began to disassociate herself from her early work, criticizing the romanticism of the Mediterranean style. The development and promotion of a new language of modern architecture became Manley's leading preoccupation for the remainder of her career. Her later scorn for the traditionalist work of the 1920s, which she characterized as "the Pseudo-Spanish era,"[50] is well documented, and the notion that Manley discarded her early drawings of countless Mediterranean houses in order to wipe the slate clean and shape the way future generations would remember her is not unfounded. Ironically, it is largely her Mediterranean residential work that remains standing today as built testament to the important architectural contributions she made in the development of the early Florida frontier.

—CP

MANLEY AND THE UNIVERSITY OF MIAMI

When Hitler invaded Poland in the autumn of 1939, Marion Manley could not have anticipated how events unfolding so far away would soon transform life in South Florida, nor could she have foreseen that Miami's role in those events was about to bring her the most important architectural commissions of her life. She had been in Miami for two decades and had survived, with difficulty, the lean years that followed the intoxicatingly optimistic ones of the 1920s. She was there when George Merrick, an idealistic real estate developer, laid out the town of Coral Gables just south of Miami, advertising it in the early 1920s, well before the fact, as "Miami's university suburb." Merrick's dream seemed on the way to becoming reality in 1925, the year he persuaded the "founding regents" of the future University of Miami to pledge to build it in his town, the same year those fifteen leading citizens secured a charter from the State of Florida for what they hoped would become a great Pan-American University.

Merrick's donation of a prominent 160-acre site for the school, his pledge of $5 million, and his spectacular images of "Spanish-renaissance" buildings to house the university figured largely in the regents' decision (figure 48). Merrick had those pictures produced by Denman Fink, an artist; Paul Chalfin, one of

FIG. 48. Preliminary study, aerial perspective, University of Miami. Paul Chalfin, Denman Fink, and Phineas Paist. Courtesy of Special Collections, University of Miami Libraries, Coral Gables, Florida.

the designers of Vizcaya; and Phineas Paist, an architect, all of whom were major contributors to Merrick's ambitious scheme for his ideal garden city planned at the new scale of the automobile. They integrated "the outdoor university," as they called it, seamlessly into the overall plan for the streets and canals of Coral Gables, arraying the school's handsome structures with great skill in a logical hierarchy around arcaded, gardened courtyards (figure 49).[1] In form, type, and detail, as illustrated in their beautiful renderings, it was all based on the classical and vernacular traditions of southern Europe that migrated so congenially to the warmth of southern Florida, as Chalfin had been instrumental in demonstrating with the dazzling accomplishment that was James Deering's mansion Vizcaya (see figure 16).

In proposals for the university, as elsewhere in Coral Gables in the 1920s, Vizcaya's influence was making itself felt as the designers and craftsmen who had come to build the great estate stayed on to work locally. Merrick, as well as many who purchased his lots, benefited from the expertise of Deering's designers and craftsmen. Houses large and small rose at a terrific pace with stylistic touches prescribed in fulfillment of Merrick's ambition to transform his father's citrus groves into a town that looked—as nearly as possible on that flat land—like a place on the Mediterranean seaside. Included among the Mediterranean-style houses, as they came to be called, were a few by Marion Manley from which she chose to distance herself in later years (see figure 28). The university soon boasted total assets, on paper at least, including pledges from 966 citizens, of nearly $10 million, an impressive sum in the mid-1920s. The metal and concrete frame for its frontispiece building began to rise on the prominence of the site Merrick had donated. The institution's regents and their architects intended this building to set a high architectural standard, rich in detail, for the campus to follow. This first building would be fronted by the university lake, which would reflect a great tower, based on the Giralda of Seville, rising to a height of two hundred feet to announce the university's presence (figure 50). On February 4, 1926, Merrick addressed the crowd gathered to lay the cornerstone for the university's Solomon

FIG. 49. Preliminary study, master plan, University of Miami. Paul Chalfin, Denman Fink, and Phineas Paist. Courtesy of Special Collections, University of Miami Libraries, Coral Gables, Florida.

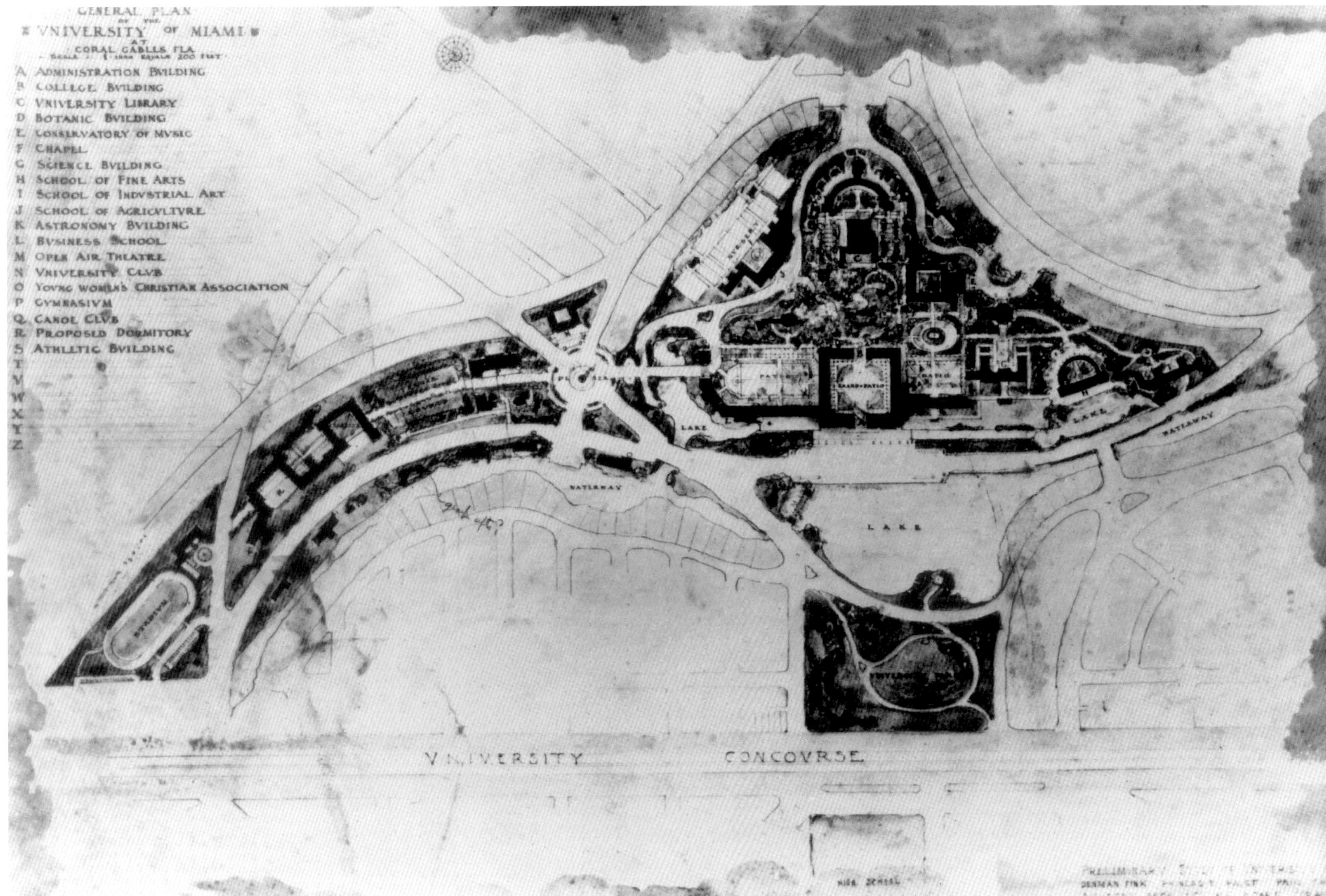
GENERAL PLAN
OF THE
VNIVERSITY OF MIAMI
AT
CORAL GABLES FLA
A ADMINISTRATION BVILDING
B COLLEGE BVILDING
C VNIVERSITY LIBRARY
D BOTANIC BVILDING
E CONSERVATORY OF MVSIC
F CHAPEL
G SCIENCE BVILDING
H SCHOOL OF FINE ARTS
I SCHOOL OF INDVSTRIAL ART
J SCHOOL OF AGRICVLTVRE
K ASTRONOMY BVILDING
L BVSINESS SCHOOL
M OPEN AIR THEATRE
N VNIVERSITY CLVB
O YOVNG WOMEN'S CHRISTIAN ASSOCIATION
P GYMNASIVM
Q CANOE CLVB
R PROPOSED DORMITORY
S ATHLETIC BVILDING
T
V
W
X
Y
Z
LAKE
WATERWAY
LAKE
LAKE
VNIVERSITY CONCOVRSE
HIGH SCHOOL

FIG. 50. Rendering, Solomon G. Merrick Building. University of Miami Historic Photo Collection, Box 16, Folder 75. Courtesy of Special Collections, University of Miami Libraries, Coral Gables, Florida.

G. Merrick Building, named for his father, a Methodist minister: "Proud as I am of what has been accomplished for Miami in Coral Gables, I am prouder of this University beginning than of everything else put together" (figure 51).[2]

Manley shared the tribulations that befell the University of Miami only seven months after that glorious moment. She lived through the infamous hurricane of September 18, 1926, that brought all its building plans to a halt, and she suffered, as did virtually everyone who had invested time and money in the region, a catastrophic reversal of her own fortunes. Everything was ruined in her architectural office when seven feet of water washed through it, as she wrote her father, lamenting, "I don't mind anything so much as the books. I have been scraping together a library of good architectural books, and saving magazine plates and other data for ten years and it's all a total loss." In the wake of that hurricane, she continued, "We lead the simple life."[3]

Well before the Great Depression that was soon to engulf the rest of the country, the collapse of the Florida real estate boom, along with the university's reversals, struck hard in the small pioneering communities just south of Miami's

FIG. 51. Dedication, Solomon G. Merrick Building, 1926. University of Miami Historic Photo Collection, Box 16, Folder 77. Courtesy of Special Collections, University of Miami Libraries, Coral Gables, Florida.

center—Coral Gables and Coconut Grove, where Manley lived. The deserted "skeleton" of the Merrick Building—the concrete and metal frame that would be sheathed only by weeds during the next twenty-three years—stood in their midst as a monument to shattered hopes. However, its stark geometry might well have resonated in a professional's eye with images on the pages of avant-garde architectural publications that showed simple unadorned forms dominated by the clear right angles of a new "international style," as the Museum of Modern Art began to call it in 1932.

As Manley's experience of resorting to cramped living quarters in the Coconut Grove home of her friend Marjory Stoneman Douglas suggests, in these hard times people in the Miami area relied closely on one another, mutual dependence strengthening bonds of friendship. By the time the war broke out, the architect numbered among her close friends Barbara Ashe, a daughter of Bowman Foster Ashe, president of the University of Miami (figure 52). He had moved from Pittsburgh, where he was an administrator at the University of Pittsburgh, to become the founding president of the newly minted institution when its prospects looked bright.

After the hurricane, Ashe's struggling little college "did not even have the promised 160-acre campus." According to a writer for the *Saturday Evening Post* who interviewed Ashe in 1949, "In the frenzied land trading of the boom, titles became inextricably tangled in a maze of mortgages and when the university finally got around to analyzing its gift, it discovered that all but the forty-odd acres on which the skeleton building sat belonged to somebody else. Of the $8,879,000 that had been promised, the school finally got about $200,000."[4] The hurricane and the collapse of the real estate bubble marked the beginning of financial deprivation that was, along with architectural trends, to weigh heavily on the university's postwar decision to build simple modern buildings, devoid of expensive traditional detailing, and to use local architects to design them.

Bowman Ashe is generally credited with nearly miraculous skill in keeping the institution afloat through painfully lean years.[5] Only a month after the hurricane, he welcomed his first 125 students to makeshift quarters in preexisting buildings near downtown Coral Gables (figures 53 and 54). This was about a mile north of the site that Merrick, soon bankrupt, had given. The University of Miami, dubbed "the Cardboard College" during those years "for its habit of expanding its facilities by setting up another fiberboard partition," briefly went bankrupt too, but Ashe's financial maneuvering and the community's support pulled it through.[6]

Just when Marion Manley became professionally involved with this institution to which her friend's father was devoting his life is not clear. The earliest record that has come to light of payment by the university to Marion Manley

FIG. 52. President Bowman Ashe looking over model of new master plan for the University of Miami, 1949 *Ibis* (yearbook). Courtesy of Special Collections, University of Miami Libraries, Coral Gables, Florida.

FIG. 53. Anastasia Building, north campus, Coral Gables. University of Miami Historic Photo Collection, Box 14, Folder 2. Courtesy of Special Collections, University of Miami Libraries, Coral Gables, Florida.

FIG. 54. Anastasia Building, north campus, Coral Gables. University of Miami Historic Photo Collection, Box 14, Folder 2. Courtesy of Special Collections, University of Miami Libraries, Coral Gables, Florida.

for architectural services is dated March 12, 1940, though what she had done for a fee of ninety dollars is not specified.[7] Two months later, she was collecting seventy-eight dollars "in connection with sketches for a proposed music auditorium," for a site on the downtown Coral Gables campus that had been growing incrementally through prolonged, though it was still hoped temporary, occupation.[8] At its founding, the university had absorbed a local music conservatory whose head, Bertha Foster, was among the board's most effective proselytizers of farsighted ambitions for the whole institution. From its earliest years her concerts drew large audiences from the community, and her courses attracted many students. Because Foster's music department was an important magnet for revenue-producing support, it is not surprising that an imposing setting for musical performance would have been proposed at this time, and a willing donor sought.

However, it is surprising, given the straight lines and right angles of Manley's earlier work (and of most that followed), that her design for a music auditorium at the university is all swoops, curves, and broad spans (figure 55). Its great rise in a single gesture seems born of engineers' calculations. Manley's "Esquisse," as she inscribed her proposal for the structure, is dated May 6, 1940; it is preserved in the university's archive as a blueprint showing the structure in plan and sections. The image suggests just how daring her architectural tastes had become.

For this auditorium, Manley proposed an unadorned, clean-lined, functional, very large shell that extended over a stage for the musicians; behind a seating area for three thousand people, another six thousand seats would have been open to the sky. Her transverse section of the shell shows a long hemi-ellipse, soaring seventy-five feet at its center. The plan is shaped like that of a household iron, an elongated triangle with smoothly curving angles. The shape conforms to the triangular site designated for an auditorium on the map showing expansion plans for the university in downtown Coral Gables published in a local newspaper in June 1940 (figure 56).[9] This site was near the athletic fields and several

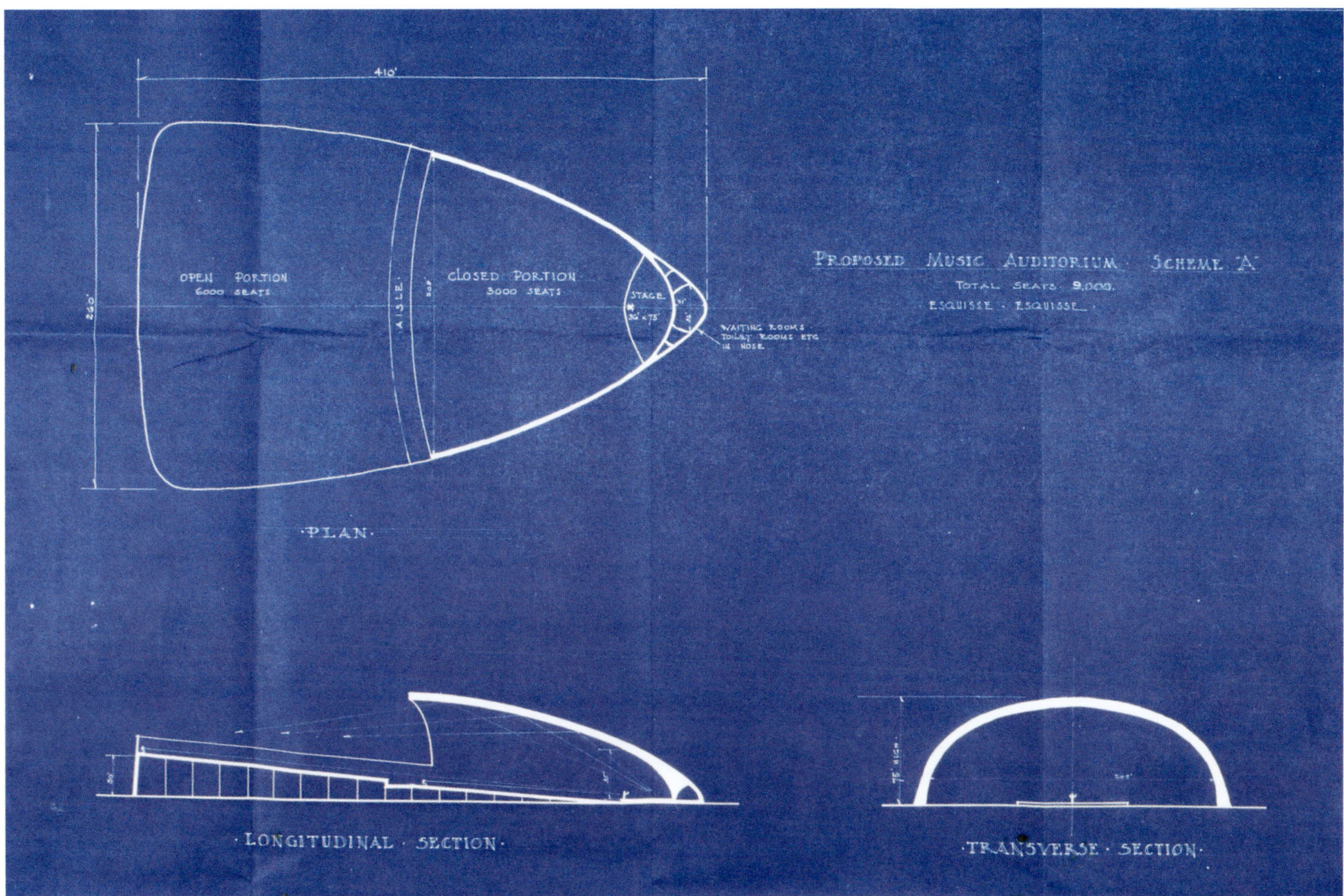

FIG. 55. Blueprint, proposed music auditorium, 1940. Courtesy of Special Collections, University of Miami Libraries, Coral Gables, Florida.

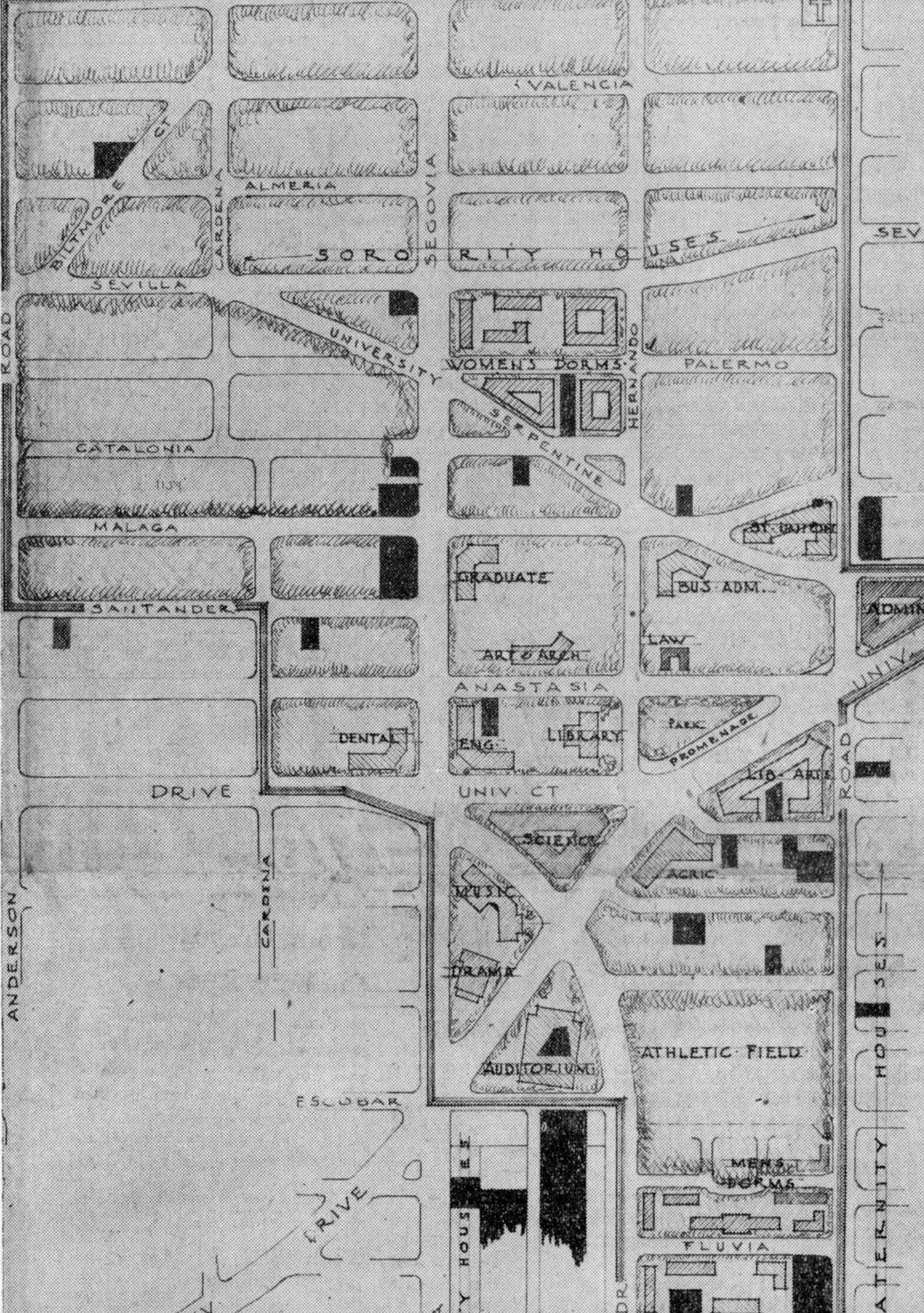

FIG. 56. North campus plan, University of Miami, 1940. Coral Gables, Riviera, June 14, 1940. Courtesy of Special Collections, University of Miami Libraries, Coral Gables, Florida.

blocks southwest of the major, very traditional buildings then occupied by the institution.

Nothing in Manley's earlier surviving work foreshadows this streamlined modern design. From the time when she must have been evolving toward such a radical form, we have no drawings that might seem to be its precursors. Although we cannot document just what she was reading at the time, we have plenty of evidence that she kept up with the professional literature, including her letter to her father lamenting the loss of her personal library in the hurricane of 1926, and a newspaper account of 1952 that notes, "When she reads, she reads the current literature that touches on any phase of architecture."[10] We can, however, speculate about her sources with some confidence informed by visual clues in the work itself. The forms she drew for the music auditorium might be traced to Le Corbusier's illustration captioned "Air Resistance of Various Forms," published in 1927 in *Towards a New Architecture* (figure 57), the same illustration that inspired so much streamlined design of the 1930s.[11] This early design for Miami's musicians is but the first of Manley's surviving drawings that bear earmarks of a disciple of Le Corbusier. It was never executed, and she was never to have anything requiring such bold engineering built on any Miami campus.

Because she does not seem to have been a theorist nor to have written at any length about architecture, at least not in any documents, published or unpublished, that have come to light, we cannot fix precisely when Marion Manley embraced architectural modernism. Nor do we know when she first began to label as "pseudo-Spanish" the buildings the university used for more than two decades in the center of Coral Gables, traditional buildings conforming to the locally dominant Mediterranean mode.[12] Her very earliest design work is unpublished. The hurricane took her earliest drawings, and she herself threw out papers that had accumulated in her office by 1968, when she moved to a smaller space.[13] She did continue to produce traditional designs for clients who wanted them, such as the house of 1938 for Denman Fink, and she valued that design highly enough to save the drawings (see figures 37 and 38). However, by 1940 her

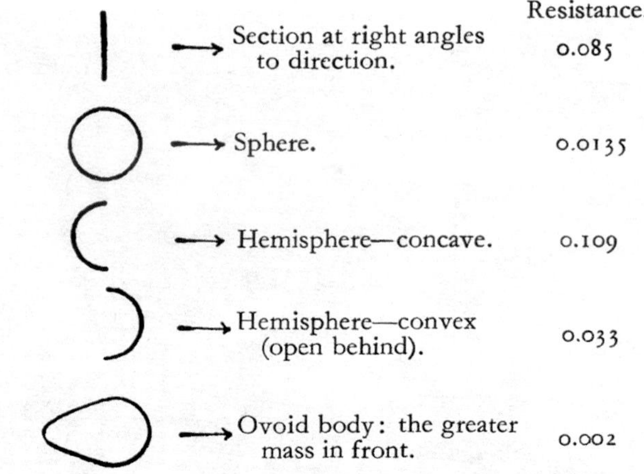

FIG. 57. "Air Resistance of Various Forms," in Le Corbusier, *Towards a New Architecture* (1927).

real enthusiasm was clearly for the modern, for staying current with her profession. And her profession was fast embracing the international style in the years leading up to the war.

By the time the United States joined the Allied cause in December 1941, Manley's blueprint for a performance shell had been permanently shelved. Well before Pearl Harbor, the university's focus had been diverted from its music school to preparations for war. The U.S. response to events in Europe brought a burst of activity to the campus that brightened the financial prospects of the little Florida college that depended so heavily on tuition to keep its doors open. In August 1940, as Americans were becoming more concerned about the European "emergency" but remained deeply divided about whether or not to commit the country fully to war, the federal government began sending army air corps cadets to the campus for twelve-week courses in long-range air navigation and meteorology. Seven months later, trainees for the British Royal Air Force arrived to take those same courses, the first of more than a thousand Brits to follow, clearly foreshadowing what lay ahead. The government's preparations to join the Allies' cause more than a year before Pearl Harbor included the U.S. Office of Education utilizing the campus for "engineering science management war training" courses.

Once the United States was fully committed to the Allied cause, there was a temporary drain on Miami's enrollment, which had grown to 1,625 at the start of the 1940–41 academic year. But just as enlistment and the draft were shrinking those numbers, crowds in uniform began to arrive for war-related courses. In March 1942 the navy's V-12 program—regular college courses with heavy emphasis on mathematics and science—swelled the ranks of student trainees. During that same year, to accommodate courses that the army air force was conducting in the Anastasia Building, unfinished but occupied since 1926, the army paid to erect a long-planned tower (figure 58).[14] By the war's end, Miami's war-related courses, including the navy's V-5 program for fliers, had brought more than

FIG. 58. Troops marching in front of the Anastasia Building, 1943 *Ibis* (yearbook). Courtesy of Special Collections, University of Miami Libraries, Coral Gables, Florida.

ninety-five hundred civilian and service trainees through makeshift classrooms on the makeshift campus in downtown Coral Gables.[15]

Marion Manley was the person to whom Bowman Ashe turned for architectural work as he squeezed in so many students. And it was during the early years of the war, as many local architects were joining the military services, that she was first elected president of the South Florida Chapter of the AIA (1941–42). Manley left Miami briefly during this period to take a planning course during the summer of 1942 at MIT in Cambridge, a city whose architectural community was astir with recently imported Bauhaus thinking. Walter Gropius and Marcel Breuer had brought their modernist ideology to nearby Harvard, where they were transforming architectural education with a model that was soon to eclipse the Beaux-Arts teaching traditions of the leading American architectural schools. Manley's course work at MIT was heavily influenced by the "revolution in planning" that Le Corbusier had ignited in Paris during the 1920s, and that Clarence Stein and Henry Wright had begun to apply and develop later in that decade at Radburn, New Jersey.[16] There, giving priority to the problem of "how to live with the auto," those most influential American planners of the period focused on separating pedestrians from vehicles and on zoning, bringing us "cul-de-sacs" and "superblocks," along with the asymmetrical placement of buildings within the free-form spaces of superblocks. Their model was soon to change the shape of American cities as well as of Miami's campus. Manley's stay in Cambridge left her with a lifelong scorn for the grid of interconnected streets, traditional blocks, and mixed neighborhoods of an earlier American planning tradition that Merrick had adapted so effectively for Coral Gables.

Meanwhile, Bowman Ashe was off to Atlanta in August 1942, called into service as director of the War Manpower Commission, a job he held for a year, during which he returned to his campus only for hurried visits. Therefore he and Manley had some correspondence that provides rare written documentation of the sorts of exchanges that normally would have been spoken and unrecorded.

It is not only revealing of the wit that was mentioned so often in stories about Manley, but also of the character of this woman's important role at the university during the war.

By February 3, 1943, Ashe's university was again paying Marion Manley for professional services, this time for "a special plot plan," almost certainly the one dated January 19, 1943, that survives in the archives.[17] Focused on the intersection of Le Jeune Road and University Drive in downtown Coral Gables, it proposes a library on the site now occupied by the Coral Gables Youth Center and a classroom building across University Drive. Although Manley was not yet on the payroll on February 10, 1943, her letter of that date suggests that she was already working as if she were an employee, acting on Ashe's behalf in dealing with both donors and their architects. She wrote that a donor, George A. Brockway, had asked her to review both the plans and the letter he had received from his New York architect about a library he was giving and to make "any suggestions I think proper." She noted that while this building was proposed in what she called a "pseudo-colonial style," a classroom building was in the works "in a style vaguely allied to the pseudo-Spanish of your acquired buildings," and she pointed out awkwardness in the relative positioning of their entrances. She warned Ashe about the school's "lack of thoughtful planning," saying it "weighed upon" and "burdened" her, and she asked for an appointment to talk about this during his next visit to Miami. When Ashe replied three days later, he agreed "that we are in danger of getting into an architectural hodge-podge around there, which would be too bad. Maybe you, in your own sweet way, can prevent too much mixture."[18]

In concluding her letter Marion Manley mentioned that she intended to close her office and "find somewhere, somehow, either a position or a job to help win the war, and the way prospects look here, I will be somewhere else." Ashe could well have known that during the First World War Manley had left Miami for Philadelphia to contribute to that war effort by designing ships and that she meant what she said. By this time, as their correspondence makes clear, he was relying heavily on her, especially since so many of the local architects were going off to war, as were about half his faculty and staff. He had many incentives to keep her in Miami, working for him. So, to Manley's announcement of her plan to leave town, Ashe replied, "I shall keep an eye out for something in the job or position line." And promptly indeed he had spotted—or perhaps created—a salaried job for Marion Manley at the University of Miami.[19]

Her somewhat amused response to his job offer is dated April 15, 1943: "Were you serious about my teaching mechanical drawing to the salty sailors? If so: (1) Will they accept me in skirts or will I have to wear pants? (2) Don't you think I'd better have someone teach mechanical drawing to me, between now and July first? It has been almost exactly thirty years since I last met the subject. (3) How much time per day and how many days per week would it be apt to take?" Ashe replied on April 19: "I suggest you go on the payroll as of about April 22. Then go over to the University and sit in on the mechanical drawing [class] and find out about it. . . . Your job will take practically all of your available time every day. They should give you an office at the University where you can do any of your own work, which will be a side line from this time on." His letter continues, "We should like to have you do some sketching in connection with building proposals, such as you have done in the past."[20]

From Marion Manley's point of view, serving a university that was so manifestly serving the armed forces must have seemed a good way to make a personal contribution to the Allies' cause, and it assured her a steady salary of $250 each month, while at the same time generously allowing her to keep her hand in her own practice using her office space on campus. In addition to Manley's role as "instructor in mechanical drawing" through the trimesters of 1943–44, she was soon busy with all sorts of minor additions and adaptations to the school's quarters near the center of Coral Gables, for which drawings survive in the archive (figure 59).[21]

Her role during these early years of the war, whether Ashe planned it that way or it evolved ad hoc, was one that had by now been well established at older

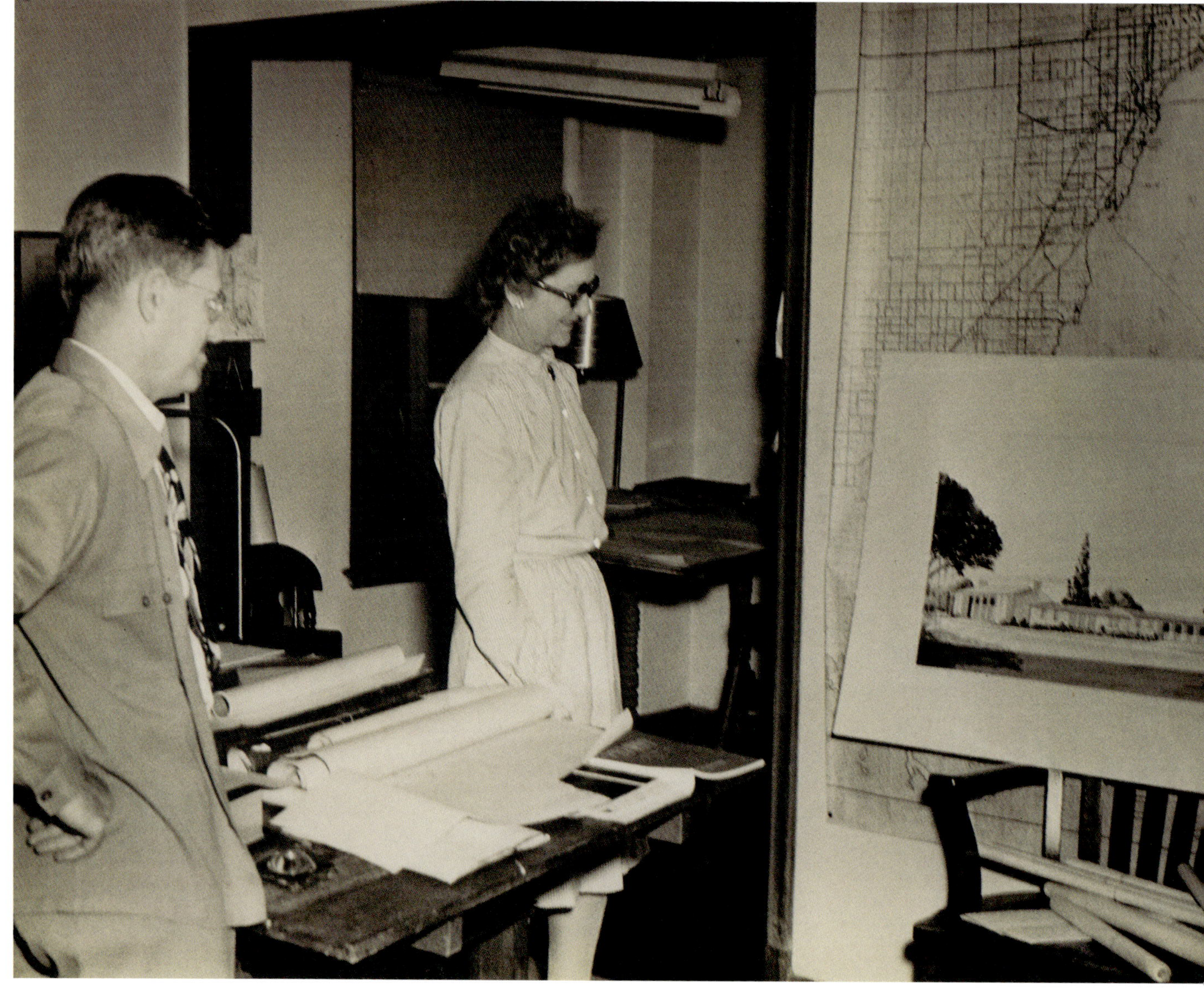

FIG. 59. Manley and an unidentified man at her University of Miami office. Courtesy of Special Collections, University of Miami Libraries, Coral Gables, Florida.

American colleges. It would have been understood that the many responsibilities of a campus architect included not only those of a designer renovating or adding to existing buildings and planning new ones, but also those of critic and coordinator of the work of others, a preplanner who expected to see, and to oversee, the more detailed design development of major buildings carried out by other architects. As university architect, Manley had an office in Room 120 of the administration building, from which, in April 1943, she wrote Ashe in Atlanta that she was "acting as your plenipotentiary-at-large," reviewing another architect's plans for a proposed library.[22]

Miami's archives include drawings and blueprints that document all manner of minor work that landed on her desk during the war. By June 1943 she was adding a kitchen porch to the main building, in July sketching a dining room for the administration building, in September making additions to a kitchen and boiler room, and in October drawing up modest athletic facilities—an open shed, boxing rings, and so on. On October 6 the university's secretary sent a memorandum to the treasurer, raising Manley's monthly salary to four hundred dollars, in compensation for her "great deal of architectural work for the University." Also in October 1943 she designed a relatively traditional, rather large classroom building for that site on University Drive that had appeared on the plan she had made earlier in the year (figure 60). The blueprints for this proposal show a structure congenial enough with the Mediterranean detailing of neighboring buildings on the campus, though its traditional forms are simplified. Its low-pitched roofs stretch over a length of 267 feet.[23] Her design appears to be a reduced version of a design by another hand, that of her former employer the local architect Harold Steward, which was already before Ashe. Ashe mentioned it in his letter of April 19 to Manley: "I may ask the War Production Board to allow us to build a classroom building almost any time now, because the Navy would like to have some additional training programs. You might sketch out one building in the location you mentioned, which would be one storey high, and

FIG. 60. Preliminary design for classroom building. Courtesy of Special Collections, University of Miami Libraries, Coral Gables, Florida.

also change the face of that two storey building which was earlier designed in Steward's office for the same location."

Marion Manley was also called upon during this period to design for an outpost of the university on Virginia Key, where a marine laboratory had been established in 1942. In 1944 its ambitious director, F. G. Walton Smith, had Manley draw up elaborate plans for a "Dade County Aquarium" (figure 61). He worked closely with her, as their correspondence of the mid-1940s reveals, especially on the technical programming and layout, evolving a scheme intended to serve the university's marine biologists and to attract tourists. Their collaboration produced an ungainly arrangement of units awkwardly joined to bend and curve as mirror images of one another about an axis centered on a square tower that rose in stages. In Manley's drawings, two open tanks form matching ovals at bayside, surrounded by observation decks, and from them low wings bend outward and landward, a little crablike, to form closed courtyards behind the central, generously glazed curve of a large entry and exhibition hall. This "Miami marine laboratory and oceanarium" would not have been out of place at a World's Fair of the 1930s.

Smith was to use Manley's illustrations first in lobbying for the county's financial support of a joint venture with the university to build "the New Miami Oceanarium . . . three times as large" as Marineland in North Florida, and "even further ahead in its ingenious modern arrangements and wealth of exhibits. It will be far and away the most magnificent show of its kind in the world." Estimating its cost in 1944 at $1.5 million, he persuaded the county to put before the voters a proposal for funding it as a bond issue. Apparently voters were not persuaded that it would in fact become, as Smith's publicity release with Manley's illustrations had described it, "a source of income for the County Government." Once it was voted down, Smith unsuccessfully pursued private support for the project into the 1950s, still using Manley's drawings in his fund-raising campaign and publishing them widely.[24]

FIG. 61. Preliminary sketches for aquarium and marine laboratory, Virginia Key, Florida, 1944. Courtesy of Special Collections, University of Miami Libraries, Coral Gables, Florida.

Manley's involvement with schemes to house the university's scientists on Virginia Key spanned more than a decade. She traveled with Smith and the county engineer to study the operation at Marineland in August 1945, and that September she went to Chicago to examine the Shedd Aquarium. When Robert Moses, the master planner of New York whose schemes included an ambitious aquarium, visited Miami to lecture in February 1946, Smith invited him out to the key for a meeting about their mutual interest.[25] And the

FIG. 62. Rendering, University of Miami marine laboratory at Virginia Key. Courtesy of Special Collections, University of Miami Libraries, Coral Gables, Florida.

aquarium project was still on Manley's mind near the decade's end, as attested by a surviving letter that begins: "Dear Walton: Although no authorization has come through on your Marine Laboratory, I have not stopped contemplating same."[26] As late as May 28, 1949, she was submitting to Smith working drawings and specifications for a less ambitious marine laboratory (figure 62).[27] But in 1953, when the university finally constructed a much more modest building, costing about thirty-seven thousand dollars, to serve as a marine laboratory on Virginia Key, John L. Skinner, not Marion Manley, was its architect.[28] The seaquarium that opened two years later on Virginia Key, though it appears to have borrowed a few ideas from Manley's design, was not hers, nor was it affiliated with the university. Hatched during wartime, Walton Smith's aquarium scheme was rather grandiose for the time, and though his campaign to realize it dragged on well past the war's end, Manley's much-publicized designs were never built.

In contrast to that prolonged and fruitless campaign to build a Manley design, the university rushed to complete her more mundane work of the mid-1940s for its downtown Coral Gables campus. She was surely called upon to adapt the "property, usually residential" that the university continued to buy and lease around the busy intersection of Le Jeune Road and University Drive in order to accommodate war-related enrollment.[29] Construction supervision was part of her task, as well as the minor design work for which documentation survives. This last included a storage building for scientific materials, for which she wrote specifications in March 1944. A month later, the university was applying to the War Production Board for authority to construct it.

As distracting as the details of stretching the capacities of the makeshift campus must have been, Bowman Ashe and his trustees had not lost sight of their original ambition to create a much larger campus to the south, on the land Merrick had donated in the 1920s. As late as 1938, Phineas Paist had submitted, in partnership with Harold Steward, proposals for that site. Their drawings are in the university archive. Stylistically and in their layout, they are much like the original "Mediterranean" campus plan on which those same architects had worked in the mid-1920s (see figures 48 and 49).

Still, the Coral Gables community remained uncertain about where the university would expand in the future. Two years after Paist and Steward's scheme for the south campus site, the newspapers published a map projecting campus growth around the downtown Coral Gables buildings that the university had occupied for nearly two decades. The appearance of this plan led logically enough to local assumption that all hope was gone for the university ever occupying the tract to the south.

But while the original Mediterranean image was fading in the minds of Ashe and his board, they were in fact refocusing on the land that Merrick had given the university in the 1920s. They had nearly lost the site around the University Lake, for which the institution then held title, because of failure to pay taxes, and outstanding liens were paid in 1941. Then, beginning in 1942 and gaining momentum dramatically in 1944, their development efforts were rewarded with increasing financial support locally, as Charlton Tebeau chronicles in his history of the university.

In 1943 Manley and Ashe had "started hunting an ideal site for the new university," according to a story about Manley published in the *Miami Herald* five years later, and by November 1944, the trustees had authorized Ashe and two other men "to choose the location, to negotiate for and acquire land, and to announce the location when they saw fit."[30] They reviewed three alternately proposed locations, all much nearer the shore but only one within Coral Gables, at Cocoplum Plaza, a little to the southeast of the present campus. After considering two other sites, both on Biscayne Bay, one to the south, the other the magnificent James Deering estate, Vizcaya, to the northeast and closer to downtown Miami, the committee fixed on Merrick's donated land in Coral Gables and began assembling adjacent parcels piece by piece.[31]

Nor had the old concrete skeleton been neglected. In September 1944 Manley submitted to Ashe a "study of old building frame, south campus," with an

FIG. 63. Solomon G. Merrick Building, 1926–49. University of Miami Historic Photo Collection, Box 16, Folder 80. Courtesy of Special Collections, University of Miami Libraries, Coral Gables, Florida.

engineer's report and an "estimate of reproduction cost of structural framework of existing building at South Campus," figured at $143,851 (figure 63). Though rusting and overgrown, the structure that had risen in the mid-1920s on Merrick's donated land was a valuable asset the trustees decided not to squander. By March 1945 they could announce publicly their intention to develop not only the original 160 acres Merrick had given but also additional acreage surrounding that core, which brought the total holdings to 245 acres.

Well before that announcement was made, Ashe and Manley had brought another local architect, Robert Law Weed, into their campus planning process (figure 64). In 1944 he was Major Weed, a forty-seven-year-old veteran of the First

World War again in uniform, this time serving the army air corps in the India-Burma sector of the China-Burma-India theater. On August 20 he was awarded a Bronze Star for "meritorious achievement" including "outstanding results in standardizing transport field requirements." In terms suggesting experience that would prove valuable at Miami, the citation specified, "With limited personnel and equipment, he has labored constantly to build according to Air Transport Command planning standards for special facility needs of air transport. The plans initiated by Major Weed have aided considerably in the augmentation of the efficiency of the bases."[32] The major's experience in standardization, and in building successfully and for efficiency within challenging limitations, was soon put to use on a campus where limitations of both time and money were paramount. His proven efficiency in the cost-cutting standardization of building components was to be much publicized.

Weed addressed the university president as "My dear Bowman" when he wrote during that same month he received the citation, and he signed the letter "Bob Weed." In 1944 using the first name of a university president on the verge of hiring the letter writer for an enormous job was not something casually done. Clearly enough, they were friends, though Ashe was a dozen years older. Weed had come to Miami in 1919, two years after the arrival of Manley, who was only four years his senior. Weed began this same letter to Ashe: "I received a very interesting letter from Marion Manley," confirming the story Marjory Stoneman Douglas was later to tell, that it was Manley who brought Weed into the project. Weed wrote in that same letter, "The confidence you have expressed in my being able to render a service in the new development as told me by Marion is appreciated. More appreciated, because I have not been forgotten while away." His words brim with enthusiasm for architecture's beginning anew after the war, and for the Miami job itself: "The opportunity offered to any architect by your project is great." And later: "What a chance for the structure to really mean something to those who use it."[33]

FIG. 64. Robert Law Weed. Courtesy of the Historical Museum of Southern Florida.

Giving credence to our understanding that a modernist vision for the campus originated with Manley and Ashe before any other architect was brought in, Weed's letter continues: "The idea expressed by Marion arouses my imagination and is stimulating." Manley afterward recalled, "Dr. Ashe gave full support to the development of a plan that broke with the antique notions of what a university plan should be."[34]

Weed's own ideas about architecture as he summarized them in this letter were doubtless of the sort he had discussed with Marion Manley when they were both active in the local AIA chapter before the war. Weed's words are especially valuable to our study of Manley since she wrote no architectural theory of her own during this period, or none that we have found, and because her choosing to bring Weed on board for this project signaled at the very least her general agreement with his basic approach to design. Weed's written words, then, are a valuable supplement to the visual evidence provided by Manley's design work, giving us some sense of her thinking.

In accord with Manley's disdain for the "pseudo-Spanish" is Weed's scorn for the traditional buildings of Coral Gables that comes through in sentences such as "I hope that the thinking in the planning and design will not be hampered by too much 'Coral Gables' and too much of the 'old school tie' type of thinking." As Weed went on, he used terms that he might well have taken from the pages of Sigfried Giedion's *Space, Time, and Architecture*, published in 1941, or from the Bauhaus masters and Le Corbusier: "Certainly in a city that is recognized as being ahead of its time and in a fast growing section of the country, the opportunity exists for the physical plant of the University to express truthfully the reason it exists. I think it would be a crime to teach our American youths Engineering in monastic halls or Renaissance libraries. At least I hope that the least that can be said is that the Engineering construction is honest and of our time." His notion that architecture must "express truthfully" and be "honest," must avoid committing an imagined "crime" by continuing old traditions, is typical of the

European modernists' habit of evaluating architecture in moral terms, making it clear enough that Weed, like them, gave precedence to architectural morality over aesthetic criteria. Weed is equally clear about his belief in architecture's obligation to express the zeitgeist—the spirit of the time: He uses those very words, "of our time" that were deemed crucial to architecture's purpose by midcentury American architects who took them from the European theorists and repeated them often during this period.

Long before the war, Weed's buildings had given evidence of his fervor to innovate, to adapt modernism to Florida's climate. For Chicago's Century of Progress Exhibition of 1933–34 he had designed, in association with Paist and Steward, a "Florida tropical house," constructed entirely of materials from the state. According to the pamphlet that was given to visitors at the fair, the model structure was aimed at clients "who saw the old be-dormered, the be-gabled dream house as a dream that belonged in a fairy tale."[35] Weed, like Manley, had catered to just such dreams earlier in his Miami career.

Major Weed was back from the Far East by April 1945, still in the army air forces, serving at air transport command headquarters in Washington, when he met in that city first with Manley "going over schemes," then wired Ashe that he thought it "important to the progress of your planning" that they too meet when Ashe was to come a few days later to the capitol. A letter to Ashe from Weed, who was still in Washington four months later, reveals that the major was already much involved in designing the new campus. He writes, "I am informed by my cohorts there that our work is progressing," work in which Manley must then have been carrying most of the burden. He lets Ashe know that it "apparently will not be necessary" to "assist" in the architect's "separation from the Army," because "it appears that I will be out within a few weeks" and, on leave, "will be in Miami about the 29th."[36]

Clearly, the university president felt it was urgent to get Weed right to the task of designing the new campus, even before his military obligation had ended. This was doubtless propelled by a realization that veterans, the first of whom had registered for classes at the University of Miami on October 8, 1943, would soon be taking advantage of the GI Bill—the Servicemen's Readjustment Act of 1944—which Roosevelt had signed into law in June of that same year. If the university was ever to grow to the size to which it aspired, and to do so on a sound financial basis, it could not miss the opportunity to collect the government-subsidized fees that men home from the war were soon lining up to hand over to every educational institution in America. Miami actively recruited veterans, relying on images of modern architecture, which was only in the planning stages, to reinforce the forward-looking message of its recruiting texts. The *University of Miami Bulletin* issued on January 1, 1945, was addressed primarily to "students from the armed forces," assuring them on page 1 that "all students who have had military training may feel confident that this institution will give them every consideration and full cooperation in their efforts to resume their studies and complete such university training as they may desire." Manley's perspective drawings of substantial modern buildings were the featured illustrations in this *Bulletin*, though none of these buildings was yet a reality and few, including the aquarium, were ever to be built. In the spring term of 1945, enrollment swelled to more than three thousand.

Bowman Ashe foresaw great possibilities for the immediate future under the GI Bill, which would pay to educate millions who had never before expected they might be able to afford a college education. He and his board did not want to miss this chance to expand enrollment to ten thousand, the goal that had been set back in Merrick's day, and they wanted to make the campus itself attractive to servicemen who, under the bill, could choose any college they liked.[37]

Robert Law Weed must have recognized that Ashe, who, with Manley's help, had already used pictures of proposed modern buildings to promote the institution, would be receptive to ideas for expanding the use of such imagery, taking it to full campus scale, as an enticement to prospective students. It would be emblematic of the aspirations of a forward-looking young institution. As Weed was negotiating his contract, jockeying for a higher-than-usual fee, he wrote to

Ashe on September 14, 1945: "Our services . . . will differ considerably from the usual architectural services in that we become virtually a part of the development department of the University." He committed himself to "be of service in the promotional work. . . . This . . . will include representation of the Board . . . before Governmental agencies, lending agencies, or with donors, other architects, engineers, and the public." A salesman oozing confidence in his personal skill as a public relations man, Weed was selling himself as more than an architect. He added that "the architects will cooperate with your publicity department in the preparation of sketches, drawings, or informational data concerning the development and construction program." And just in case his intention was not clear—to get a relatively obscure college into the newspapers and magazines by dazzling the country with pictures of a campus like nothing seen before—Weed added, "It is my idea that the present construction program and the overall plan for development should be given maximum publicity and be kept constantly before the public."[38]

The strategy Weed spelled out was embraced by the university's board. They hired him, and they did indeed expand the use of Manley's and Weed's modernist designs to sell the school to prospective students, donors, financial institutions, and the government. The architects' drawings reinforced the image of a university of the future, if not one with much of a past. Miami successfully launched itself on the course that was to attract thousands of GIs with federal funding in hand, and to bring the co-eds with them, even before the new campus was built.

In November 1945 Weed returned to Miami and reopened his office, "expanding his organization over its pre-war size . . . associated with . . . other veterans," with "Miss Marion Manley associate architect for the University."[39] Not only did a contractual arrangement for professional services between the university and Robert Law Weed then become effective, but so too did the university's new arrangement with Manley. As of November 13, 1945, she ceased to be an employee, the university became her client, and soon her name appeared on a new letterhead: "Robert Law Weed and Marion I. Manley, Associate Architects-Engineers, Miami, Florida." Weed and Manley signed a contract with the University of Miami on October 1, under which she was to receive $5,000 in annual fees, which came to $416.66 monthly, so she realized only $16.66 more than her old salary.[40] Weed's annual fee, $10,000, was double hers. The contract specified "services in connection with zoning, site planning, preliminary sketches of various structures and groups of structures," on what their new office was calling the "University of Miami Expansion Project." This project soon involved the architects not just in the building of permanent buildings on a new campus, but also in the arrangement of temporary buildings there, and perhaps in the university's adaptation of an old military base for temporary use, along with the continuing adaptation of the "north campus"—the old buildings in the center of Coral Gables.

We can follow the evolution of the architects' ideas through several schemes that had to be drastically altered when the university refocused its building program to qualify for a sudden bonanza of federal funding. Yet alongside the changes, we can see that the architects retained fundamental features from what appears to be the earliest scheme for the "new campus"—after September 1946 to be called the "main campus." This first plan took shape during 1945, and one suspects that Manley, as the person on the spot while Weed was still in the military through most of the year, took the lead in the design drawn up as the "new campus—bird's-eye view" (figure 65). This illustration is nearly diagrammatic: Most of the buildings are low, unadorned slabs—long rectangular bar shapes—with the exception of gymnasiums, field houses, and the Merrick Building. This last has a higher wing, and a tower—now a thin, straight-sided, flat-topped one, replacing the 1920s image of the Giralda. Landscaping is summarily suggested, largely by hasty broad strokes, although plantings appear to dominate the land surface.

It is difficult not to contrast this fundamentally dreary sketch with the eloquently conceived plan of the 1920s. Differences are certainly striking, both in

FIG. 65. Bird's-eye view of University of Miami campus. Courtesy of Special Collections, University of Miami Libraries, Coral Gables, Florida.

the architectural style and in the size of a layout expanded to cover newly acquired acreage to the south and west, where much of the campus now has frontage on Ponce de Leon Boulevard. Several major buildings—dormitories and athletic facilities—have been located on that new acreage. The lake has been enlarged and moved to the new land, so it no longer fronts and reflects the Merrick Building, the fixed landmark, largest on the plan, but now with a modernist skin and without its tower.

This modernist Merrick Building has become the frontispiece for the "central group" of buildings marked by a very thin unadorned tower near a library, part of the central group that dominates the original 160 acres (figure 66). That group also includes classroom and administration buildings. In the orthogonal layout of the slabs within this original part of the site, the imprint of the geometry of the 1920s is still apparent. Here administrative offices and classrooms are parallel with the Merrick Building or set at right angles to it and to one another, forming a broken grid. Within that grid, very narrow bars are extended by even lower covered walkways. Placed at right angles to the longest buildings are shorter slabs, to which additional transverse slabs are sometimes added, enclosing courtyards,

FIG. 66. Rendering, central group (colored pencil on board, 16′ x 26′). Courtesy of Special Collections, University of Miami Libraries, Coral Gables, Florida.

though more often the exterior spaces formed by the attached bars are open-ended, if still defined, outdoor rooms. The underlying geometry of the grid in this area is rational and orderly. While that geometry has not moved very far from that of Miami's campus plan of the 1920s, the stripping away of traditional detail and of the few circles and ovals of the old landscape are crucial. As in Merrick's plan, courtyards abound, though shorn of arcades. But the rich articulation, not to say the unity, of the old plan is almost entirely gone.

Right-angled geometry is retained for some of the dormitories on the new parcel extending south to Ponce de Leon Boulevard, where about half the structures shown are undifferentiated slabs or bars arranged in U-shaped configurations and oriented along the straight line of the public street. Other dormitory slabs are more randomly disposed along curving roads within the campus.

On the northern shore of the lake, edging part of the original Merrick tract, buildings of more distinctive and erratic shapes are shown—a theater, as well as a "student club and cafeteria" that extends over the lake, as does the stage of an amphitheater to its west. Nearby, drama and music departments appear a little inland. The road patterns here meander asymmetrically from the central group, and the placement of additional slabs within this area is also visually more random. The sites for buildings become even freer of geometric symmetry in much of the new parcel.

This early layout perhaps records attraction to two quite different models of modernist American campus planning available in the mid-1940s: Mies van der Rohe's plans of 1940 for his Illinois Institute of Technology (IIT), and Frank Lloyd Wright's for Florida Southern College, begun in 1938, both of which had been published before Weed and Manley began their work for Miami. But their campus plan appears to owe even more to Clarence Stein's town plans. The visual evidence that Stein's work increasingly influenced Manley and Weed's campus planning as it developed through two later iterations is reinforced by the fact that Stein delivered a lecture titled "The Form of Future Cities" at the University of Miami's Winter Institute of Arts and Sciences on January 15, 1945.[41]

In Manley and Weed's scheme for the central group, the tight geometric rationality of the modernist campus plan for IIT may have been remembered, if at some distance: The plan retains a memory of the clear visual coherence of Miesian place-making with generic bar buildings, toward which the decision to retain the old Merrick Building's skeleton provided an extra push. Beyond that core, the more random siting of object buildings perhaps owes something to Wright's plans for relatively nearby Lakeland, as might the covered walkways. However, the developing schemes for the University of Miami look much more like town plans by Stein, where zoning separates functions and the placement of buildings is relatively casual and is justified in "functional" rather than compositional terms. The Miami architects said again and again that the orientation of their structures was dictated by the prevailing breezes or by proximity to roadways.

"Roads circle the campus, rather than run through, with parking places situated near the walks," a student reported in the university's yearbook, the *Ibis*, published in the spring of 1946. Reserving large swathes of parklike land for foot traffic within the encircling road systems calls to mind Clarence Stein's emphasis on the separation of pedestrians from moving vehicles. The University of Miami's car-free interior is reminiscent of Radburn's superblock reserves of greenswards. By the time this early scheme was illustrated in the *Ibis*, it had been superseded at the architects' offices. Sketches for individual buildings also appear in the yearbook of 1946, developed in ways not anticipated on the overall campus plan they accompanied, and with a text that sometimes wanders so far from both plan and sketches that one suspects imaginative student misunderstanding of them. "The architecture is severely functional with simple lines and many windows," it says truly enough, going on to devote space to the "dormitories and fraternity and sorority houses." Miss Manley is quoted, "We tried to anticipate student requirements and take care of them." The text notes appreciatively that "sheltered walks between the buildings will protect students from sudden showers." Sure that the plans to accommodate ten thousand students would be realized by 1949, the *Ibis*'s reporter prophesized that the new campus would attract so many students that "then the next problem will be what to do with the extra 10,000 who will have to be turned away."[42]

Though much of this plan was soon to be abandoned, some of it apparently went through modifications intended as development toward construction. An undated illustration labeled "master plot plan" seems to record an intention to simplify this early scheme, eliminating many of its buildings as well as the covered walkways, so that the scheme might actually become something the university could afford to build.

In February 1946 Weed and Manley presented to Bowman Ashe their much-revised "University of Miami Expansion Program, Original South Campus Site Coral Gables, Florida," which was publicized in Miami during the subsequent months with a bird's-eye view captioned "dormitory and fine arts groups" (figure 67). Here the "fine arts group" north of the lake and the "central group" in the distant background remain much like those of the earliest plan, but the dormitories in the foreground are no longer slabs (figures 68–69). They have become cross-axial structures with plans whose debt to Le Corbusier's cruciform skyscrapers in his "Voisin Scheme for Paris" is visually apparent. However, for Miami's campus, the designers rather awkwardly chopped Le Corbusier's sixty-story skyscrapers down to four stories and fiddled with his patterning of floor plans in their design. They shifted their projecting units, typically three to a side, flanking the spines of each cross's arms. Rather than lining up these projecting units back-to-back across each cross's arms, as Le Corbusier had done, Weed and Manley staggered their units on either side of the arms, which became narrow corridors in the dormitory plans. The positioning of those corridors was also shifted so that they do not quite meet at the center.

For these dormitories the Miami designers appear to have taken the idea of the standardized "cells" and "flats"—living units Le Corbusier intended for low-rise dwellings with "set-backs"—and inserted them into a rift on his plan for skyscrapers "designed purely for business purposes," whose cruciform he valued for "doing away with an internal court and giving a maximum stability." In elevation, the conflation of the office type with the residential type still yielded

FIG. 67. Pencil rendering, dormitory and fine arts group. Courtesy of the Historical Museum of Southern Florida, Marion Manley Collection.

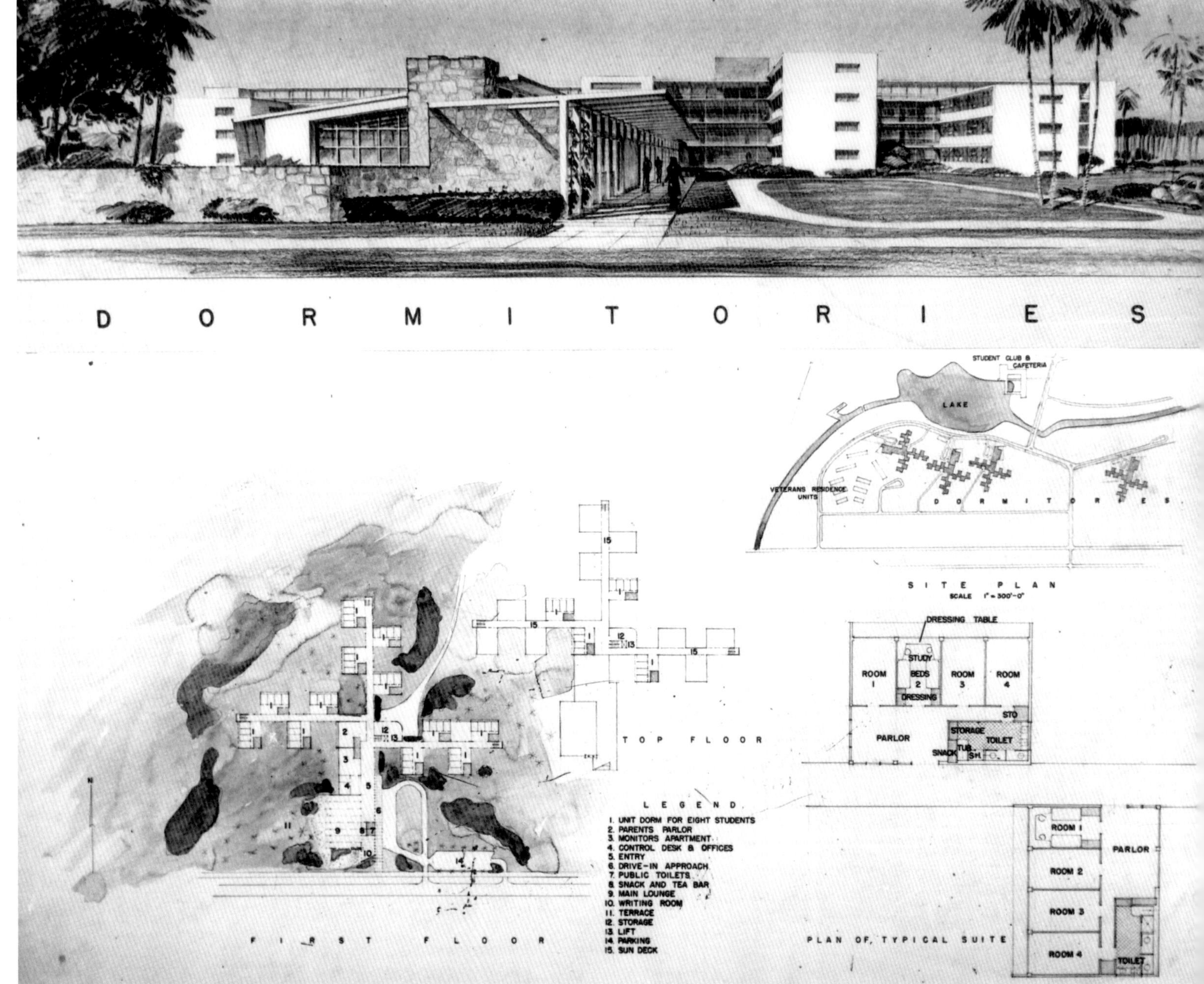
D O R M I T O R I E S
STUDENT CLUB & CAFETERIA
LAKE
VETERANS RESIDENCE UNITS
D O R M I T O R I E S
S I T E   P L A N
SCALE 1" = 300'-0"
DRESSING TABLE
ROOM 1
STUDY
BEDS 2
DRESSING
ROOM 3
ROOM 4
STO
PARLOR
STORAGE
TOILET
SNACK
TUB SH
T O P   F L O O R
L E G E N D
1. UNIT DORM FOR EIGHT STUDENTS
2. PARENTS PARLOR
3. MONITORS APARTMENT
4. CONTROL DESK & OFFICES
5. ENTRY
6. DRIVE-IN APPROACH
7. PUBLIC TOILETS
8. SNACK AND TEA BAR
9. MAIN LOUNGE
10. WRITING ROOM
11. TERRACE
12. STORAGE
13. LIFT
14. PARKING
15. SUN DECK
F I R S T   F L O O R
PLAN OF TYPICAL SUITE
ROOM 1
ROOM 2
ROOM 3
ROOM 4
PARLOR
TOILET

facades for Miami that, as Le Corbusier described his, "are deeply serrated and form veritable traps for light."[43]

Ashe could not find financing for any of the dormitories envisioned in these two sets of plans, and he rightly anticipated that veterans with young families were about to descend on his campus in the thousands, with government money in hand not only to cover tuition and most other direct educational costs, but also to contribute fifty dollars a month to their living expenses. As a writer for the *Saturday Evening Post* told the tale in 1949, Ashe was able to find a way to house the veterans by taking the timely advice of a mortgage broker, Thomas O'Toole, who told him about a pending bill. Under it, the Federal Housing Administration "could guarantee loans to educational institutions of good repute." Ashe is said to have moved quickly in 1945, with O'Toole's help, to secure the largest loan to that time—$4.969 million from the Trust Company of New Jersey—90 percent of the sum needed to build twenty-seven buildings with a total of 533 apartments. Each of these would be planned with a kitchen, living room, and bathroom, and could accommodate three to seven people. Although on-campus student apartments represented a radical departure from traditional American collegiate dormitories, "The FHA insisted on this arrangement to protect the loan, figuring that if the project failed and the university fell on its face again financially, they could foreclose on a property easily convertible into public housing."[44] As early as September 14, 1945, Weed wrote to Ashe, "The work is well under way on the G.I. housing," though it was not until December 21, 1946, that announcement of the "biggest loan ever insured by the Federal Housing Administration on a single mortgage" appeared in the *Miami Herald*, which predicted that they would not be ready for occupancy until fall term 1947, a prediction that proved to be overly optimistic.

Well before the papers carried news of the loan for the veterans housing, Weed and Manley were redrawing their master plan to accommodate the apartment buildings that were to be substituted for dormitories (figure 70). In 1947 Marion Manley was able to include these changes in an elegantly printed and

FIG. 68. Perspective rendering, dormitory and fine arts group. Courtesy of the Historical Museum of Southern Florida, Marion Manley Collection.

FIG. 69. Plans, dormitory and fine arts group. Courtesy of the Historical Museum of Southern Florida, Marion Manley Collection.

bound presentation of their "planos en desarrollo," when she served as the AIA representative to the Pan American Congress of Architects' meeting in Lima, Peru. As the Spanish title indicated, these designs for the university were still in development; nonetheless, they represented near finality for the major phase of the architects' master plan for the institution. The accompanying text introduced the site "located at the economic capital of this explosively growing region," asserting that "the Architectural Planning of campus and plant of the new University of Miami cannot fail to express, in a certain boldness and freshness of attack, these unique circumstances." Applying the principles of modernist planners to their campus, they explained that they had established patterns of "broad zoning . . . for four basic uses: Education and Administration, Housing, Athletics, Student and Community Activities." The scorn that Manley and Weed shared for the architectural traditions of the era so recently past is articulated for their South American colleagues: "Having outgrown the pseudo-Mediterranean romanticism of twenty years ago, Caribbean Florida has become the center of some of the most vigorous development of contemporary architectural design and planning on the continent of North America." They characterize their own response to the South Florida landscape as "obedient to the first law of shelter-adaptation," emphasizing that their buildings, generally described using terms such as "clean simplicity" and "light and rhythmic linearity," are "oriented primarily to the flow of the South-East trade winds."

This latest iteration of their master plan published for the meeting in Lima lays out the apartment buildings over the sixty acres south of the lake extending to frontage on Ponce de Leon Boulevard. A system of roadways and parking lots more elaborate than that of earlier plans is shown within the housing area, where groups of apartment buildings are distributed along the roads. The architects reserved as much open-ended space as possible between each group. The structures are standardized, relatively undifferentiated two- and three-story bars configured and linked variously at right angles to one another, or paralleling one another within discrete groupings, but never paralleling a roadway (figure 71).

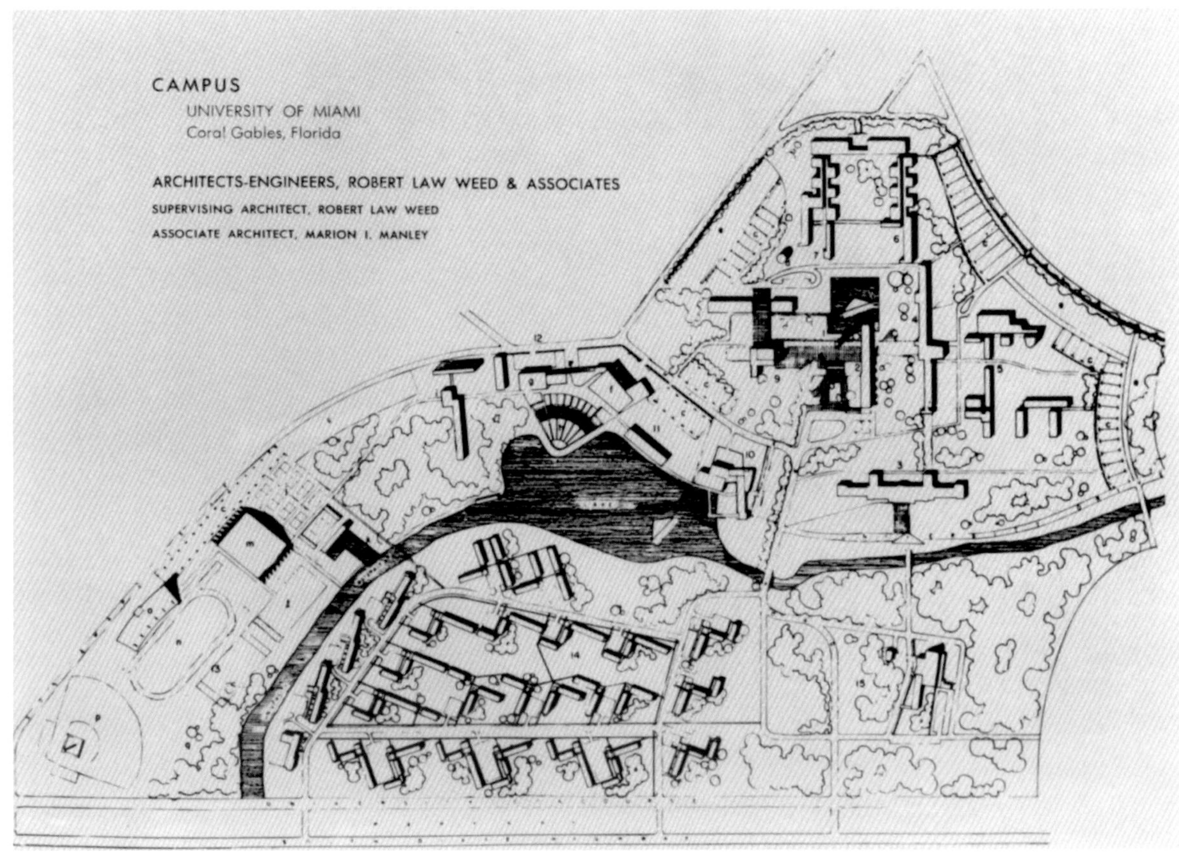

FIG. 70. Master plan, University of Miami, *Florida Architecture and the Allied Arts* (July 1948). Courtesy of Special Collections, University of Miami Libraries, Coral Gables, Florida.

While orientation to the prevailing breezes is a major announced rationale for the placement of campus buildings, the random alignments of the bar shapes here appear inconsistent with that rationale. It seems to give priority to orienting the buildings where ready access by cars can be provided. A parking lot is indicated beside each apartment group. "One hundred percent parking has been provided," a press release boasted. This part of the plan betrays an aversion to lining up the wall of any building with the edge of a roadway, distaste for any

FIG. 71. Rendering, typical veterans housing units.
Courtesy of the Historical Museum of Southern Florida,
Marion Manley Collection.

gesture that might acknowledge traditional patterns of orientation to the street. As in their first campus scheme, town planning like that at Radburn remains a clear model for preserving as much green space as possible within roadways that surround the housing groups. The text prepared for Lima is emphatic about one goal for the campus as a whole: "The Pilot Plan for the development of this site has one basic purpose—to be flexible, to leave the pathway open for different times and changing methods." The results in the housing area were, and remain, disorienting—they made no identifiable place. But in 1949 a writer for *Architectural Forum* recorded the prevailing consensus that Weed and Manley had developed "a site plan suitable to contemporary architectural treatment" where "informal grouping is the rule," a plan that could only have been introduced on a virgin site "uncorseted by yesterday's bi-axial symmetry."[45]

While Manley and Weed were adjusting the master plan, developing their designs for the apartment buildings, and completing drawings for a Memorial Classroom Building, on which construction began in June 1946, President Ashe pushed his own administrative staff to put twenty-eight temporary wooden buildings into service before the fall term began (figure 72). These were of a design later characterized as "obviously . . . borrowed from military barracks," perhaps because war surplus buildings had been promised to the university earlier that year. But by July, when their delivery was still delayed, the university ordered new lumber, "lumber . . . so green and new that the hot sun forced the resin from it," according to the university's historian.[46]

In their hurry to have teaching space put in place by September 1946, the administrators inadvertently complicated the architects' plans for more permanent buildings. In a memorandum of August 12, Weed registered his dismay after learning that "a number of temporary types of buildings were being erected to the east of the new classroom buildings in an area generally held for some time for this use." Weed's complaint records the fact that no drawings were made for siting these small one-story structures, which were lined up to form tight rectangles around a series of small open courtyards (figure 73). The contractor,

FIG. 72. On-site construction of temporary wooden buildings. University of Miami Historic Photo Collection, Box 16, Folder 109. Courtesy of Special Collections, University of Miami Libraries, Coral Gables, Florida.

according to Weed, had only been told where, in terms that were too general, to place "the Shacks," as the students were soon calling them (figure 74).

Marion Manley seems to have been the architect on the spot on the new campus, facing practical problems, responding when, as she put it in a memorandum that summer, Weed was "needling me to needle the University on certain questions."[47] In his long memorandum about "the temporaries," Weed reported to Ashe that Manley's attempts to have one temporary building moved because it had been strategically misplaced had been blocked by a university administrator. Weed concluded the memorandum, "It would have been simpler for us to

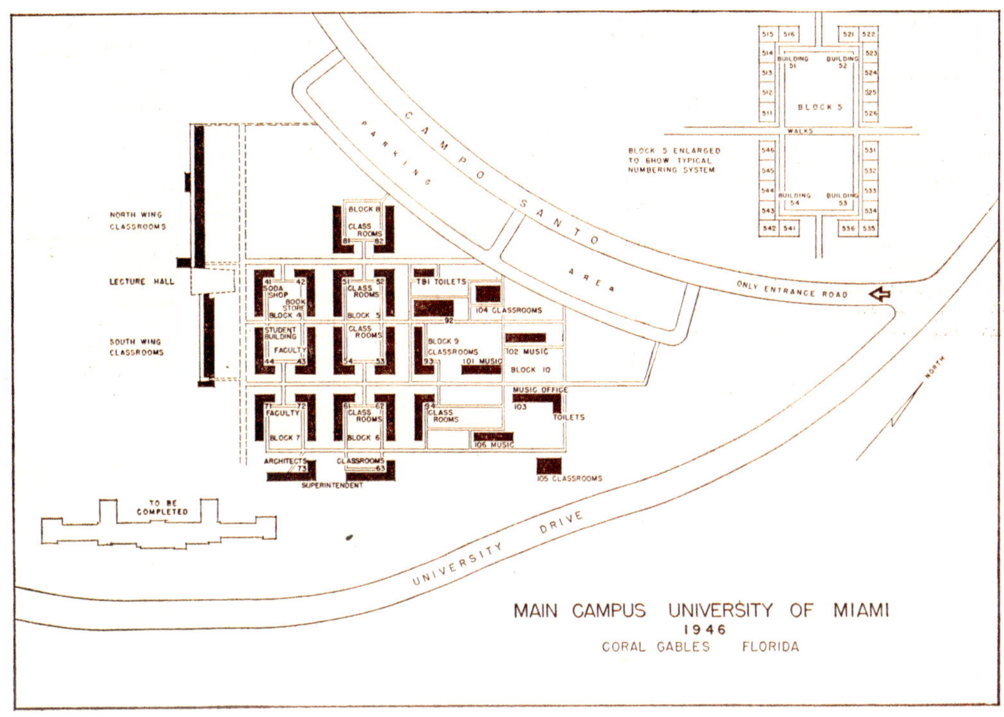

FIG. 73. Master plan, temporary wooden buildings, 1946. Courtesy of Special Collections, University of Miami Libraries, Coral Gables, Florida.

FIG. 74. "The Shacks." University of Miami Historic Photo Collection, Box 15, Folder 66. Courtesy of Special Collections, University of Miami Libraries, Coral Gables, Florida.

have prepared a simple set of installation drawings, together with a site plan, which would have been sufficient for the installation of these minor temporary buildings (and would still have tied in with the scheme as it is planned) than it is to have to actually measure the conditions in the field and make record drawings."[48]

Now Manley was installed in an "architect's office" in one of the shacks, Temporary Building 73, with at least two assistant architect-draftsmen. They shared the building with a "construction office." In the fall of 1946 enrollment increased by more than five thousand, surpassing all expectations, and the shacks were less than adequate. Ashe had to make hurried arrangements for many of the veterans to be housed at a nearby army air field and a naval base, and to be shuttled by bus between the several sites now serving them. To manage all that, he had expanded his administrative staff.

A perspective drawing by Manley showing a "proposed office building for University of Miami" and bearing the date December 12, 1946, probably represents her suggestion to Ashe for a building to house his expanded administration. No credit is given to Weed or his firm on this drawing, which is signed "Marion I. Manley, Architect" (figure 75). It was, however, a proposal the school could not afford to build. Fortunately, a gift from the U.S. government was soon to obviate the university's need to construct expensive new office space, even as it had to add administrators to cope with yet more record-breaking enrollment: seventy-two hundred by March 1947.

Construction started that month on four semipermanent, largely prefabricated buildings at the same time major permanent structures—the Memorial Classroom Building and the veterans apartments—were being built on the new main campus. The minutes of the Commission of the City of Coral Gables for March 18, 1947, record Miss Marion Manley's submission of "a plot plan showing a proposed location of four temporary wooden buildings." They were "to be furnished by the U.S. Government for the Veterans Educational Program [and] . . . erected at no cost to the University." Both the *Miami Herald* and the

FIG. 75. Rendering, proposed office building, University of Miami, 1946. Courtesy of Special Collections, University of Miami Libraries, Coral Gables, Florida.

PROPOSED OFFICE BUILDING
FOR UNIVERSITY OF MIAMI
CORAL GABLES FLORIDA
MARION I. MANLEY, ARCHITECT
DEC. 12, 1946

Miami Daily News reported that "an outlay of approximately $350,000 is represented in the structures given the University of Miami." While the university consistently referred to them as "semipermanent," thereby distinguishing them from the "temporary" shacks, the commission in granting its permission seems to have been impressed by their temporariness. In applying for their approval, Miss Manley had explained that "the length of time that they will be used will depend upon the length of time that the Veterans Educational Program will be in effect."[49]

For the *Miami Herald* Manley described the mutually beneficial arrangement between the university and the federal government that had put the semipermanents in place by September 11, 1947, when an article about them was published: "The Army had a double problem after the war. They had to demolish the temporary wartime structures, and at the same time they wanted to help universities with the veterans' training programs." At the naval station, about twelve miles to the south, where eleven hundred students were being housed, a fifth structure, about which little has come to light, was also pieced together from materials recycled from military bases, this one for botany classes. Adapting "surplus navy property from Daytona Beach and Lake City" as well as from other nearby military bases to the university's needs must not have been an exciting assignment for Marion Manley.[50] However, she turned what was probably a dull task into the creation of a stylish frontispiece for the new main campus under construction (figure 76). Though the original drawings for these buildings bear the Weed firm's name, Manley was at the time clearly credited with their design.[51] Transforming the military's cast-offs was a job of secondary importance to that of designing the major, permanent buildings, and it probably landed on her desk because she was the architect on the spot dealing with day-to-day practicalities.

FIG. 76. Wooden administration building, main campus, 1948 *Ibis* (yearbook). Courtesy of Special Collections, University of Miami Libraries, Coral Gables, Florida.

Manley combined the materials she was given to make up four wooden buildings, the most important of which was an administrative building. She used the rest to build a cafeteria and two smaller laboratory buildings—one for chemistry, another for physics. She placed them all at the far northern corner of the original Merrick tract in a spot where the two largest would, for the foreseeable future, present an important public face to prospective students and, no less important, to the Coral Gables neighbors (figure 77). The university was mindful of the necessity of sustaining the goodwill of those who lived in the surrounding residential area since neighborhood opposition might have influenced local politics and complicated such essentials as the approval of building permits.

These semipermanent wooden buildings were to be much bigger than the little one-story structures that had been arrayed in rigid rectangular groupings during the previous summer. While they were consistently designated semipermanent, they were not expected to survive, as three of them have, for half a century. This time the university turned the job of siting and designing the nonpermanent buildings over to the professionals and supported the architect's creative, if rushed, manipulation and restrained adornment of unpromising raw materials.

During this period just after the war, on other campuses across the nation, lumber and buildings were also being salvaged from military installations and hurriedly reused. However, few of those campuses were to benefit from such clever handling of recycled war surplus as Miami's was or to see military barracks so effectively transformed by a few simple devices to convey an image of architectural modernism. As Henry Cavendish recognized at the time, writing in the *Miami Daily News* on September 10, 1947, "Where the Coral Gables institution differed from other institutions receiving similar gifts . . . was in redesigning the structural reassembly so that the re-erected buildings would conform to the general outlines of the functional type architecture which is being followed in the construction of permanent buildings on the university's new campus." By involving its architects in this project, the university was avoiding siting problems like those of the previous summer. But it was also acknowledging that even in its ad hoc arrangements, architectural imagery mattered, that it was worth the extra time and expense to support designers who could endow vernacular

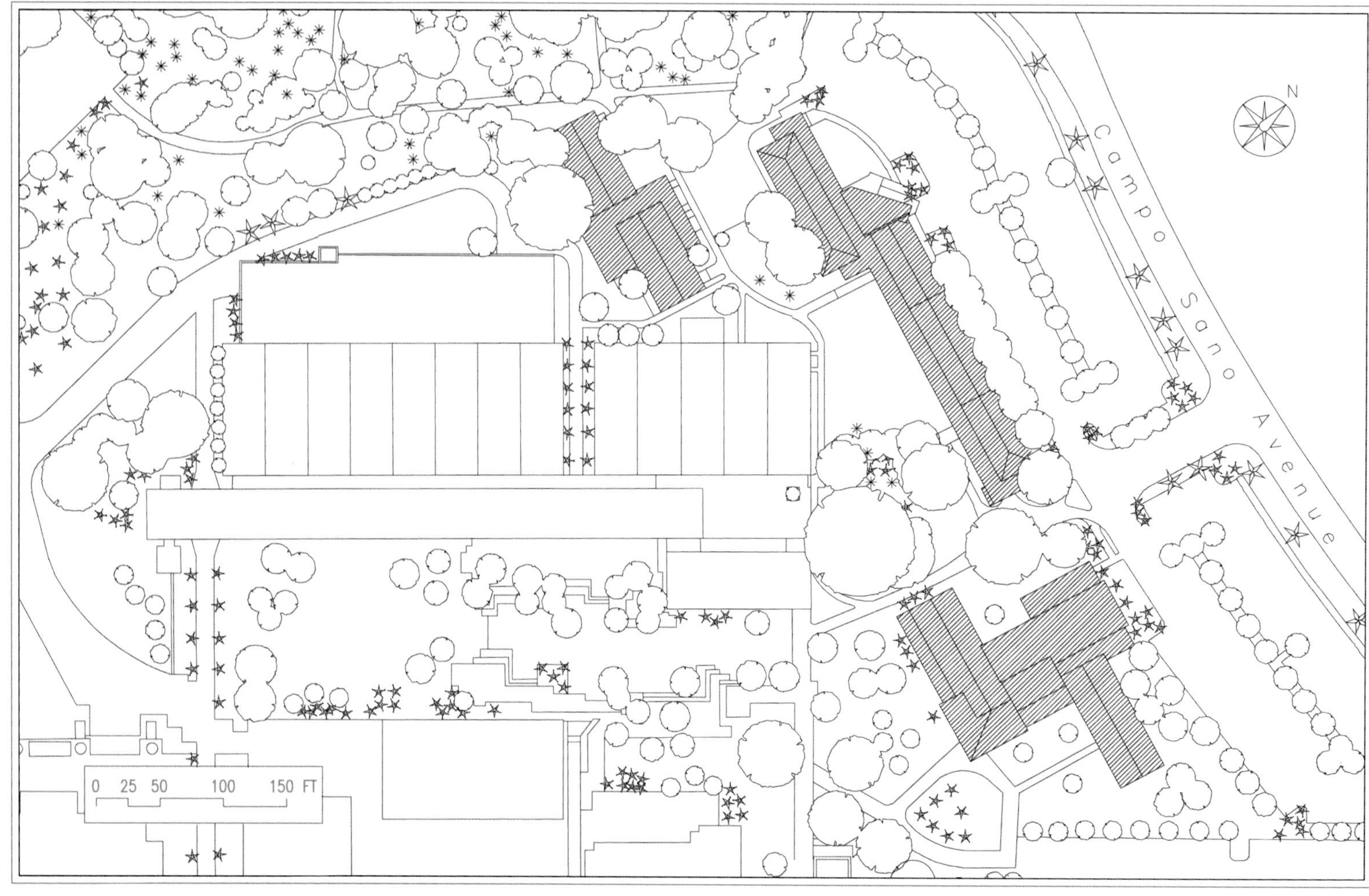

FIG. 77. Site plan including original wooden administration building, cafeteria, and laboratories. Drawing by University of Miami School of Architecture faculty: Carie Penabad; students: Leticia Acosta, Marcus Chaidez, Elisa Cuaron, Krista Kasprzyk, Gorata Magdiele, Christina Miller, Alice Oliveira, Elena Romero, and Jose Venegas.

wooden structures with a veneer of stylish modernity, visible testimony to the institution's full commitment to innovation.

The largest and most imposing of these wooden structures was the two-story administration building. It was put into service in September 1947, a month before most of the Memorial Classroom Building was ready for use (figure 78). The parti—the basic design concept—for the temporary building is strikingly similar to that for the permanent one. Manley stretched the administration building to an exaggerated length of 308 feet, putting it together from wood-frame building

FIG. 78. Wooden administration building, main campus. University of Miami Historic Photo Collection, Box 16, Folder 100. Courtesy of Special Collections, University of Miami Libraries, Coral Gables, Florida.

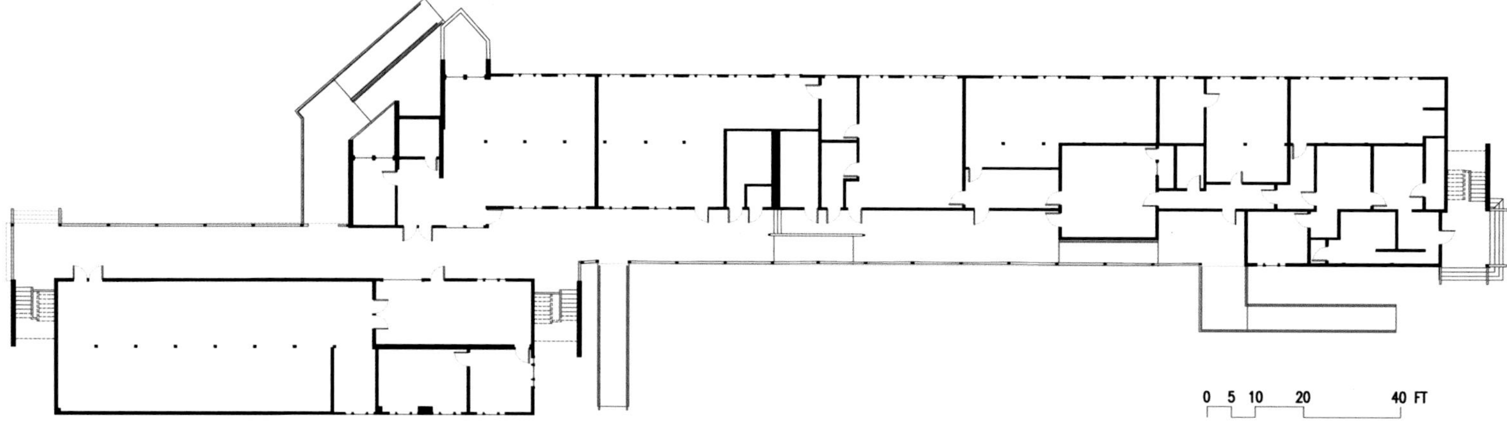

FIG. 79. Wooden administration building, first-story floor plan. Drawing by University of Miami School of Architecture faculty: Carie Penabad; students: Leticia Acosta, Marcus Chaidez, Elisa Cuaron, Krista Kasprzyk, Gorata Magdiele, Christina Miller, Alice Oliveira, Elena Romero, and Jose Venegas.

parts that were shipped in by rail from military bases (figure 79). By cleverly arranging the individual units as building blocks within a larger structure, she produced a much more fitting entrance to the university than another gaggle of small wooden buildings would have been had the unhappy precedent devised by campus administrators the previous summer been repeated. She joined several of the small surplus buildings in two parallel lines, a longer line in front, a shorter one just behind, to the southwest, to form two-story bars that slipped just past one another at the breadth of an open-air porch, again of two stories. The porch forms a long spine running through the building for its full length, connecting the two discrete parts as one structure. The site has a slight rise, and to deal with it at two points Manley simply created a step up where one unit met another. She edged the porch with square posts and simple board railings that formed a bold right-angled pattern, a long horizontal screen for the two major facades. From ground level the porch suppressed the view of low-pitched roofs, forms associated with things ordinary and old-fashioned and therefore disdained by modernists. More practically, with its open stairs at each end, this porch eliminated the need for interior circulation spaces by giving shaded, open-air access to each of the major rooms. The efficiency of this arrangement, which assured cross ventilation of each room, was readily apparent in the semitropics in the age before air-conditioning.

Near the center of the building, where the two long structures slid a little past one another, Manley fronted it all with an impressive modernist entrance piece, its walls rising a few feet above the low-pitched roofs of the adjacent reused building parts (see figure 77). At this focal point, on the side facing the town, she brought four taller walls just a few feet forward, at right angles to the long facades. These walls, much like ones the architects referred to as "fins" on the east elevation of the permanent classroom building under construction at this time, supported a flat roof that cut across the rectilinear plan as a bold diagonal. The projecting walls created strong vertical elements that divided the generously glazed facade of this entry piece into three bays stepping back under the diagonal of the roof. President Ashe was installed here in an office on the second floor, central to everything. Manley's modernist gesture fronting the vernacular bulk of the semipermanent wooden administration building signaled clearly enough the role of its glass double doors as the principal place of public entry to the entire campus. It apparently impressed the students who pictured it proudly on the frontispiece of their student yearbook for 1949. Makeshift though it might have been, this administration building has survived to the present day. It is at this writing a sad and shabby sight, but it was remarkably little altered in any fundamental way while it served for several decades as the art building. It now stands as a tangible link not only with the university's most dynamic period of growth, but also with Florida's pivotal role in wartime America.

To lend a look of modernity to the major campus-side facades of the nearby cafeteria, another large wooden structure put together at this time from war surplus, Manley wrapped a high, flat-roofed projecting porch around the southeast corner, facing it with an oversized grid of boards—"modernistic grill work," the *Miami Herald* called it on September 10, 1947 (figure 80). This simple wooden screen with its big open squares caught the eye, distracting it from the rather jumbled assemblage of reused building parts that were joined in a more centralized cross-axial arrangement of a single story, a plan complicated by additional wings. Again, as in the administration building, tall porches suppressed the view of the pitched roofs of its several wood-framed building units. Manley achieved the cafeteria's bold veneer of modernity very simply and cheaply using a few wooden sticks arranged in a novel way. Though shorn of the east-facing portion of its distinctive grid screen, this cafeteria building of 1947 has also survived largely intact, and most recently has been known as the communications building.

FIG. 80. Temporary buildings. Courtesy of Special Collections, University of Miami Libraries, Coral Gables, Florida.

Only one of two additional semipermanent wooden buildings from that same campaign of 1947 on the main campus is still standing. These two smaller structures, built as laboratories, were sited near the administration building and cafeteria within the same northwestern corner of the campus, though in subordinate positions, and they revealed quite forthrightly their origins on military bases. One was a little larger than the other, but both were made up of two barrack-like gable-roofed single-story buildings linked to one another by flat-roofed connectors. Surviving plans for the laboratories specify that their windows were to come from "B.O.Q. [bachelor officers quarters] surplus." A third science building was put up on the temporary south campus, the naval station; its fate is unknown.[52]

Manley's work on the semipermanent wooden buildings was well received. As an account in the *Miami Daily News* put it, "You'd never guess, though, that the structures were refabricated out of old army encampment buildings . . . and equipped to a considerable extent from war surplus materials obtained from the War Assets Administration."[53] Wooden war-surplus buildings, briefly ubiquitous on American campuses, are now extremely rare in those contexts. Miami's therefore are important surviving examples of the structures rapidly put up on Florida's military bases, training facilities that had important roles in winning the Second World War. The physical fabric of these buildings was then recycled on college campuses, and the few left on Miami's now stand as physical evidence of the federal government's postwar campaign to democratize higher education. Moreover, they are rare documents of early experimentation with the image of architectural modernism on American college campuses. And not least, they are the key surviving examples of some of the most important design work of South Florida's first female architect, the only major examples from the postwar building campaign on the university's campus for which there is firm documentation that she alone took the design lead.

Since she was a member of the campus design team within the office of the associated architects Weed and Manley, Manley's precise contributions to the design of their major permanent buildings at the University of Miami are more difficult to pin down. A typescript in the archives, "University of Miami Statement of Architectural Costs from June 1944 to Sept. 30, 1946," shows that she was paid fees of $13,934 for "new architectural & planning" during this period, while Weed's individual fees in the same category were only $8,388.07 (slightly less than the fee listed for another member of the office, Frank H. Shuflin), though Weed was paid a great deal more in expenses. Manley's itemized expenses on this same statement include sums for "Classroom Unit No. 1" (the Memorial Classroom Building), as well as for the "veterans housing units," "marine laboratory," and "temporary buildings," further suggesting that she personally participated in the creation of them all, including the student center and a maintenance-facilities building (recently used as a sculpture studio and ceramics lab). Accounting for the student center and the maintenance facility was normally lumped into that for the veterans housing, since these two were financed as part of the government-subsidized veterans housing project.

Manley's friends and associates long ago put on record their opinions that she was undercredited for this work. Marjory Stoneman Douglas acidly commented in her autobiography, *Voice of the River*, "The reason she's never been given enough credit is that she brought in big time collaborator Robert Law Weed, who proceeded to elbow her out. To hear him talk—and he talked a great deal—you'd think he was the primordial architect of the university. It wasn't true." Trip Russell, an architect who worked with Manley at the university, also defended Manley's role during an interview in 1990 with Emily Perry Dieterich: "Robert Law Weed claimed the lion's share of credit 'although Marion selected him as the person she would like to work with. Towards the end, she felt he hogged the publicity and the profits to a large degree, and from my own experience, I believe she was right.'"[54] Whatever the case, within their office, several architects worked as a team under Weed and Manley on these major projects, and the drawings for the permanent buildings each bear a title block prominently displaying the

FIG. 81. Memorial Classroom Building under construction. University of Miami Historic Photo Collection, Box 16, Folder 80. Courtesy of Special Collections, University of Miami Libraries, Coral Gables, Florida.

words: "Office of Robert Law Weed, Architects Engineers, Marion I. Manley, Associate Arch."

The first major architectural design product of Weed and Manley's association was the very long, very large—63,400 square feet—Memorial Classroom Building, on which construction began in June 1946 (figure 81). It was given priority by a university for which teaching and learning were the central concerns. Nowhere in the neighborhood were there ready-made classrooms and auditoriums large enough for all the new students. On the other hand, temporary housing could be and was—if a little awkwardly—arranged, much of it in quarters that were rapidly being abandoned on nearby military bases. This situation reinforced the logic of first building classrooms to anchor the future campus.

FIG. 82. University of Miami Memorial Classroom Building. Pencil rendering. Courtesy of Historical Museum of Southern Florida, Marion Manley Collection.

Manley's work on the design for the Memorial Classroom Building probably inspired her organization of the surplus wooden units in the semipermanent administration building a year later. Both were long bars of modular units with major entrances and activities projecting near the center and with open porches or galleries that substituted for hallways and were served at each end by open stairways (figure 82). While the wooden structure was put up within the space of six months, it took nearly two years to finish the permanent building with its reinforced concrete frame sheathed largely in exposed concrete and its galleries cantilevered beyond its west wall.

The architects sited this narrow bar building at a right angle to the still skeletal frame of the Merrick Building, stringing out its forty-six classrooms in a line, shifted slightly near its midpoint, running northwest from the old structure, and separated from it by more than two hundred feet. The siting conformed to the underlying grid of "the central group" shown in the earliest published campus plans (see figure 71). A slope accommodated three stories in the shorter, southernmost wing, while raising the roof height only a little in the longer two-story wing to the north (figure 83). The designers emphasized that they had made "exhaustive studies" before placing the major axis where "ideal light and prevailing breeze," from the southeast, would flow past the building. And they pointed to "high-up windows on the gallery or hot [west] side of the building," which, with what they called "fins," that is, "structural supports on the exterior wall of the classroom side," succeeded in "scooping the breeze through the rooms" (figure 84).[55] All this was especially important since the classrooms were not air-conditioned, though the three-hundred-seat lecture hall and, beneath it, a student reading room and lounge were.

Functional, innovative responses to structural challenges and to South Florida's climate are main themes both in publicity about this classroom building that was generated by the architects themselves and in the national press's response to it. The architects detailed the functionality of their every form in their press release about the Memorial Classroom Building, and its "handsome

FIG. 83. Memorial Classroom Building. Ezra Stoller © Esto.

FIG. 84. Memorial Classroom Building. Courtesy of Special Collections, University of Miami Libraries, Coral Gables, Florida.

and economical structural system" was the focus of a major article about the campus in the *Architectural Forum* of July 1948. Weed's press release described how "a rigid concrete bent was designed, enabling the long galleries of the west to be cantilevered far beyond the west wall of the building." Unfortunately the original "light steel sunshades, protecting the galleries from the western sun and the rain" have been replaced by panels that distort the intended effect of the design (figure 85). *Architectural Forum*'s piece elaborated on the structural system: "Instead of the conventional beam-and-column, the architects have used a series of rigid bents, spanning the building transversely . . . and cantilevered out 10½ ft. . . . to carry the galleries. These bents are tied together laterally by integral floor and roof slabs." The architects were proud of the protection the building's

own form afforded itself from sun and rain because each story overhung the one below. Those "vertical fins" on the eastern side, they said, "control the sun at each bay so that direct sunlight does not penetrate any rooms after 9 o'clock in the morning." The architects not only took advantage of the semitropical climate to leave major circulation spaces—the galleries and stairs—open to the air but also designed an open-air lounge below the lecture hall, which they faced with stonework (figures 86 and 87).[56]

And for Florida, color seemed more appropriate than the white surfaces of much European modernism. The architects wrote that "a great deal of thought has been given to the color of the exterior walls," recording that they had left the concrete frame a light gray "except that walls and sides of fins facing north are painted a lemon yellow." Color was also introduced to "the interior gallery walls facing west," which were painted slate blue, while the interiors of stair towers were "a dull terra cotta." They asserted that "by maintaining a uniform color on the envelope of the building, and using strong color within the enclosed spaces, the building is colorful and interesting, without loss of dignity, necessary to its proper use." Additional color appeared, "ranging from grey to buff to rose" in the Tennessee sandstone facing of the east and west walls of the lecture hall and in the "buff red" of coral rock on the stairs of the main foyer and elsewhere (figure 88).[57]

The *Architectural Forum* for July 1948 called the university's campus the "only completely new, completely contemporary, educational plant in the country," when it ran four photographs of the "biggest veterans' housing group in the country insured by FHA." The pictures show the student apartments still under construction.[58] Actual building of the 533 units in twenty-seven bar-shaped

FIG. 86. Memorial Classroom Building, rendering of foyer from the south. Courtesy of the Historical Museum of Southern Florida, Marion Manley Collection.

FIG. 85. Memorial Classroom Building, open galleries, circa 1948–49. Ezra Stoller © Esto. All rights reserved.

FIG. 87. Memorial Classroom Building, first-floor outdoor lobby. Ezra Stoller © Esto. All rights reserved.

FIG. 88. Memorial Classroom Building, vintage postcard. Courtesy of the State Library and Archives of Florida, Postcard Collection, Tallahassee.

structures had, according to the university's historian, begun in the summer of 1947, and by January 1948 some were complete enough to be occupied, while the remaining ones were finished by May 1948.[59] Fewer than half survive (figure 89).

Manley's precise role in the design of the apartment buildings themselves is unclear. A press release about the veterans housing units issued by Weed's office on January 24, 1947, seems to belittle it: "The project planning and design has been accomplished under the direction of Robert Law Weed. . . . Miss Marion Manley is Associate Architect for the University. Architectural and engineering plans have been executed by Weed's office of Architects-Engineers, with development of design largely attributed to Frank E. Watson, Associate in the firm."[60]

We can only speculate that Manley's primary contributions to design of the veterans group came in the planning stages, in determining the overall form of

the individual two- and three-story buildings and of their siting, since planning was an area in which her interest and expertise were emphasized at this period, and because the planning here is consistent with the models she admired. The very simplicity of the forms adopted for the veterans apartments conforms to that of her other projects that were in the works about this time and were based on early international style models (figure 90). Then again, perhaps the emphasis in this press release on the role of Weed's own office is one of the instances of overclaiming credit that Marjory Stoneman Douglas resented on her friend's behalf.

The evidence suggests that Manley bore primary responsibility for construction supervision on this massive project. She was then working every day right on the building site, housed in Shack 73, and was an architect who, well into her old age, enjoyed a reputation among her peers for being a meticulous construction supervisor who demanded of contractors that they execute architectural plans precisely as designed. The university's archives retain a number of memoranda from and to Marion Manley as she worked out details crucial to the efficient performance of facilities associated with the project, including a community building and a management and maintenance building, as well as electrical, gas, and water facilities and a sewage disposal plant.

Manley's usual approach to landscape, consistently conserving a site's natural topography and native plants by nestling structures as gently as possible within little-disturbed settings, was frustrated on the vast veterans housing project. This happened despite the fact that William Lyman Phillips, a Harvard-trained landscape architect whose approach to design was sympathetic to Manley's, had joined the design team. Phillips's work—in collaboration with Frederick Law Olmsted Jr. for several projects, and on his own at Fairchild Tropical Gardens in Coral Gables—argued successfully that the native landscape had, as Joanna Lombard has noted, an important place in the designed landscape. In a letter to Manley on October 25, 1946, Phillips mentioned a "slight sinkhole at the easterly end" of the classroom building. "I have the impression," he continued, "that in

FIG. 89. Aerial view of main campus from the south, January 1948. Courtesy of the Historical Museum of Southern Florida, Marion Manley Collection.

FIG. 90. Rendering, veterans housing project. Courtesy of the Historical Museum of Southern Florida, Marion Manley Collection.

general there is a lot to be said for not reducing the surface of this campus to a series of level or inclined planes, but to retain the natural surface wherever there is no strong reason for doing otherwise. Any slight relief, such as we see here is a rather precious thing in Dade County." Manley replied a few days later that she was "very glad" Phillips was "ruminating on the future of the campus" and that she agreed with his "desire to retain whatever of the natural irregularities of the ground surface we can."[61]

While they were able to preserve the rocky imprints of two sinkholes and a few other outcroppings of native stone where grade levels changed, they could save little more of the site's natural topography or indigenous vegetation. With its new Lake Osceola, acres of grass, paved roads, and parking lots, along with allées of exotic palms, the campus became a highly artificial construction. By July 1947, in a letter to a friend, Phillips could only lament what had happened to the university grounds. After pointing out that the "vegetation that already exists . . . may be as valuable, or more so, as the vegetation that may be introduced," Philips went on, "In this bulldozer age . . . the construction boys will have the site swept clean before you know what is going on. That is what has happened on this University of Miami housing project that I am connected with."[62]

Publications touting the veterans housing relied heavily on press releases issued by Weed's office. They emphasized the economy, functionality, and efficiency of the standardization and methods of mass production applied in construction here, the sort of thing for which Weed had been awarded a Bronze Star in 1944 when he built for the air transport command's India-Burma sector. A release issued by his office on January 16, 1947, went on for nine of its twelve pages detailing ways that "construction of the buildings has been simplified for economy—designed to use local materials and stock sizes." The structural system in the veterans housing was indeed a simple one: "Bearing walls of [eight-inch] concrete block run across the building to serve as room divisions as well as to support the weight" (figure 91). The fabrication of the blocks on site "at approximately 65% of the prevailing retail market price," along with "shop fabrication of typical unit parts as much as possible" were among the ways these architects were proud of having cut construction costs "by design of the buildings," as they put it. Among other cost-cutting devices much touted in the publicity were what they called "storagewalls," units "used to define the spaces, at the same time eliminating solid partitions for this purpose" (figure 92). Floors of "2 × 8 joists throughout, 12' long and spanning between partitions," were used, as the architects explained, to take "all floor and roof load off of the exterior walls" and permit "opening the full width of the room, the necessary tie-beam being used as shelter and overhangs to protect the exterior window screen walls." The resulting sun shades were a prominent visual feature of the elevations, as well as an important element in the much-emphasized concern for the "functional

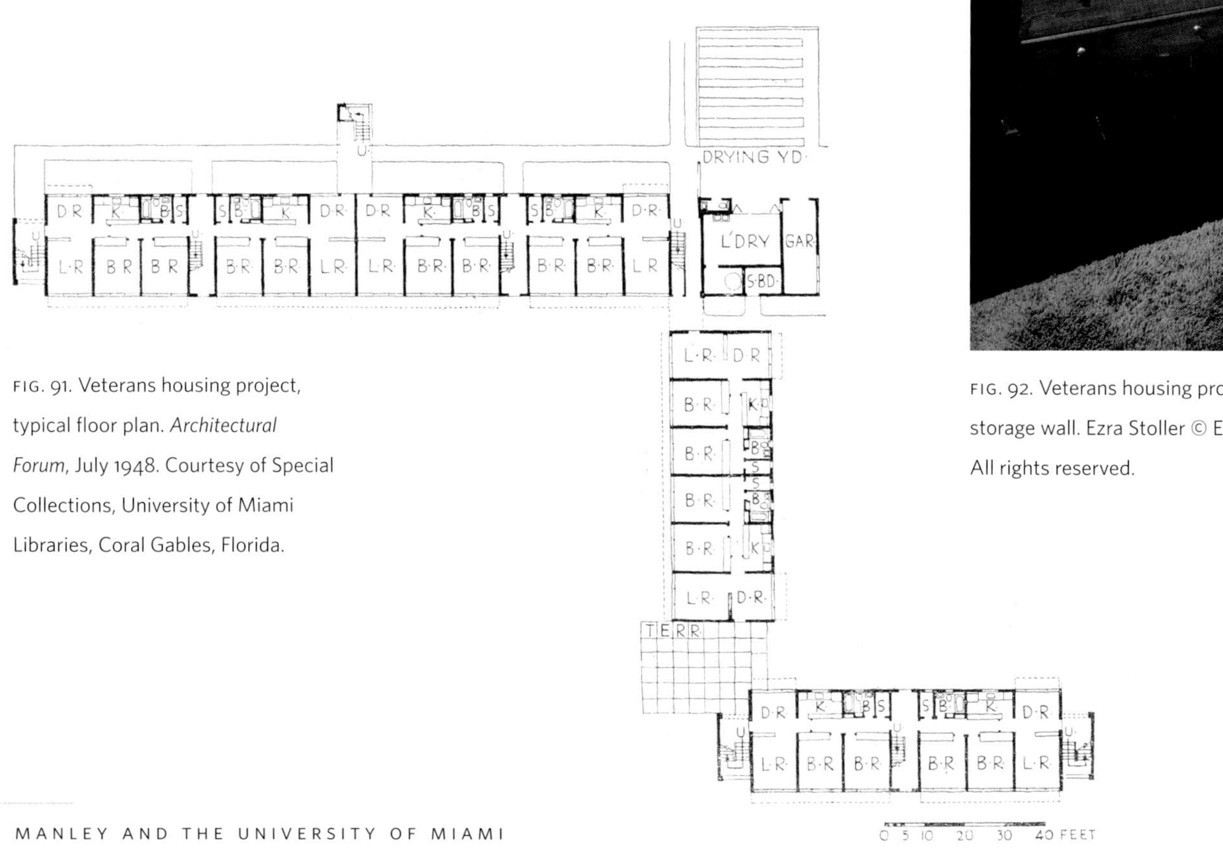

FIG. 91. Veterans housing project, typical floor plan. *Architectural Forum*, July 1948. Courtesy of Special Collections, University of Miami Libraries, Coral Gables, Florida.

FIG. 92. Veterans housing project, storage wall. Ezra Stoller © Esto. All rights reserved.

FIG. 93. Veterans housing apartment building.

and practical arrangement of all facilities incident to healthful, enjoyable indoor and outdoor living" (figure 93). As in nearly every published piece about the veterans housing, the architects' own press release of early 1947 emphasizes that "in orientation, maximum advantage has been taken of prevailing breezes, sunlight and view—of utmost importance in the Florida area." They oriented these apartments, they said, so that the "prevailing breeze may be caught and its free circulation assured," even in the rain, when windows could be left open because the exterior walls of each room were protected by overhangs and "a screen of projected steel sash."

Decoration of the veterans housing is a topic succinctly addressed in the same twelve-page press release, in a paragraph that highlights "the use of various materials, such as local stone and terra cotta" to achieve it. Again, as in the Memorial Classroom Building, the plain white wall of so much European modernism of the day was apparently eschewed here, for the text records that there was a "great variety in painting. These colors are in solid masses and none in small areas. Thus, to the largest degree possible, unnecessary decoration and details have been eliminated." No historical record of what colors were chosen or where they were introduced, nor any surviving physical evidence of them has yet come to light.

A multifunctional community building was also part of the veterans housing project (figure 94). However large the government loan, here the architects had to stretch it to take care of many pressing needs—including those for a cafeteria to serve fifteen hundred to two thousand, a faculty dining room, a screened patio, a general store, a book store, a snack bar, club facilities, and a reading room standing in for the library, which was yet to be built (figure 95). Given this complex program, they produced a much more interesting form than the boxlike bar they repeated so often for the student housing and gave it a fine site at the center of the campus, right on the northern edge of the newly dredged lake (figure 96). They housed many of its multifarious functions within the two stories of a reinforced concrete structure, an irregular L-shape in plan, and then expanded its capacities outside to serve crowds on patios and porches (figure

FIG. 94. Aerial view of main campus depicting Memorial Classroom Building, student lounge, and veterans housing project, 1949 *Ibis* (yearbook). Courtesy of Special Collections, University of Miami Libraries, Coral Gables, Florida.

97). The most impressive of these was a narrow, L-shaped covered patio that they sent out over the lake, raising it above the water on pilings. This "tropical student club" became one of the most photographed buildings on the new campus. Sadly, its most interesting feature, that part of the patio that extended out over the water, was eliminated, and the original form was subsumed within vast additions made in 1963. The building as it was completed in 1948 is now unrecognizable (figure 98).

It is largely Weed's voice that rings through articles about Miami's modern campus in local, national, and even international publications that appeared as it was taking shape. He had followed through on the promise he made to Bowman Ashe in 1945 "to be of service in the promotional work." Weed acted aggressively on the idea he had put in writing "that the present construction program and the overall plan for development should be given maximum publicity and

FIG. 95. Rendering of community building and cafeteria. University of Miami Historic Photo Collection, Box 16, Folder 95. Courtesy of Special Collections, University of Miami Libraries, Coral Gables, Florida.

TUDENT CLUB-UNIVERSITY OF MIAMI-OFFICE OF ROBERT LAW WEED-ARCHITECTS-ENGINEERS-MARION I MANLEY-ASSOCIATE ARCHITECT

FIG. 97. Students on the outdoor patio of the student club. University of Miami Historic Photo Collection, Box 18, Folder 183. Courtesy of Special Collections, University of Miami Libraries, Coral Gables, Florida.

FIG. 96. Rendering of student club. Pan American conference booklet, 1947. Courtesy of the Historical Museum of Southern Florida, Marion Manley Collection.

be kept constantly before the public." Within the press releases that his office issued, Weed's design principles and priorities are imbedded, and they clearly influenced the journalists who wrote about the campus.[63] Weed also talked about the project to reporters. So it is he, rather than Manley, who is most frequently quoted and most prominently credited in the regional architectural press, such as *Florida Architecture and Allied Arts* for July 1948, as well as in major articles that appeared in professional journals with national circulation during the late 1940s and early 1950s. *Architectural Forum* followed the Miami campus especially closely, featuring a photograph of the Memorial Classroom Building on its cover in July 1948, and following construction on the campus into 1953 with two more articles (figure 99).[64]

The foreign architectural press also took an interest in the university's ambitious modernist project. Its progress was reported in an article on Miami that appeared in *El Arquitecto Peruano* in 1948, and in December of the same year *L'Architecture d'Aujourd'hui* carried even more extensive coverage of the new Miami campus.

The wonders of this modernist artifact were also pictured on the pages of America's most widely read magazines of the postwar period. For December 27, 1948, *Life* reported on the "modern college," finding that "Miami's new buildings set new campus style," and in November of the following year the *Saturday Evening Post* assured its readers that "they love it at Sun-tan U," in a major article featuring the new campus. In a long piece about the city of Miami in *National Geographic Magazine* for November 1950, William H. Nicholas also focused on the campus: "Suddenly I saw before me a streamlined mass of steel, concrete, glass, and fieldstone—a group of spectacular and distinctly modern-type buildings rising in open pineland and rubbing shoulders with several low wooden structures resembling army barracks." He found it "startling to an observer accustomed to cloistered halls and ivy-covered walls on a university campus."[65]

FIG. 98. University of Miami student club overlooking Lake Osceola. Ezra Stoller © Esto. All rights reserved.

While such nationally published attention to Miami's campus was doubtless gratifying, its creators could well have been even more pleased by the success of

FIG. 99. Cover of *Architectural Forum* featuring Memorial Classroom Building, July 1948. Courtesy of Special Collections, University of Miami Libraries, Coral Gables, Florida.

their experiment in modernity as an enticement to enrollment. Its appeal to undergraduates, even at the height of construction in 1947, was made clear in many of the responses to an on-campus survey made that year for *Ibis*, the yearbook. Student reporters asked freshmen, "What appeals to you most at the University of Miami?" Ray Welch of Southwick, Massachusetts, replied that it was "watching the girls with their nice new convertibles driving by." But many others focused on the architecture. For Joan Cramer of Harrisburg, Pennsylvania, it was the "cool new buildings"; for Robert Rich of Miami, "the new modern buildings." Joe Byrne of New York City said, "The new campus is swell, the new buildings are definitely unusual," and Toni Lopez of Miami added that he had "even heard Yale men say they'd like to go here."[66] *Ibis* photographers for 1949 and their campus-beauty-queen subjects revealed their infatuation with the new buildings in a series of pictures in which the girls embrace the structures lovingly, beaming in their shared luster (figures 100, 101, and 102).

FIGS. 100–102. University of Miami campus beauty queen, 1949 *Ibis* (yearbook). Courtesy of Special Collections, University of Miami Libraries, Coral Gables, Florida.

Additional confirmations of the architecture's immediate professional impact arrived in the mail. Manley reported to Bowman Ashe on August 13, 1948, that she "had correspondence with architects and planners for the University of Denver, North Carolina State College, Michigan State College, University of the Philippines, and perhaps some others, who are interested in what we are doing here. You may be amused to know that, while their comments are complimentary, their chief question is, 'how do you get permission to use contemporary architecture?'"

That letter was written as she was packing up her campus office. August 1948 marked the end of Marion Manley's most intense involvement with the University of Miami as well as her formal association with Weed for their most important work on the campus. News that she was vacating Temporary Building No. 73 to make way for the ever-swelling crowd of students and was setting up an independent office in the post office building in Coconut Grove ran in the *Miami Herald* under the headline "Campus Farewell for Miss Manley." There was also a smaller headline, "But It's Not Goodbye," and indeed Manley, working independently, was soon to design chapels and student centers for the Baptists in 1949 and the Episcopalians in 1951, and to see them executed on campus. They were built on what has become a very prominent site, but then was a lesser one, fronting the part of Miller Road that is now Stanford Drive, near the southwest corner of the present main campus entrance from Ponce de Leon Boulevard. The university's board deeded sites on Miller, flanking Levante Avenue, to the denominations, who, rather than the university itself, were Manley's clients.

The Baptist student center was a restrained and simple construction of concrete block and stucco, with protruding bays clad in limestone veneer (figure 103). Instead of designing a single large volume accommodating classrooms and meeting rooms, an auditorium, a hobby room, a kitchen that served those gathering places, and living quarters for the center's director, Manley accommodated each in a separate structure. She arranged these discrete parts around courtyards, a patio in one case, a lawn in another, and joined them with covered walkways

FIG. 103. Baptist student center. Courtesy of the Historical Museum of Southern Florida, Marion Manley Collection.

for circulation. Her strategy here, responding to a program by housing its parts in small built elements, closely follows that for houses she was designing at the time. She gave the largest volume an asymmetrical sloping roofline, which rose to cover a two-story meeting room, lending interest to the relatively low building, which now blends unobtrusively into lush tropical foliage. Some of Manley's sensitive use of outdoor space was lost when one of the courtyards was later filled by a two-story structure.

In 1951 the Episcopal Diocese of South Florida asked Manley to design an Episcopal church center for the university (figure 104). She responded with a U-shaped structure of brick and stucco, housing an array of facilities much like those of the Baptists, as well as a small chapel, dedicated to Saint Augustine,

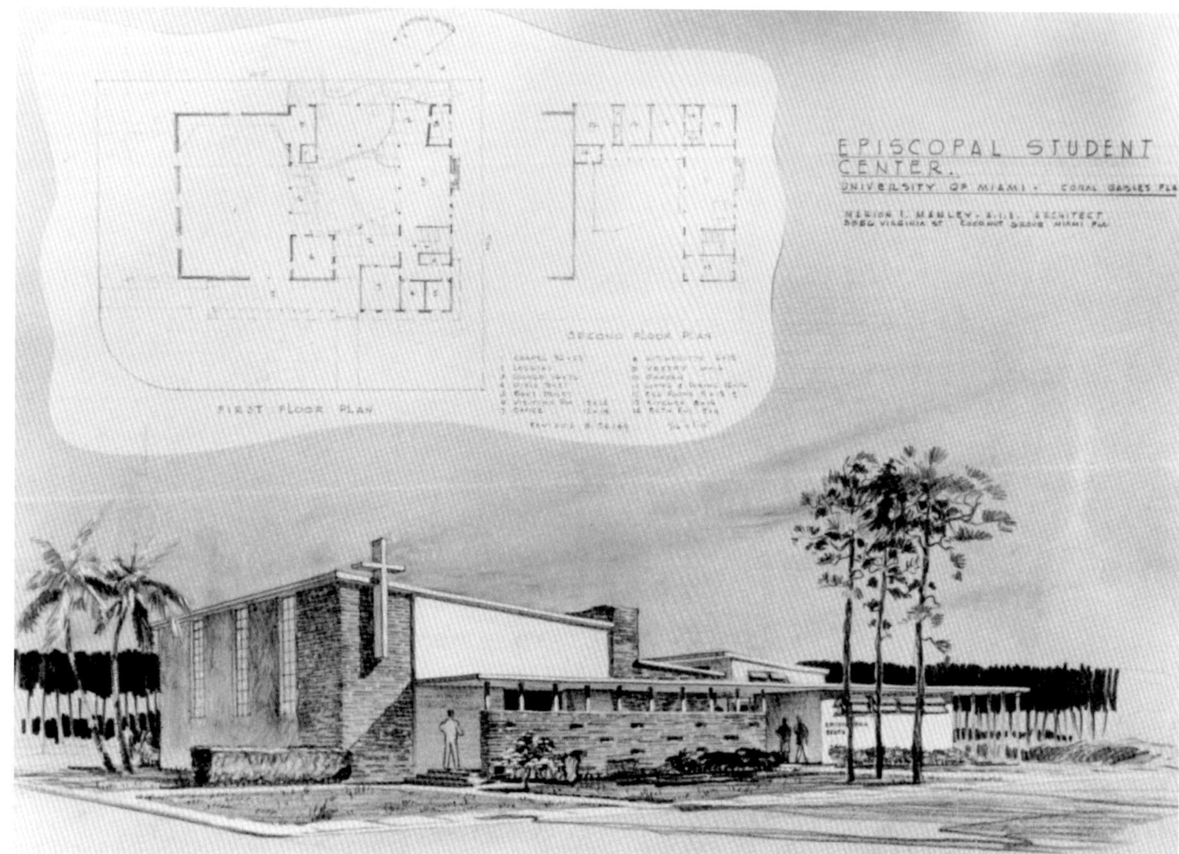

FIG. 104. Rendering, Episcopal student center. Courtesy of Special Collections, University of Miami Libraries, Coral Gables, Florida.

on its second floor. In 1958 the Episcopalians again turned to Manley when an enlargement of this campus center was made possible by a donation from Jean Flagler Matthews, a granddaughter of Henry Flagler, Florida's rail baron. Working with a larger budget, Manley produced a chapel that was more flamboyant than its predecessor, giving it a very rough coral rock veneer penetrated by exuberant triangular doorways and windows. When completed in 1960 it was dedicated to Saint Bede, a scholar.

Working for the university itself in 1948, only five months before she was to depart, Manley, apparently independent of any associates, had submitted preliminary designs for a "conservation and angling building" rather wonderfully sited on Lake Osceola on the Coral Gables campus, but her designs were never realized (figures 105, 106, 107, and 108). However, in 1951, again working for the university, but off campus this time, she undertook design work to adapt the Koubek mansion in downtown Miami, which had been given to the university in 1942, for use as an adult educational center.[67]

FIG. 105. Rendering, conservation and angling building (colored pencil on board, 20′ x 30′). Courtesy of Special Collections, University of Miami Libraries, Coral Gables, Florida.

FIG. 106. Rendering, conservation and angling building (colored pencil on board, approx. 20′ x 30′). Courtesy of Special Collections, University of Miami Libraries, Coral Gables, Florida.

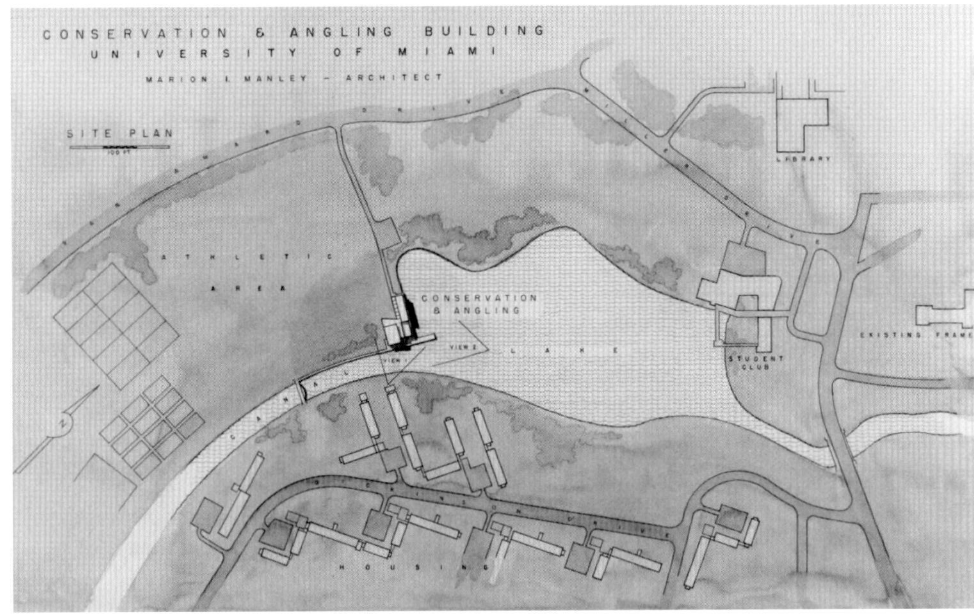

FIG. 107. Site plan, conservation and angling building (pencil on board, 20′ x 30′). Courtesy of Special Collections, University of Miami Libraries, Coral Gables, Florida.

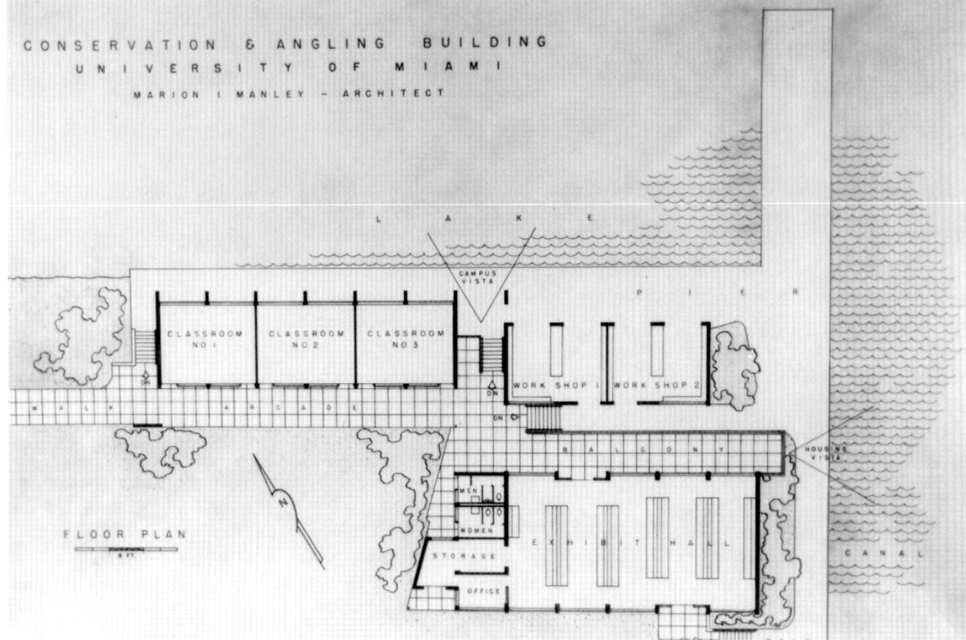

FIG. 108. Floor plan, conservation and angling building. Courtesy of Special Collections, University of Miami Libraries, Coral Gables, Florida.

In 1951 she was also working on her last important commission from the university for a building on its Coral Gables campus, again in association with a local architect who had returned to Miami after the war, Robert M. Little (figure 109). The two were asked to replace the tent in which the drama department had recently been staging its productions, to give it instead a totally flexible and permanent performance space, and to do it on a very tight budget, "less than $10 per square foot." Robert Little later credited Manley as the lead designer

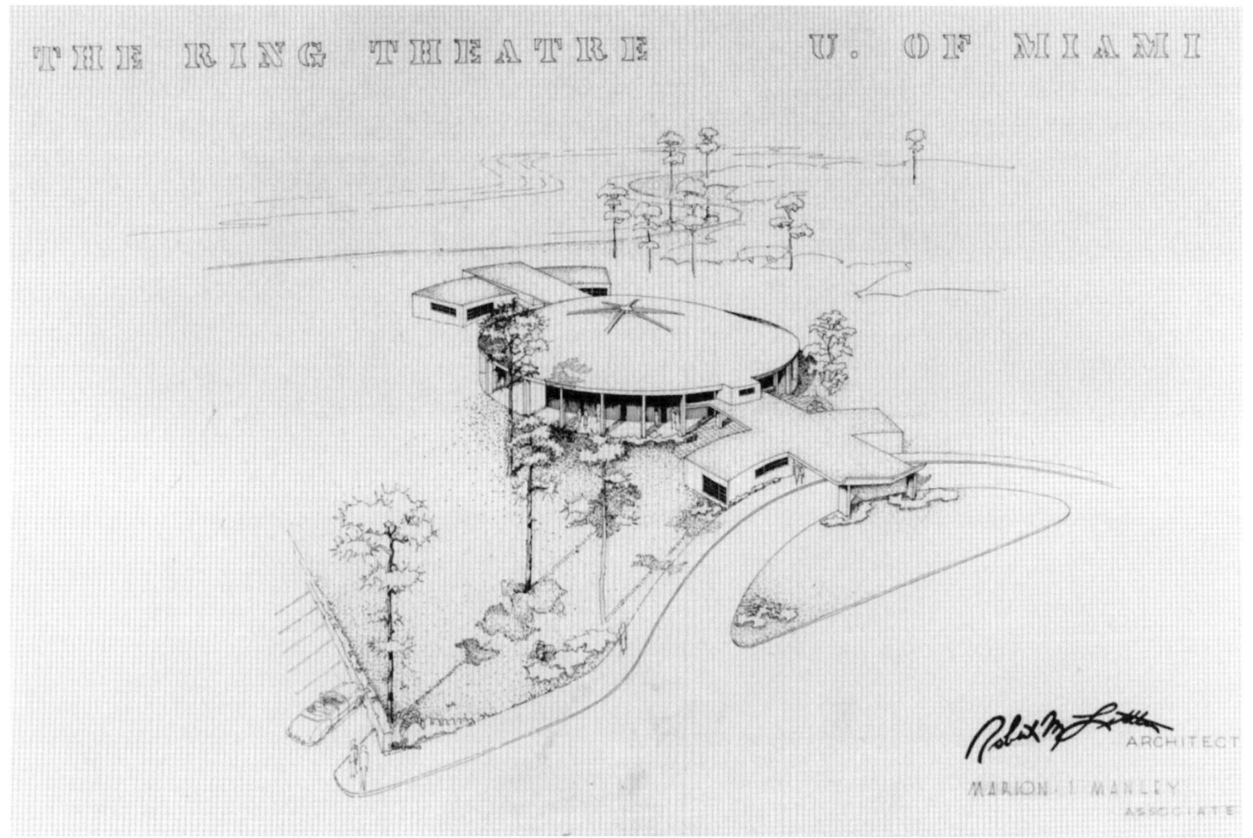

FIG. 109. Rendering, Ring Theater (ink on board, 20′ x 30′). Courtesy of Special Collections, University of Miami Libraries, Coral Gables, Florida.

FIG. 110. Ring Theater. Courtesy of the Historical Museum of Southern Florida, Marion Manley Collection.

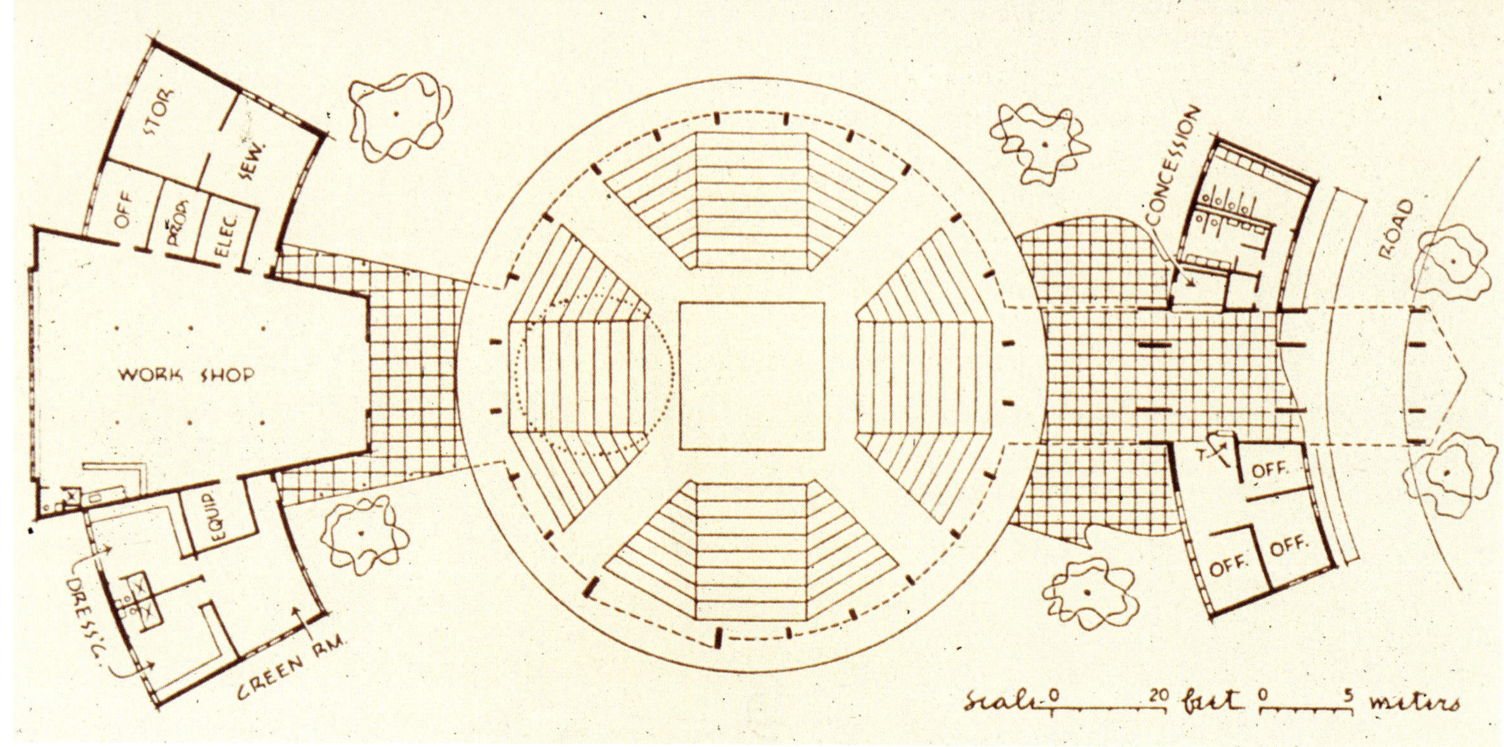

FIG. 111. Ring Theater, floor plan. Courtesy of Special Collections, University of Miami Libraries, Coral Gables, Florida.

here, writing in 1955, "I proudly acknowledge and respect her as the author of the design of the Ring Theater. It was somewhat of a challenge due to limited knowledge of problem and budget. The straightforward truthful philosophy of Miss Manley resulted in . . . simple, pleasing, and functional results as reflected in most of her work."[68]

They designed an exposed-concrete theater-in-the-round with a low dome, a hundred feet in diameter and five inches thick (figure 110). *Progressive Architecture* illustrated this experimental "Ring Theater" in great detail in 1953, describing as "kite-shaped" the plan of the central performance space and its two semi-detached structures, one—fronting the lake—that housed the usual back-of-stage facilities, another—on the land side—that contained the ticket booth and concession stand. The original "screened-aluminum jalousies" that the magazine noted were "set around the perimeter for the maximum ventilation in the subtropical climate" were replaced with solid walls when the theater was later air-conditioned. The magazine published diagrams of the "five seating arrangements for 400 people and two positions for a revolving stage" (figure 111).[69]

While Manley was associated with Robert M. Little on this theater, she had not participated in his work to complete (in 1950), the "skeleton" of the Merrick Building, for which she and Weed had roughed out suggestions in their master plan, suggestions to which Little generally adhered. Despite her years of work and her ideas about laboratories and aquariums for the marine scientists on Virginia Key, John L. Skinner was commissioned to design the marine laboratory there in 1955.

Manley, like Rosie the Riveter, was not much needed by her wartime employers when the fighting ended. Having taken over a traditionally male role as campus architect while the men fought the war that Hitler had started, she found herself treated by the University of Miami in much the same way the women who had worked in the munitions plants were by the captains of industry: When the boys came home, the men in charge gave them the big jobs.

—CL

DESIGNING POST–WORLD WAR II SOUTH FLORIDA

When her responsibilities for the University of Miami dwindled in the late 1940s, Manley reopened her independent practice. It was essentially a one-person operation, though she took on a small staff when she had too much work to handle alone, and she often collaborated with other Miami architects. This new office was much like her office of the 1930s, but the product was radically different: It now represented what Manley believed to be a new and appropriate architecture for South Florida. Significantly, for most of her later work, Manley did not employ the language of the international style that she had used at the university. Instead, she looked to the vernacular traditions of the early Florida pioneers for inspiration. This later work provides visual evidence that she found in the buildings of South Florida's pioneering American settlers authentic responses to the region's unique climate and geography. The austere, lightweight wooden architecture, in which construction and materials were clearly expressed, accorded with Manley's newly minted modernist sensibilities.

FIG. 112. Wylie house, South Miami, carport and second-floor master bedroom. Courtesy of the Historical Museum of Southern Florida, Marion Manley Collection.

Like other regional architects who brought academic models derived from classical precedent to many parts of the country during the 1920s and 1930s, by the mid-1940s Miami's architects were importing a new academic model, one heavily influenced by modernist architectural theories. They were eager to break with tradition. Economy and efficiency were paramount in an era recovering from the ravages of war, and the modern movement, having banished expensive ornamentation and being preoccupied with function, offered forms well suited to meet society's new demands. Modernism had been slow to affect American architectural practice, much less the building trades and the public in general, during the 1920s and 1930s, but that changed in the postwar years, as its influence became increasingly felt.

In 1947 the South Florida Chapter of the American Institute of Architects resumed publication of its magazine, *Florida Architecture and Allied Arts*. A group of prominent Miami architects made up the editorial board; these included Robert Law Weed and Robert M. Little, with whom Manley was working closely at the university. The journal became a powerful tool for disseminating new architectural ideals throughout the state, and while the majority of the magazine's pages were devoted to examples of traditional architecture, modern projects were increasingly featured. These projects included contemporary residential designs by the board members Little and Weed, as well as by Alfred Browning Parker, another preeminent Miami architect.[1]

Manley's own residential designs received local as well as national attention and were often featured in publications alongside the work of her male peers. In the later part of her career, she designed not only well-publicized houses but also numerous public buildings, and she ventured into town planning as well, focusing on the creation of an "ideal" residential neighborhood. While maintaining a successful practice, Manley served on numerous local and state boards. Her life of service to the profession, coupled with her body of accomplished work, earned her national distinction within her profession, confirmed in 1956 by her election to the prestigious College of Fellows of the American Institute of Architects.

RESIDENTIAL ARCHITECTURE

Manley's house for the well-known writer Philip Wylie was heralded as a "perfect object lesson on how to beat the Southern Florida climate" by *Architectural Forum*.[2] It is her best-known house of the period, in large part because of *Architectural Forum*'s ongoing series of articles documenting the residential work of leading South Florida architects (figure 112). The fact that this important professional journal presented her work alongside that of her more famous local male colleagues led to national recognition and local prestige.

The relatively modest house that Manley designed for the Wylie family was demolished in 2003 and replaced by an outsized, overscaled, latter-day Mediterranean revival mansion. Manley's plans for the Wylie house reveal many themes characteristic of her later work. Her evolving sense of style is in evidence here as she pursued her ambition to create a new and modern architecture in response to South Florida's climate and geography. The house was built in South Miami, a municipality three miles south of downtown Miami that was incorporated in 1927.[3] The architect and her client worked together to select the site on Erwin Road, a lot covered with mature oaks, pines, and palmettos. This lush indigenous landscape was well suited for developing the concept of an "outdoor house" that seamlessly interacted with South Florida's climate, inviting nearly year-round indoor-outdoor living.

The only surviving preliminary sketch for the Wylie house reveals Manley's initial focus, which was to forge a relationship between the building and the existing landscape. She plotted all of the mature trees on the site in order to insert the building carefully into the existing canopy (figure 113). As was the case for most of her residences of the period, the preservation of existing trees mandated the building's location on the site.

Manley's original working drawings for the project depict the house at the center of the densely wooded lot. She composed a plan of three detached pavilions, joined by a large screened porch (measuring approximately eighteen by thirty-five feet; figure 114). One pavilion was a study for the writer; another, a bedroom wing for guests and children. The third and largest pavilion had a living room with a dining area, the kitchen, and a carport on the ground level and, upstairs, a master bedroom. The living room, with its large retractable door, served as a seamless extension of the screened porch and was the most important indoor-outdoor room in the house (figure 115). The openings were choreographed to frame carefully selected views of the surrounding landscape. The large windows on the east and west walls guided the eye to the mature oaks on either side of the house, and the south-facing retractable door opened onto an expansive new lawn with a backdrop of pines and palmettos. For privacy, and to capture the prevailing breezes, the master bedroom suite was set above the carport at the northern end of the building. Here, large operable windows filled the entire length of the east and west walls, allowing an uninterrupted view into the canopy of surrounding oaks. Early morning and late afternoon sunlight filtered through the trees, providing the interior with light.[4]

Screened windows and deep overhangs, found throughout the house, protected it from rain and insects and permitted each space to remain open to the outside even through frequent afternoon showers. Large masonry walls, typically placed to the west, protected the interior from the harsh afternoon sun, and large windows on the east and southeast facades captured the prevailing southeasterly breezes. In describing the house, Philip Wylie told an interviewer, "This is the most livable, easy-to-keep, bugless house I've seen. . . . It does what a house should do. It's efficient." This was high praise coming from a prominent writer of the era who was known in part for his scathing critical abilities. The landscape played an important role in suggesting a carefully

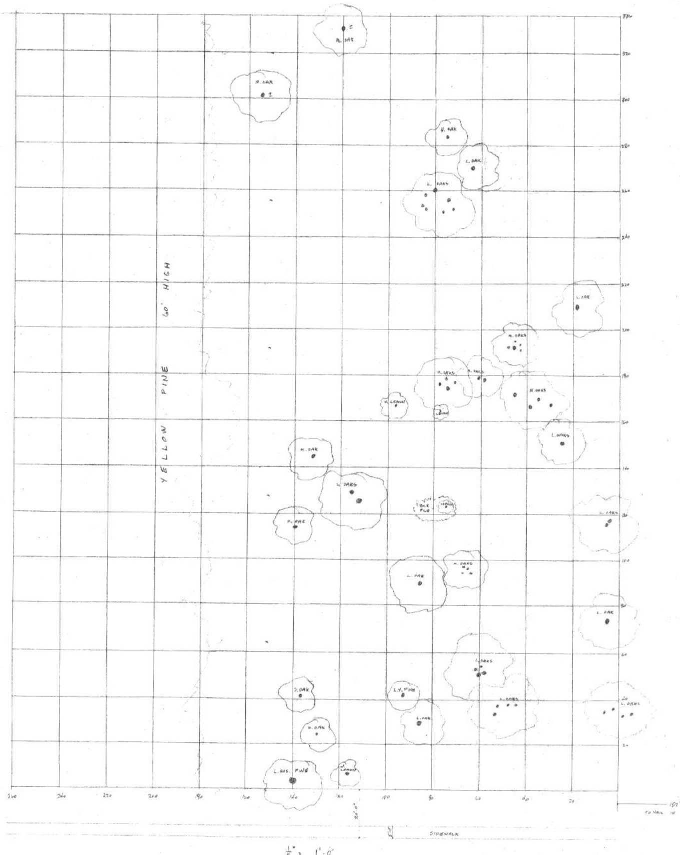

FIG. 113. Wylie house, South Miami, sketch of lot plotting location of existing trees (pencil on trace). Courtesy of the Historical Museum of Southern Florida, Marion Manley Collection.

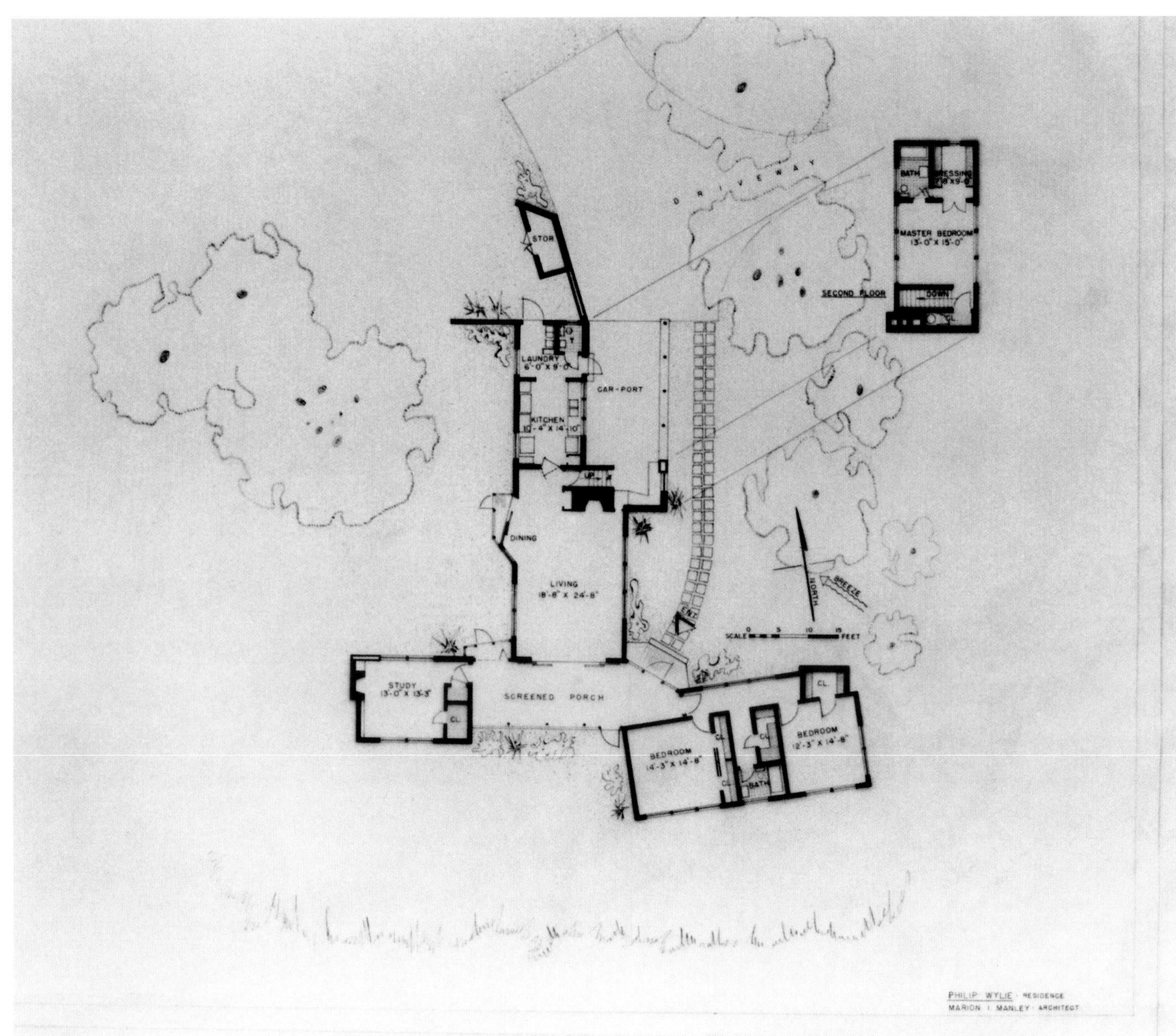

FIG. 114. Wylie house, South Miami, first-story floor plan (ink on vellum). Courtesy of the Historical Museum of Southern Florida, Marion Manley Collection.

conceived exterior color scheme for Wylie's house. Although no color photographs remain of the house in its original condition, a 1953 description in *Florida Architecture and Allied Arts* reveals that overhangs, seen against the expansive South Florida sky, were painted a "mild" blue; brick walls, with their varying shades of red, served as accents complementing large expanses of stucco walls painted "chartreuse," a pale green hue that served to integrate the pavilions visually with the surrounding landscape.[5]

Manley was interested not only in every detail of the overall design of the building but also in its construction. For her, it was important that the house be built of durable materials that could withstand the hot, humid, often violent climate of South Florida. To this end, she specified concrete floor joists and concrete walls, faced in stucco, brick, or cypress throughout, as well as terrazzo floors with brass joints that were not only resilient but also kept the building cool during the harsh summer months.

It is clear from the work itself, as well as from many people's recollections of her, that for Manley architecture was not only an act of drawing but also an act of building. She told a *Miami Herald* reporter that "architecture demands the whole man or the whole woman. The hand, the heart, and the brain are involved and no matter how strong our sex may be on heart and brain, we often lag when it is a matter of fitting bricks, making T-squares, handling masonry in the raw. Architecture isn't merely knowledge of Gothic arches, rose windows, building Florida rooms or fitting restrooms in a skyscraper. Lots of it is good, hard manual work."[6]

Manley certainly did not "lag behind" her colleagues in matters of construction; in fact, she played an active role in her projects from the drawing table to the jobsite. The same article goes on to describe Manley as "tall, brisk and overpowering. . . .Skilled in everything pertaining to building, [Miss Manley] takes complete charge of the workmen, masons, plumbers, carpenters and bricklayers, who swarm over a house under construction. She is not above taking the shovel or the hammer right out of their hands."[7]

FIG. 115. Wylie house, South Miami, view from living room toward screened porch. Courtesy of the Historical Museum of Southern Florida, Marion Manley Collection.

Themes prominent in the Wylie house are emphasized in another house built in South Miami six years later for Robert Hector and his family. The residence is still owned by the Hector family. Manley situated the house near the center of its lot, and in siting it, she was again careful to preserve as much as possible of the existing landscape. The house's major functions are, as in the Wylie house, dispersed into separate zones.

The primary living spaces, placed at the center of the plan, are composed around a large, L-shaped, screened passage. The living room, with its large, retractable wood panels (each eight feet wide), opens seamlessly onto the screened passage and provides an uninterrupted view of a triangular garden that is defined by the house itself and a lush wall of dense vegetation to the west.

The clear separation of public and private spaces in the Hector house is a recurring theme in other Manley houses from this period. The master bedroom suite is isolated to the west of the main living room, and a separate children's bedroom wing is located to the north of the primary living spaces, accessible only from the screened passage or the maid's quarters. An attached carport extends the house to the east (figure 116).

Manley's plan-making strategy here reflected international trends that sought to redefine the character of the contemporary home. Her generation of American designers took to heart the analyses by their profession's acknowledged masters, especially as they had been publicized by the Museum of Modern Art in an influential exhibition and accompanying catalog titled *Built in USA, 1932–1944*. Alvar Aalto was one of those practitioners whose pronouncements about the ways architecture should accommodate modern lifestyles were especially influential, and his ideas were showcased by the museum. The exhibit's curator, Elizabeth Mock, cited Aalto as the architect "who made many of us more conscious of the strongly differentiated character of the modern family," noting that "his charming sketches suggested recognition of the private lives of the individuals as well as their membership in the group." By so clearly differentiating the separate spaces to which Wylie and Hector family members might retreat at some distance from

FIG. 116. Hector house, Coconut Grove, plan. Drawing by Alvaro Briganti.

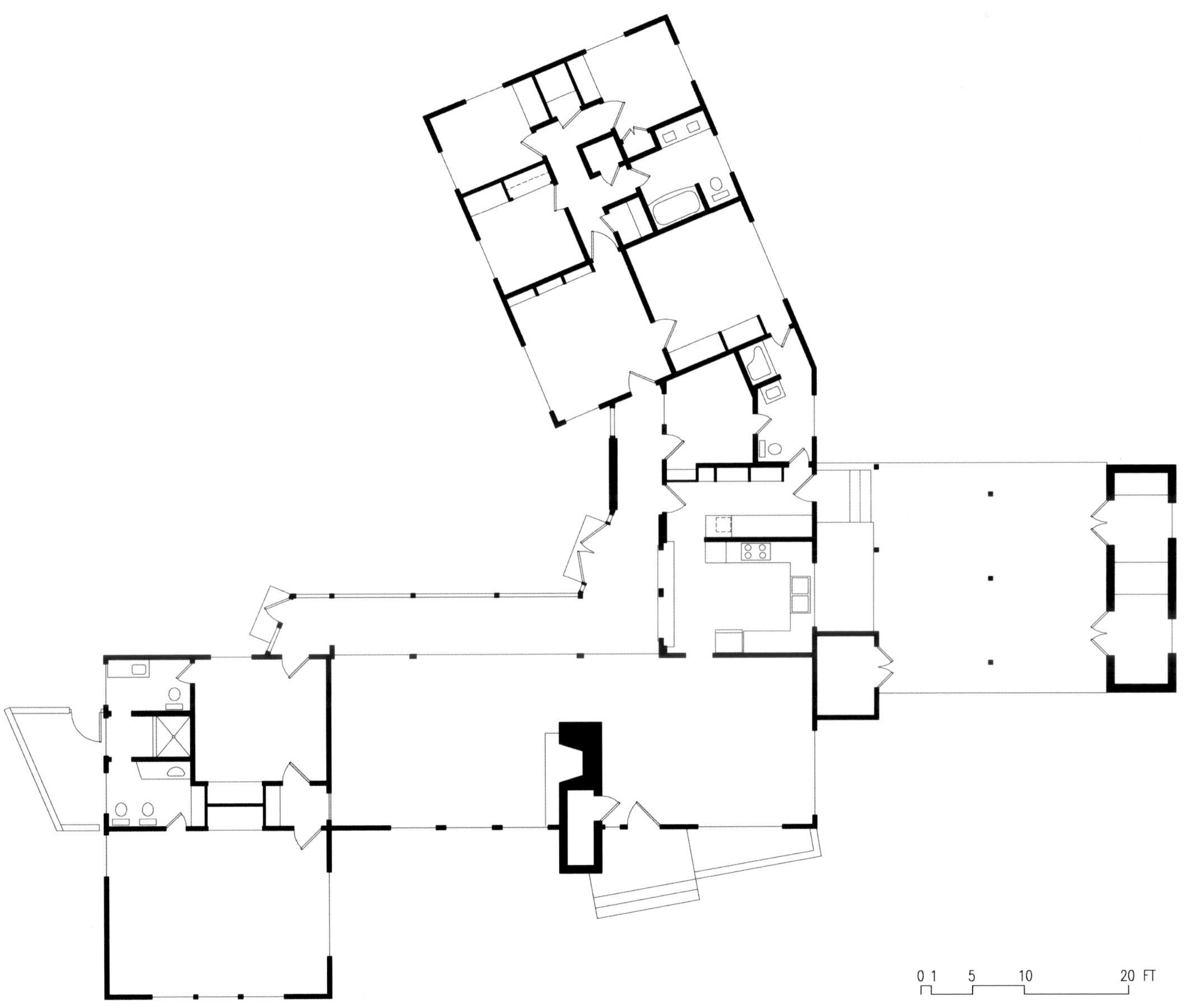
0 1 5 10 20 FT

the more public rooms of their houses, Manley physically drew into these house plans her own consciousness of that "strongly differentiated character."[8]

Today the unassuming profile of the Hector house, barely visible from the street, is nestled under mature oaks and native hardwood trees. Many of the original details, including exposed concrete block, terrazzo floors, and interior wood paneling remain unaltered. The house is virtually intact with the exception of a few minor interior alterations and the glass enclosure of the screened passage.

Even while designing these 1950s houses that express her personal responses to modernist ideals, Manley was developing several more direct, contemporary interpretations of Florida's vernacular architecture. She gave her ideas their most articulate form in a 1952 house that she called her cracker-style cypress cottage. As the early Floridian pioneers had done, she set this house within a clearing in the landscape, hovering above the damp ground on masonry piers.[9]

Manley designed this cracker-style cottage for Peyton Wilson in Homestead, Florida. The second-oldest city in Dade County, Homestead, located approximately thirty-five miles southwest of Miami, was incorporated in 1913. As an area opened up for homesteading at the turn of the twentieth century, the place had become the nameless construction camp at the end of the Florida East Coast Railway's line while it was being extended to Key West, and materials and supplies for the railroad workers were simply addressed to "Homestead Country," a designation shortened to "Homestead" by the engineers who later mapped the area.[10]

The modest cracker-style cottage is a reinterpretation of the typical vernacular dogtrot, a two-room structure with a large front porch, its nearly freestanding rooms separated by a breezeway but joined by one common roof (figure 117). The dogtrot developed from the one-room house that any pioneering homesteader typically built before adding an extra room. The dogtrot type, which can be seen throughout the country, was especially popular in Florida during the nineteenth century because it generated an abundance of covered outdoor space.

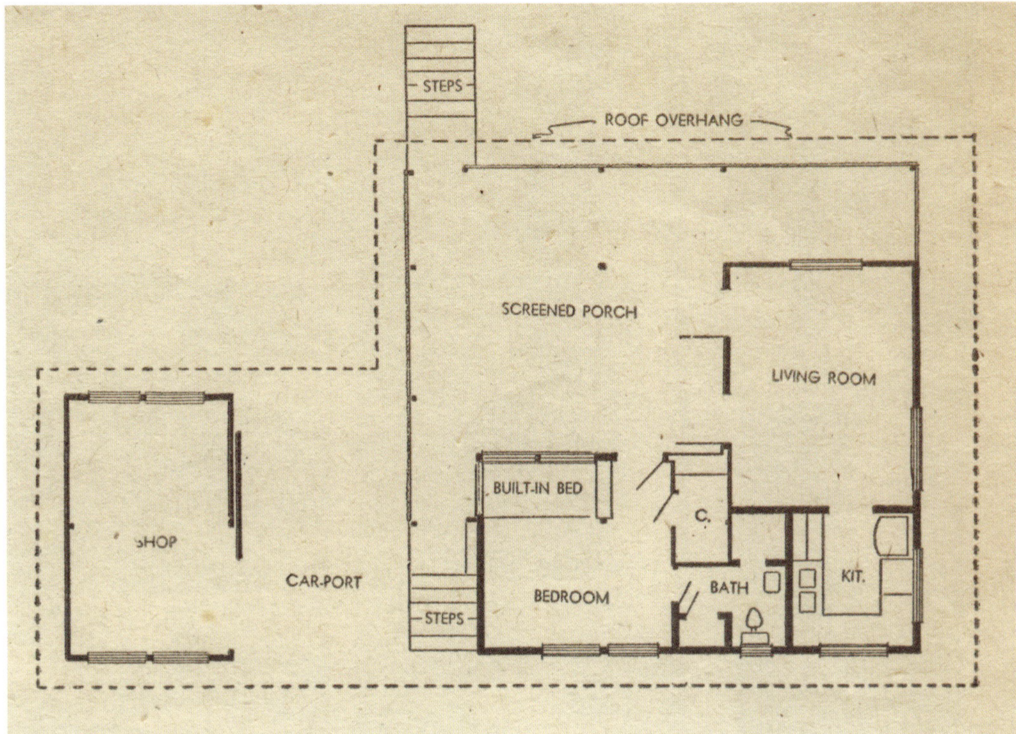

FIG. 117. Cracker-style cottage, plan. Courtesy of the Historical Museum of Southern Florida, Marion Manley Collection.

The original drawings illustrate how Manley transformed the traditional breezeway of the dogtrot house into a carport that separates a workshop from the primary living spaces. In sharp contrast to the compact interior, Manley expanded the traditional porch to become a large open room that serves as an extension of the main living space, capturing the southeasterly breezes and providing an uninterrupted view of the lush surrounding landscape (figure 118). That porch is arguably the most important room in the house and the ideal place for "hammock living."[11] Large enough for hanging a hammock from end to end, it is a place where one could sit, eat, read, or sleep throughout the day (figure 119).

FIG. 119. Cracker-style cottage, living room. Courtesy of the Historical Museum of Southern Florida, Marion Manley Collection.

FIG. 118. Interior, built-in bed, cracker-style cottage. Courtesy of the Historical Museum of Southern Florida, Marion Manley Collection.

The well-publicized Sam Bell house (1951–52) is another of Manley's designs that evokes the architectural sensibilities of Florida's early settlers. Although the typological reference is less specifically apparent here than in her cracker-style cottage, the Bell house again demonstrates the architect's fundamental desire to create a building responsive to the vagaries of the Florida climate (figure 120). The Bell house was built in the Moorings, a small subdivision within Coconut Grove approximately four miles south of the Miami River along Biscayne Bay. Coconut Grove is the area's oldest settlement, with roots dating to 1806 when a Bahamian emigrant began cultivating land there. Homesteaders took advantage of provisions of the congressional act of 1862 that granted title to as many as 160 acres after five years of residence.[12]

FIG. 120. Bell house, Coconut Grove. Courtesy of the Historical Museum of Southern Florida, Marion Manley Collection.

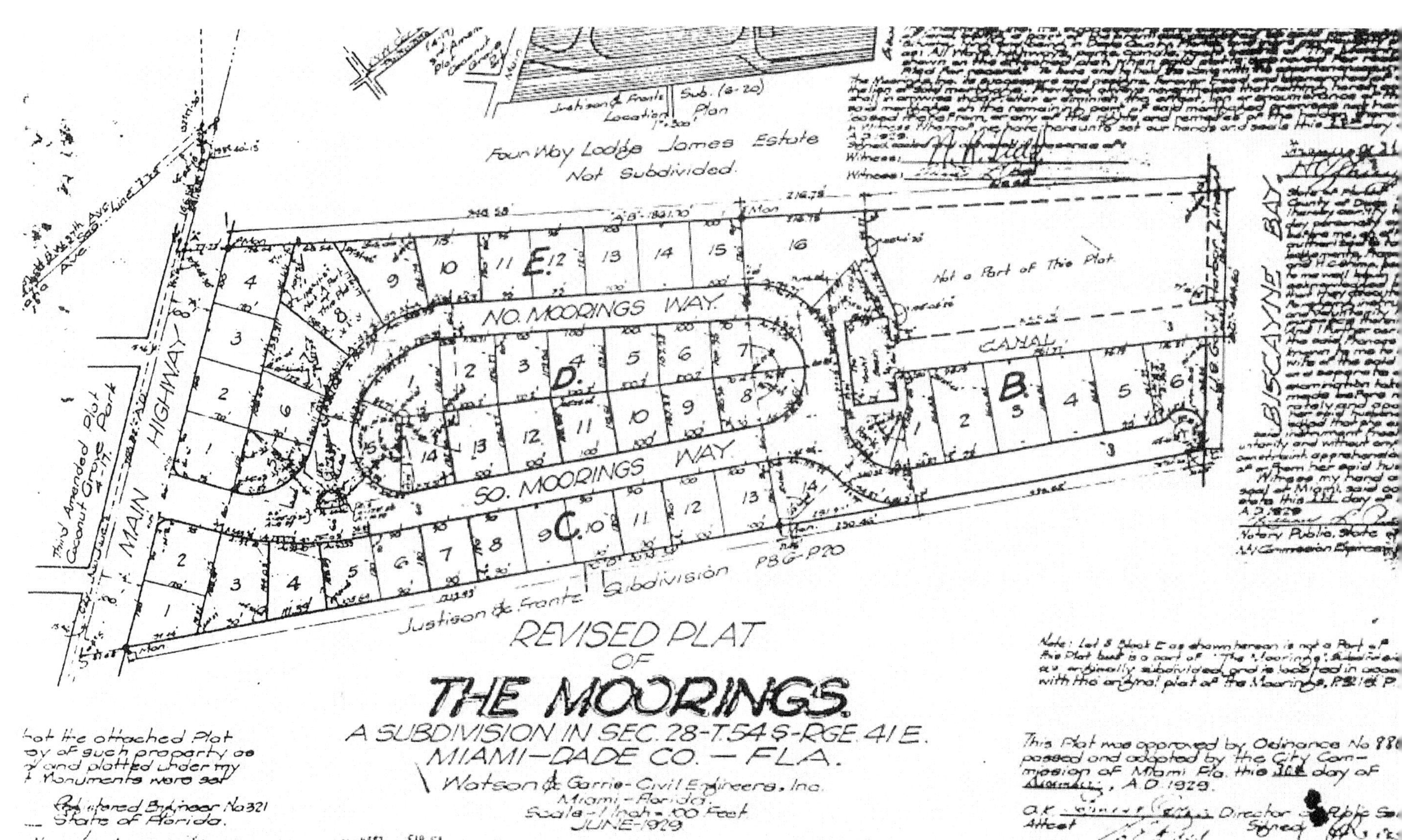

FIG. 121. Revised plat of Moorings subdivision, Coconut Grove, 1929. Courtesy of the Arva Moore Parks Collection.

In the late nineteenth and early twentieth centuries, Coconut Grove attracted artists and intellectuals from the North, who shaped it as a distinctive local community; the old homesteads were subdivided as residential developments. One of them, the Moorings, was named after a house with that name owned by Mrs. Jessie S. Moore, a widow from Massachusetts who was a founding member of Coconut Grove's Second Christian Science Church. Her home, built about 1897, was a large vernacular wooden structure with deep overhangs and wide verandas; its name was adopted by the subdivision platted in 1929, of which her land became a part.[13] Manley's Sam Bell residence was located on a prominent waterfront site within the subdivision (figure 121).

Like the early settlers who raised their homes above the ground to protect them from the frequent rainstorms, Manley elevated the Bell house to avoid water damage during the inevitable hurricanes. Manley's early drawing showing a section through the house depicts the floor of the second level set above the high-water line of the 1945 hurricane (figure 122).[14] This "house-on-stilts" prototype

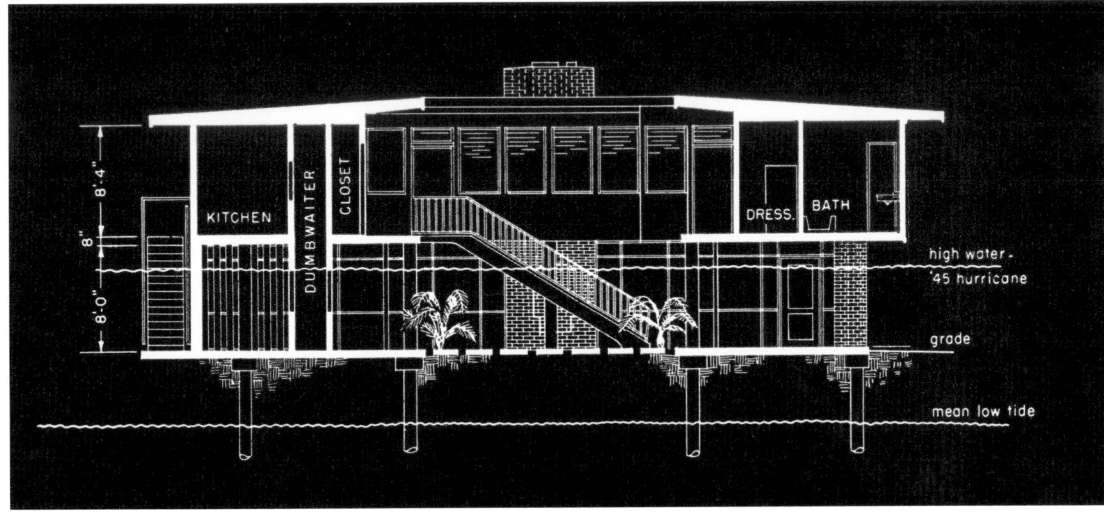

FIG. 122. Bell house, Coconut Grove, cross section indicating "high-water" line of the 1945 hurricane. Courtesy of Special Collections, University of Miami Libraries, Coral Gables, Florida.

FIG. 123. Bell house, Coconut Grove, first-floor screened lounge. Courtesy of the Historical Museum of Southern Florida, Marion Manley Collection.

was becoming popular among Florida architects for waterfront homes. Other examples include the Adler house (1951) in Miami, designed by Rufus Nims, and the Collins residence (1961) in Coconut Grove, designed by Peter Jefferson.

Anticipating future storm surges, Manley fortified Sam Bell's house below the high-water line with concrete construction and with brick in the chimneys and plumbing-stack enclosures. The only lightweight element below that critical line was the screen wall that defined the perimeter of the inhabitable first floor. This thin architectural screen blurred the boundaries between indoors and out, defining what could be regarded as a giant covered porch at grade level (figure 123). Within that space was a double-story court open to the sky. Architectural journalists of the day called this open court a "patio in the air" (figure 124).[15] The description was, however, misleading, for in the Bell residence this feature did not function as it would have in a traditional patio house with an inhabited patio at grade, a patio spatially defined within that tradition by the most important rooms in the house. Manley saw the patio here as part of the open ground floor, extending the garden horizontally under the house and then rising up through it to serve as the primary circulation space. The vertical court enhanced the passive cooling of the structure by allowing warm air to rise through the center and draw replacement air in from below, creating a cooling evaporative effect throughout (figure 125).

During the mid-1950s, in addition to the houses that brought attention to Manley in the local and national press, she also designed her own house in Coconut Grove, as well as numerous wooden cottages throughout the city, none of which were published. All of these give ample evidence of her commitment to and belief in vernacular methods of construction as the most reasonable ones for building in the tropics. In these houses her compact plans that cross ventilate, her ample exterior spaces, and her use of wood all hark back to the pioneer models.

About 1955 Manley built for herself a modest two-bedroom house along Battersea Road in Coconut Grove, which she shared with her companion, Lillian Fly. The house is placed at the center of a large lot, measuring about 100 × 140 feet, and is rotated off the reticular street grid to capture the prevailing southeasterly breezes. Like the Hector house, it is almost hidden from the street, masked by a screen of mature trees including sea grapes, pines, and palmettos (figure 126). Once again, the preservation of existing trees was Manley's primary concern when siting the building. The house remains standing today, but both the building and landscape have been badly neglected.

In this, her own home, Manley demonstrated the possibilities of building for a life in close proximity to nature, devising a plan that allowed her to experience the landscape and its wildlife very directly. The plan is T-shaped, placing

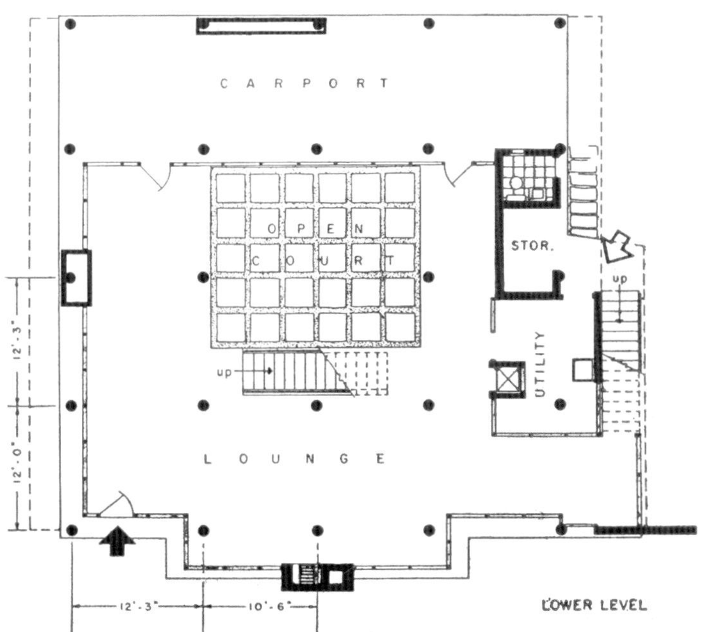

FIG. 124. Bell house, Coconut Grove, floor plans. Courtesy of Special Collections, University of Miami Libraries, Coral Gables, Florida.

FIG. 125. Bell house, Coconut Grove, courtyard. Courtesy of Special Collections, University of Miami Libraries, Coral Gables, Florida.

FIG. 126. Manley house, Coconut Grove. Photograph by Carie Penabad.

the primary living spaces (including the living room, screened porch, and bedrooms) to the east and perpendicular to the kitchen, carport, and toolshed (figure 127). Large, operable, screened windows throughout the house provide uninterrupted views of the surrounding landscape and ample cross ventilation. Perhaps in the interest of economy, or because she had no children, she did not opt for a scheme of separate pavilions for public and private activities, as she had done at the Wylie house. Instead, she produced a more compact plan, reflective of her own needs. She lived in the house until her death in 1984.

Manley's reverence for the landscape, manifested in the design of her own house, involved a great deal more than the simple act of saving a few trees. She was concerned with the preservation of the shady canopy that made life outdoors not just bearable but pleasurable. She was also concerned with preservation as a function of protecting the natural habitat for wildlife.

Marjory Stoneman Douglas surely fostered Manley's preoccupation with preservation, and as was their habit, they shared their ideas in an ongoing exchange.

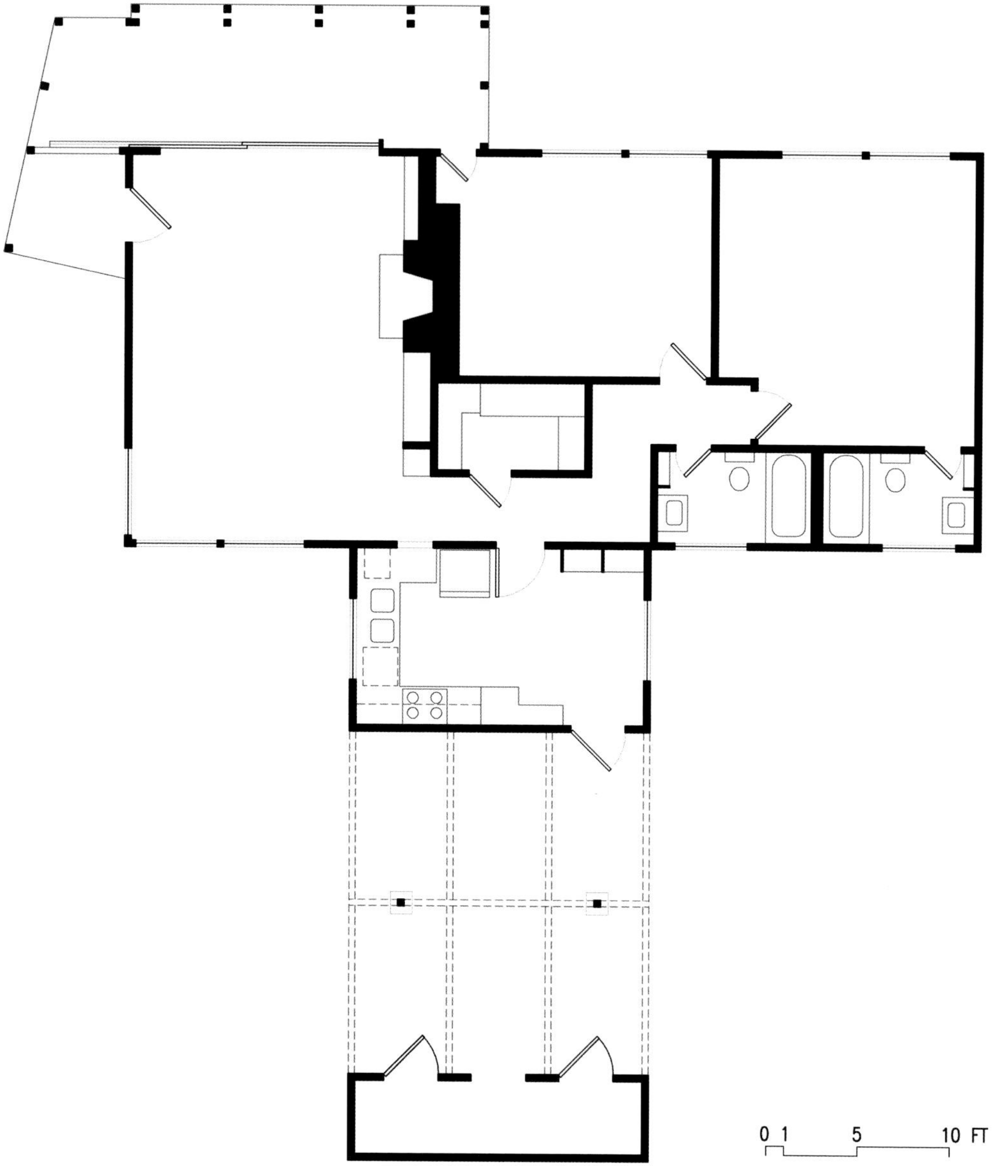

0 1 5 10 FT

FIG. 127. Manley house, Coconut Grove, floor plan. Drawing by Alvaro Briganti.

In the 1920s, when their concerns ran parallel, they engaged in a prolonged and fruitful dialogue as Manley designed various Mediterranean modes and Douglas wrote about the Mediterranean style in Coral Gables. Such was the case throughout the 1950s—the built forms of the one continued to correlate with the ideas about which the other wrote.

Douglas published countless articles and numerous books on both the natural and man-made history of the state. In 1947, in her seminal work, *The Everglades: A River of Grass*, she poetically described the nature and history of the state's unique swampland and eloquently appealed for its preservation for future generations. In her book *The Joys of Bird Watching in Florida*, Douglas wrote: "You will never forget the pleasure of meeting suddenly, walking through some shadowy hammock among live oaks, the imperious stare of a Barred Owl from his tree branch, or, by a little stream, [catching] sight of two of three Anhingas, spreading out their dark wings to dry in the air from a little bush. . . . And to look up and suddenly behold, over the tops of the small white cypress or an open Glade, the splendid flying of a pair of Bald Eagles, is to experience an excitement that cannot be bought with money."[16]

For Douglas, the birds and the landscape were intimately connected; one could not be appreciated without the other. Manley shared this sensibility. She kept for many years a notebook in which she recorded each season's first sighting of every species that visited her yard. A page from it reads like that of an amateur ornithologist's. It carefully lists not only particular species but also the number of times they were spotted.[17]

The most elegant examples of the group of small wooden cottages Manley built from the mid-1950s into the 1960s include the cottage designed in 1957 for Ray Sadler and built in Miami, as well as two structures designed in 1963 for the Quatrefoil Corporation and built on Jackson Avenue in Coconut Grove.[18] Original drawings depict compact structures situated on thin, rectangular lots measuring approximately 50 by 135 feet.

Each cottage, which had a primary living space with an open kitchen, a small bedroom, and a bath, was approximately eight hundred square feet. Each also had a large screened porch that played a vital role in these designs, nearly doubling the size of usable space. All were wood-framed constructions, built predominantly of Douglas fir with cedar board-and-batten siding. Each was covered by a steeply pitched gabled roof with deep overhangs that provided protection from the incessant tropical rains. Certain architectural details, including large wood-lath lattice grills, flared ridge beams, and upturned rafter ends, were inspired by traditional Japanese roof assemblies, producing far more elegant profiles than were commonly associated with her other cottages of the period. Inside, exposed wood rafters not only revealed the building's structure but also created a more expansive sense of space (figures 128 and 129). Sadly, none of these buildings remain standing today.

In addition to these small wooden cottages and her larger individually commissioned residences, during the early 1960s Manley also designed inexpensive speculative housing for the new Miami Lakes community built by the Graham family. Ernest R. Graham (1886–1957), the family patriarch, had moved to Dade

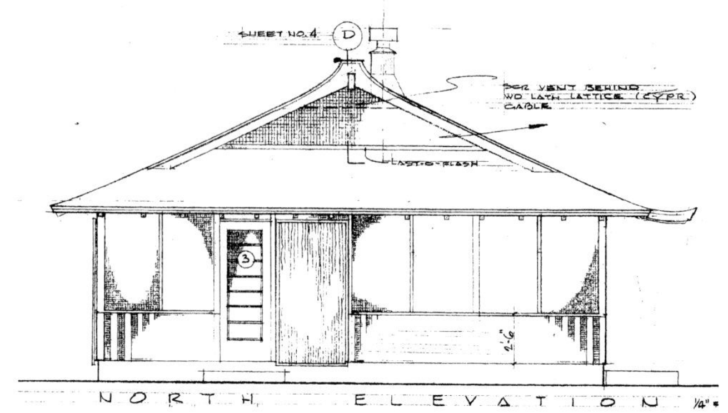

FIG. 128. Sadler cottage, Miami, north elevation. Courtesy of the Historical Museum of Southern Florida, Marion Manley Collection.

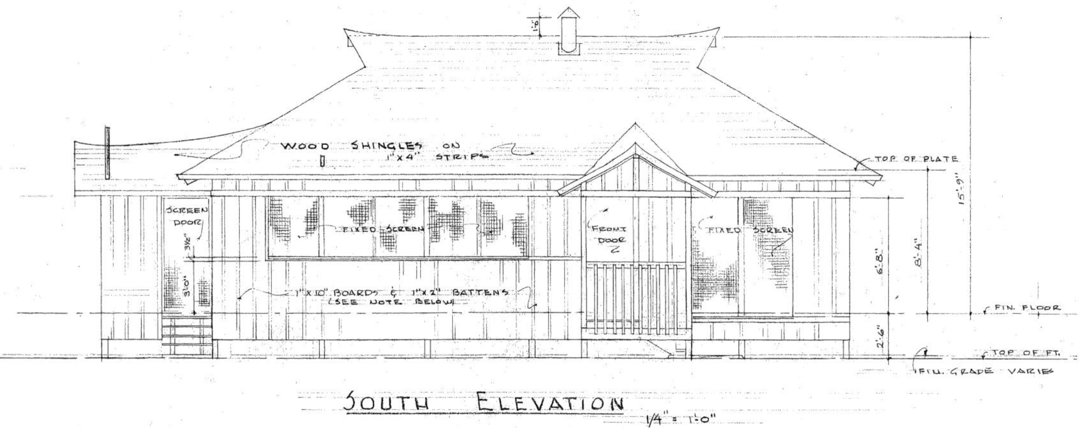

FIG. 129. Quatrefoil Corporation cottage, Coconut Grove, south elevation. Courtesy of the Historical Museum of Southern Florida, Marion Manley Collection.

County from South Dakota in 1921. In Florida he farmed, dealt in real estate, and served in the Florida senate from 1937 to 1944. His son Philip Graham (1915–63) was the publisher of the *Washington Post* from 1946 until his death, and his youngest son, Daniel Robert (Bob) Graham (b. 1936), was governor of Florida from 1979 to 1987 and a U.S. senator from 1987 to 2005.[19]

In the 1930s Ernest Graham purchased the land for dairy farming that was to become the site of the town of Miami Lakes, located approximately twenty miles northwest of downtown Miami. As the city grew, the Graham family created the Sengra Development Corporation and hired the well-known Chicago firm of Collins, Simonds, and Simonds to develop a master plan for the twenty-four-hundred-acre parcel. During the 1960s and 1970s this Chicago firm, specializing in large-scale land-use planning, designed nearly twenty major Florida communities including Fisher Island, Weston, and Pelican Bay. It pioneered the concept of the planned unit development, a system of planning that promotes the clustering of development in order to ensure the conservation of natural resources.[20]

For Miami Lakes, Collins, Simonds, and Simonds proposed a variety of residential units, including single family houses, town houses, and apartments, grouped around twenty lakes. The project also had a championship golf course, an industrial district (developed beside the Opa-Locka airfield), shopping areas at the center of the town, a complex of resort hotels, and various churches and schools.[21]

The Grahams' Sengra Corporation hired three architects—Marion Manley, Joel Myer, and Robert Little—to design the prototypes for the first three hundred houses within the larger plan produced by Collins, Simonds, and Simonds. Manley contributed schemes for three models in this development. Each is L-shaped, with the primary living spaces and an enclosed garage along the street and a perpendicular volume behind with three bedrooms and a shared bath.[22]

Manley's prototypes are low to the ground and horizontally proportioned with very little architectural detailing. She omitted, or more probably was asked to omit, any important exterior spaces including porches and screened passages—features that had figured so prominently in her earlier residential work (figure 130). Participating in this corporate project was a trying experience for Manley, but she was able to amuse herself by using the process as the inspiration for a witty little poem she wrote in 1965 and called "Ode to Owner Builds." In her poem, the architect voiced her dissatisfaction with the corporate design-construction process. Her verses ridicule the shifts of direction during the lengthy planning and building process, blaming much of the confusion on frequent hiring and firing of construction staff, as in these lines:

They're changing the guard at Miami Lakes
Its hard to remember how many this makes
First was McCammon assisted by Mix
They started the building with concrete and bricks
With all sorts of labor and all kinds of gear,
Threw the plans in the corner and played it by ear.
The air hammers came with their beautiful song
To pound out the concrete they'd put in all wrong
These instruments stayed and they jammered and yammered
They left, then came back and still hammered and stammered.
With Jernigan gone and Mix disappearing
Is it possible another new crisis is nearing?[23]

Despite the difficulties, Manley was to see a number of her models realized at Miami Lakes.

Manley returned to the house-on-stilts prototype, as she had done more than a decade earlier at the Sam Bell house (1951–52), for two designs of the mid-1960s, one that was not realized and another that was built. While the Zims were never to build the house she designed for them in 1964 (figure 131), Eugene and Gwladys Scott did build—quite literally with their own hands—the house that

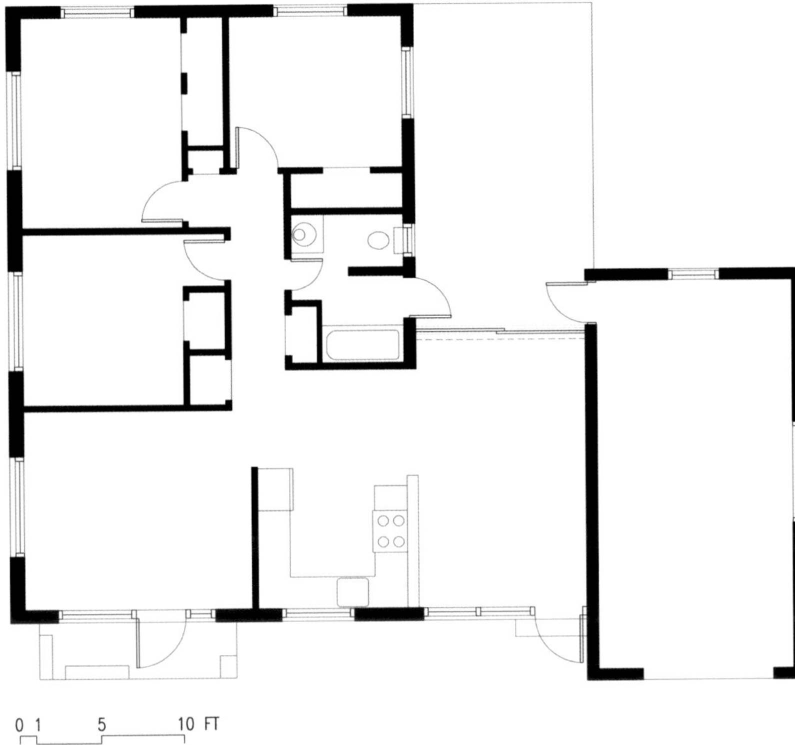

FIG. 130. Miami Lakes housing prototype. Drawing by Alvaro Briganti.

in 1967 they first asked Manley to design for their lot in Palmetto Bay. This was a newly developed subdivision twenty miles southwest of Miami (figure 132). When the Scotts approached Manley, who was by then seventy-four years old, they feared she would turn them down because they did not have enough money to pay her fees. However, as they recalled in 2008, Manley sat patiently through the young couple's description of the densely wooded lot they had recently purchased.[24] It occupied a transitional area between two natural habitats—pineland and seasonally wet prairie. As is often the case when two diverse habitats meet,

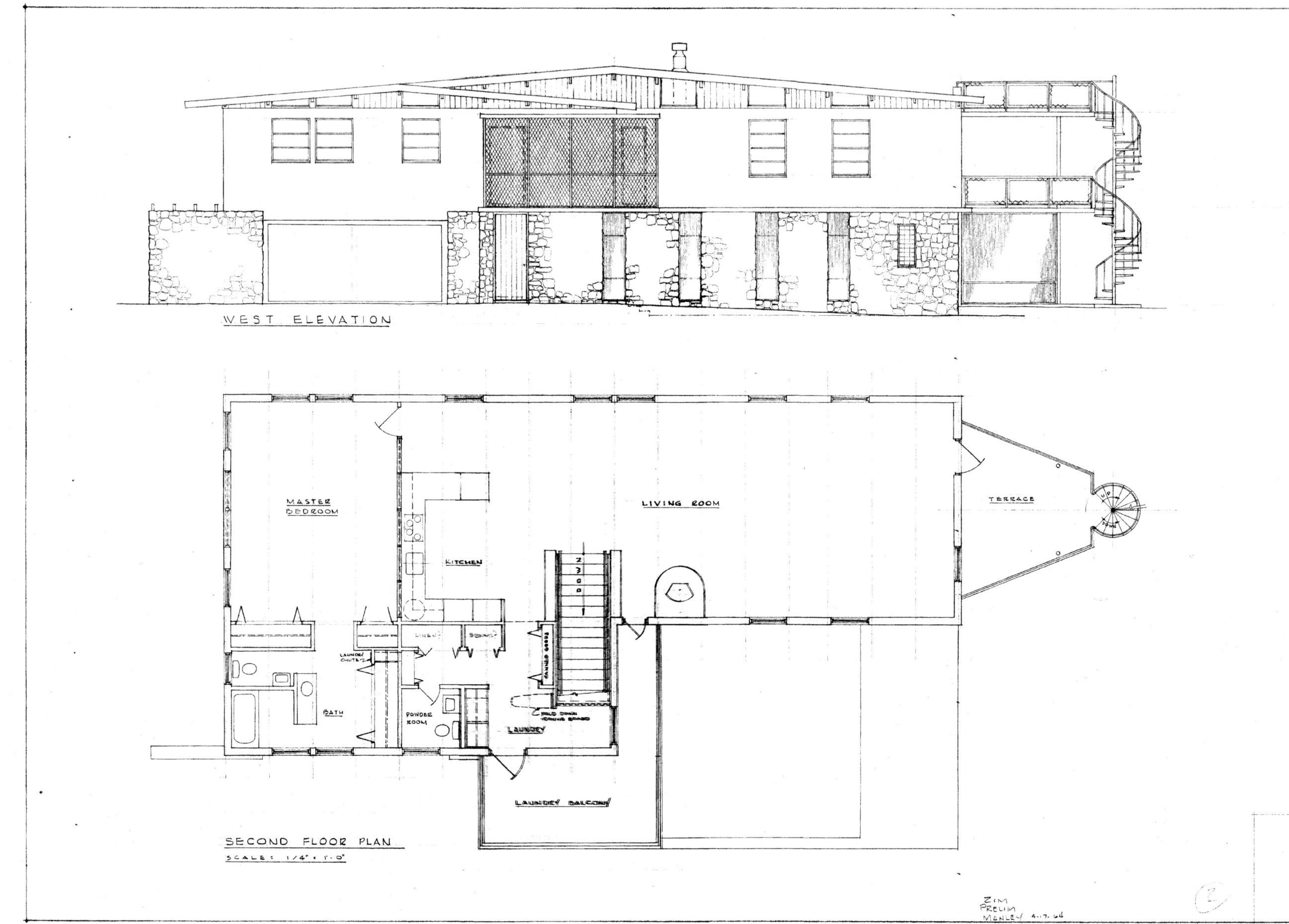

FIG. 131. Zim house, unbuilt project, plan and elevation. Courtesy of the Historical Museum of Southern Florida, Marion Manley Collection.

native plant diversity on the site was extraordinary; the Scotts wanted to protect it by gently fitting into the verdant landscape a house with as small a footprint as possible.[25]

Their reverence for the place resonated with Manley, and she agreed to work with them. On their first site visit, the elderly architect stepped out of the car and charged into the center of the thick hammock—something the Scotts themselves said they, though young and curious, had never done. According to Eugene Scott, "She was strong, fearless, and full of energy."[26] In that instant, they knew she was the best architect for the job.

At one of the earliest design meetings, Gwladys Scott showed Manley a copy of *House Beautiful* that she had saved since its publication in August 1960 for its articles about the beauty and simplicity of traditional Japanese domestic architecture and the many lessons it had to teach about the design of a contemporary American house. Again the Scotts' interests resonated with Manley's.[27] Nearly a decade earlier, she had adapted a variety of Japanese roof details for the Sadler and Quatrefoil Group cottages (see figures 128 and 129).

The elements of the traditional Japanese house that most appealed to both Manley and her clients were the open columnar plan and the layered system of sliding wall panels that could be used singly or in combination with one another to respond to varying social and climatic conditions. When open, these movable panels provided framed views of the garden, extending the interior (both visually and physically) into the surrounding landscape. The steep pitch and deep overhangs of the Japanese roof were also especially appealing, as they seemed well suited to protect a Miami house from intense heat and rainfall.[28]

The Scotts constructed Manley's Japanese-inspired design from salvaged Dade County pine and cypress with the help of Manley's talented and trusted carpenter Chuck Wilcox. Eugene acted as contractor, pouring concrete columns and beams for the first floor, while Gwladys and their four children worked on interior wall paneling for the upstairs. Manley stopped in on a regular basis to make sure things were being done properly.[29]

FIG. 132. Scott house, Miami. Photograph by Patrick Farrell.

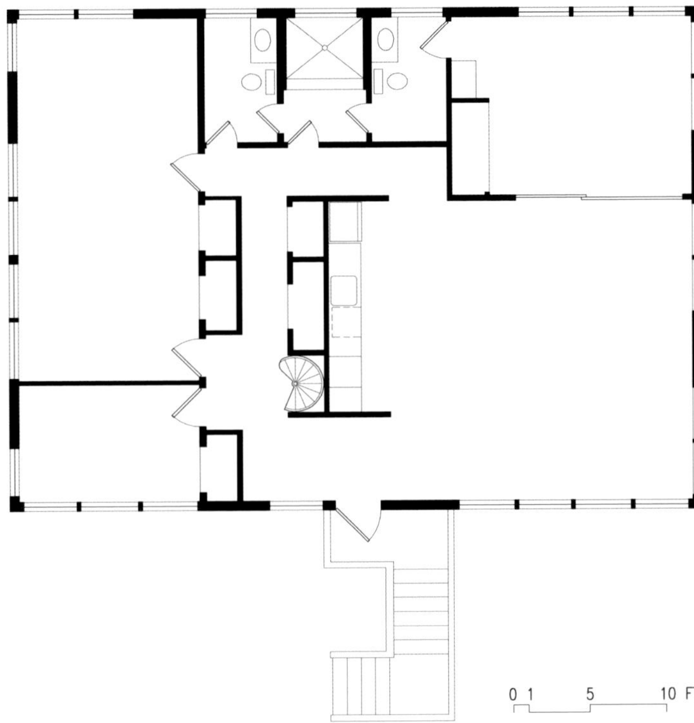

FIG. 133. Scott house, Miami, second-story floor plan. Drawing by Alvaro Briganti.

The primary living spaces hover over the columnar concrete structure (which has since been enclosed) and are accessed by an exterior wooden stair. The living room, kitchen, master bedroom, and bath, along with an open children's wing, fill the upper floor, largely constructed of local pine and cypress. The living room walls, sliding wood glass-and-screen panels, can be opened on all sides to provide panoramic views of the midlevel canopy (figure 133). Interior wall panels can be moved to create varying plan configurations. Most notably, the children's wing can be partitioned into four smaller cells or opened to create one large room.

The Scotts still live in the house that Manley designed for them nearly four decades ago. It is nearly intact and the surrounding native landscape has grown

FIG. 134. Scott house, Miami, living room and surrounding landscape. Photograph by Patrick Farrell.

and endured. "Watching the way that landscape functions and changes and what birds and insects arrive and thrive are the most appealing aspects of living here," says Gwladys Scott (figure 134).[30] Their lot preserves one of the last vestiges of indigenous hammocks in the area; the remainder have been cleared by local developers.

PUBLIC BUILDINGS

In the later years of her career Marion Manley won a variety of commissions for public buildings in Florida, well beyond the confines of Dade County. They range from modest structures, such as the Quaker meetinghouse in South Miami, to more high-profile work, most notably dormitories for Florida State University in Tallahassee and the Asolo Theater in Sarasota. As in the 1930s, she collaborated with leading architects of the region on many of these jobs. However, while her earlier male collaborators had received the lead credits, by the late 1940s and through the 1960s, she had earned a fine reputation that had spread across the state, and she was listed as the principal architect of these designs.

In 1948 Manley worked with Guy Chandler Fulton, one of the most notable of her later collaborators, on a project for three men's dormitories for Florida State University in Tallahassee, though they were never built. Fulton, who held the post of university architect for the State Board of Control for the University of Florida from 1944 to 1956, was largely responsible for the architectural and urban vision of its post–World War II campus. The architects sited the proposed dormitories on a large, sloping, rectangular parcel at the corner of Jefferson Street and Wildwood Drive in Tallahassee, along the northeast corner of the current campus. They drew three independent object buildings that broke with the reticular grid of the existing campus. Set at varying angles to one another, the buildings were loosely joined by a new curvilinear driveway from Wildwood Drive (figure 135).

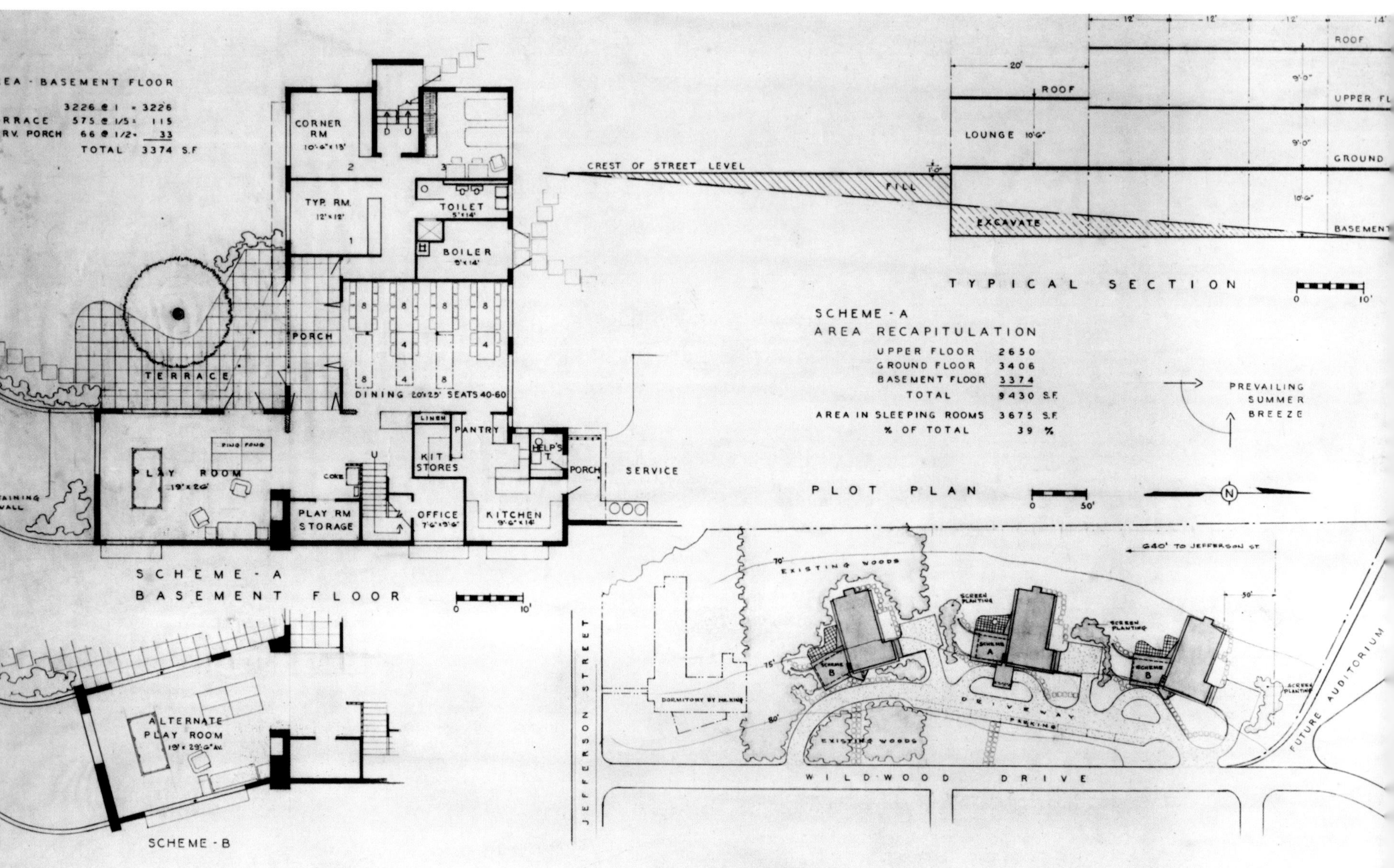

REA - BASEMENT FLOOR
3226 @ 1 = 3226
RRACE 575 @ 1/5 = 115
ERV. PORCH 66 @ 1/2 = 33
TOTAL 3374 S.F
CORNER RM
TYP. RM.
TOILET
BOILER
PORCH
TERRACE
DINING 20'x25' SEATS 40-60
PANTRY
KIT STORES
HELP'S T
PORCH
SERVICE
PLAY ROOM 19'x 26'
PLAY RM STORAGE
OFFICE
KITCHEN
TAINING WALL
SCHEME - A
BASEMENT FLOOR
ALTERNATE PLAY ROOM
SCHEME - B
ROOF
UPPER FL
GROUND
BASEMENT
LOUNGE 10'6"
CREST OF STREET LEVEL
FILL
EXCAVATE
TYPICAL SECTION
SCHEME - A
AREA RECAPITULATION
UPPER FLOOR 2650
GROUND FLOOR 3406
BASEMENT FLOOR 3374
TOTAL 9430 S.F.
AREA IN SLEEPING ROOMS 3675 S.F.
% OF TOTAL 39 %
PREVAILING SUMMER BREEZE
PLOT PLAN
640' TO JEFFERSON ST
EXISTING WOODS
JEFFERSON STREET
DORMITORY BY MR. KING
DRIVEWAY
PARKING
WILDWOOD DRIVE
FUTURE AUDITORIUM
THREE MEN'S DORMITORIES
FLORIDA STATE UNIVERSITY
TALLAHASSEE, FLORIDA
MARION I. MANLEY - ARCHITECT
COCONUT GROVE, FLORIDA
IN ASSOCIATION WITH
GUY C. FULTON, ARCHITECT TO THE STATE BOARD OF CONTROL

This site-planning strategy accorded fully with contemporary planning theories that called for the abandonment of the traditional city, with its dense network of well-defined streets, preferring instead free-standing modernist forms, objects set on expansive greens. The leading advocate of such schemes was the formidable European architect Le Corbusier. Manley, an enthusiast of all things new, specifically, as the visual evidence of her work indicates, of Le Corbusier, adopted similar plans in many of her larger-scaled projects. Among these the most significant was the University of Miami master plan (see figure 70), and Manley relied on a similar scheme in her unbuilt Town Shores housing project of 1949 in Miami (figure 136).

FIG. 135. Florida State University, Tallahassee, men's dormitories. Courtesy of the Historical Museum of Southern Florida, Marion Manley Collection.

The Florida State dormitory buildings would have been modest two-story masonry structures with underground basements. The plans showed communal rooms on the first floor, including a lounge, kitchen, dining hall (seating forty to sixty), and a screened porch and outdoor terrace; the upper floors consisted of typical twelve-foot-by-twelve-foot rooms for students. While maintaining a minimalist aesthetic here, Manley and Fulton abandoned the more usual flat roofs, emblematic of the international style, in favor of a series of gently sloping roofs better suited for providing protection from Florida's rains. In addition concrete eyebrows and operable awning windows replaced the more iconic horizontal openings of the European precedents and were utilized to promote cross ventilation and protect the interiors from the harsh sun (figure 137).

Nearly a decade after that joint effort on a never-realized project, Manley and Fulton again worked together, this time on an addition to the John and Mable Ringling Museum of Art in Sarasota, a project that was completed in the mid-1950s and opened to a great deal of national publicity.[31] The addition was constructed specifically to house what has repeatedly been called the "gemlike" Asolo Theater. This is an eighteenth-century Italian structure, a precious antique object that the museum had acquired in 1950 (figure 138).

Manley and Fulton designed their building as an addition to a Renaissance villa of the 1920s, its forms derived from several Italian models reinterpreted for

FIG. 136. Aerial perspective, Town Shores, unbuilt housing project. Courtesy of the Historical Museum of Southern Florida, Marion Manley Collection.

FIG. 137. Rendering, Florida State University dormitories, Tallahassee. Courtesy of the Historical Museum of Southern Florida, Marion Manley Collection.

FIG. 138. Asolo Theater. Courtesy of the Historical Museum of Southern Florida, Marion Manley Collection.

Florida. John Ringling (1866–1936), one of the founding partners of Ringling Brothers Circus, built the museum between 1925 and 1928 to designs by John H. Phillips, a relatively unknown New York architect. Phillips designed an imposing building from which loggias extended to embrace a generous courtyard within a verdant tropical setting.[32] This villa housed Ringling's art collection in a setting that fulfilled his wish to make his collection available to the people of Florida so that they might study art without leaving the state.

The museum commands a prominent site within a grand architectural complex that the circus impresario had begun creating in 1912, when he acquired sixty-six acres of waterfront property several miles north of the city center. Ringling's own residence, Cá d'Zan, dominated that complex, looking like a grand Venetian palace. It was designed by another New York architect, Dwight James Baum. Begun in the same year that construction started on the museum, it was completed two years sooner, in 1926. Cá d'Zan stands before a one-hundred-foot-long terrace overlooking Sarasota Bay. In 1927, just after completing his palatial home, Ringling made Sarasota the winter home for his entire troupe, annually installing his employees and their menagerie nearby.[33]

Ringling was to enjoy this new home for less than a decade; he died in 1936, bequeathing the site and its buildings to the people of Florida. Extensive litigation prolonged the settling of his estate for nearly a decade.[34] In 1946 the Florida State Board of Control was given responsibility for the property and A. Everett Austin (1900–1957), former director of the Wadsworth Athenaeum in Hartford, Connecticut, was named director of the Ringling Museum. Four years later Austin persuaded the State of Florida to buy the Asolo Theater for its new museum.[35]

The Asolo Theater is a small horseshoe-shaped playhouse built between 1796 and 1798 in Asolo, Italy, in memory of Caterina Cornaro, a fifteenth-century queen of Cyprus who held court in the castle of Asolo for twenty years. The theater remained in its original setting until 1930, when it was dismantled and replaced by a movie theater. It was purchased by a Venetian antiquary who kept it in storage for nearly twenty years; the museum purchased it in 1950.[36]

Soon thereafter the Asolo Theater, all crated up, arrived by boat in Tampa. In 1952 part of it was temporarily installed in a gallery of the Ringling Museum of Art. However, the room was not high enough to accommodate the theater's staircases and upper boxes, essential parts of its design. Two years later, the Florida Board of Control commissioned Manley and Fulton to design a larger structure to house the entire theater so that it could be properly restored and used for performances.[37]

FIG. 139. Rendering of addition to John and Mable Ringling Museum, Sarasota; historic building seen at the far right. Courtesy of the Historical Museum of Southern Florida, Marion Manley Collection.

In hiring Manley and Fulton, the overseers of Ringling's legacy made it clear that although they felt an obligation to preserve the Italian baroque paintings and decorative objects in John Ringling's collection, they felt no responsibility to maintain the architectural character of the estate he had created. The Florida Board of Control had hired architects who were admired for their modernist designs. When those architects drew up a simple container for the ornate and finely detailed theater, the board approved and built their design, although it was utterly devoid of fine architectural detailing comparable to that of Ringling's own constructions. The contrast must have been stark.[38]

An early rendering and two photographs, taken shortly after the building's completion, document important discrepancies between the architects' original scheme and the executed structure. As built, it was much simpler and smaller than originally planned. The rendering illustrates a head-tail scheme in which the head piece housed a two-story lobby connected to the museum by a long covered walkway, behind which was another proposed structure (figure 139). The only piece of this scheme actually executed was an unadorned masonry shell immediately surrounding the Asolo Theater. Much of Manley and Fulton's design focused on the development of the front facade, with its large expanse of glass that brought light into the two-story lobby. On the exterior, the lobby's window wall was capped by an undulating concrete eyebrow that became the signature element of the new building.

The addition, which opened to great fanfare on January 10, 1958, was featured in *Life* magazine on February 17, 1958, perhaps the surest proof in America during that era that an object or event had achieved national importance. Manley and Fulton's addition housed the Asolo Theater for nearly forty years but ultimately proved to be only a temporary resting place. In February 2001, the building was officially closed to the public and subsequently demolished to make room for a larger building complex in which the theater is now housed.

In 1960, two years after the inauguration of the Asolo Theater, Manley designed the modest Quaker meetinghouse along Sunset Drive in Coral Gables (figure 140). This was not Manley's first religious building—during the early 1950s, she had designed a variety of projects for religious groups at the University of Miami including the Baptist student center (1949) and St. Bede's Episcopal Church (1951) (see figures 103 and 104). For Baptists, Episcopalians, and Quakers alike, Manley had similar architectural solutions. In each instance, she housed their several programs within small independent buildings, grouped around a central patio that promoted interaction among congregants (figure 141).

In the case of the Quaker meetinghouse, the meeting room, classrooms, library, kitchen, and bathrooms are organized around an exterior screened patio

FIG. 140. Quaker meetinghouse, South Miami.
Photo by Emily Adams Perry.

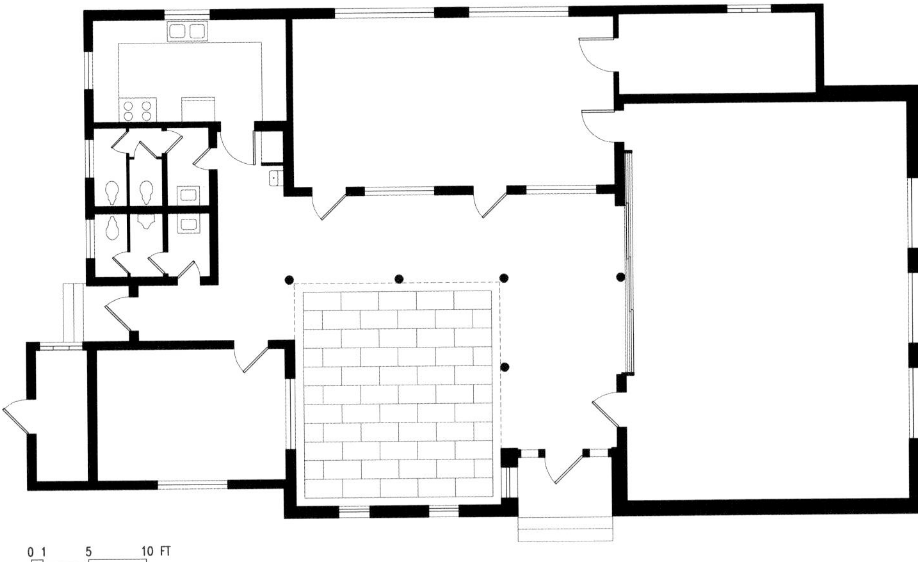

FIG. 141. Quaker meetinghouse, South Miami, cross section and floor plan. Drawing by Alvaro Briganti.

that becomes the most important outdoor gathering space. As in many of Manley's public buildings, this one-story structure is simple in its organization and detailing. Here, Manley utilizes local Douglas fir for the roof and oolitic limestone—a porous local stone—to clad the primary walls.

NEW PLANNING IDEALS AND A COMMITMENT TO SOCIAL SERVICE

While maintaining an active architectural practice, Manley also honed an interest in planning that she had pursued since before World War I, when she took courses on the subject at the University of Michigan. She updated her expertise in this field during World War II at MIT. The city planning courses there had a profound impact on her development as an architect. Upon returning to Miami in 1942, she immediately began applying modernist city planning theories to the design of a new master plan for the University of Miami.

Signaling a stylistic and ideological rift that fundamentally challenged George Merrick's original image for the campus, Marion Manley and Robert Law Weed devised a new plan for the university that promoted a thoroughly modern urban and architectural agenda. Their rejection of historical precedents and their emphasis on function and flexibility, while foreign to the architectural culture Merrick had so carefully nurtured during the 1920s, seemed to them, and to the university's administration, to be well suited for meeting the challenges of designing the new campus. This radical shift was linked in part to the transformations American higher education experienced in the years following World War II, as well as to the recent revolutions in architecture and planning ignited by early modernists such as Le Corbusier, Walter Gropius, and Frank Lloyd Wright.

In addition to her responsibilities at the University of Miami, Manley served on various local planning boards. For the remainder of her career she carefully balanced a busy office with an active life of public service. Her first civic responsibility was as a member of the Coral Gables Board of Supervising Architects from 1939 to 1946. This was a powerful group that reviewed architectural plans for all new buildings in the city.

These years marked a period of transition for Manley; her architectural views were radically changing. Despite the fact that she herself had designed numerous Mediterranean-inspired houses during the 1920s and 1930s, by the mid-1940s she was openly criticizing the use of any traditional precedent and promoting a new language of architecture for the building of the city. In a meeting of the city commission during 1946, she contended that architectural styles could not be frozen, and she faced harsh opposition from her colleagues when she pushed to allow modern architecture in Coral Gables and argued for doing away with the legal requirement that permitted only proposals in Mediterranean styles. The minutes of one meeting in 1946, at which the issue of style was hotly debated, record that Denman Fink, Manley's former client and a leading local architect, declared his opposition to the City of Coral Gables becoming a "guinea pig" for changing architectural styles. The city, he continued, "had become world renowned because of its original and distinctive Mediterranean architecture and should not substantially depart from its original ideas regarding architectural styles."[39]

Frustrated by the ongoing debate, Manley resigned from the Coral Gables Board of Supervising Architects in 1946. After nearly seven and a half years of service, she voiced her frustration to a reporter, "There were too many rules left over from the Pseudo Spanish era [with] no chance for anyone to produce a distinguished piece of architecture."[40] Despite giving up her position on that board, within a year she was willing to serve as a member of the City of Coral Gables Joint Committee to complete a rezoning study of the city.

Overlapping her service to Coral Gables, Manley also sat on the City of Miami's Planning Board from 1942 to 1945. But she also resigned from it with some dismay, this time because "it bore no relation to planning and I could not convince the other members of that fact."[41] Years later, Manley lamented that Miami was one of many cities that had grown unplanned and unguided. As she told a reporter in 1973, "Now, we are beginning to see the need for real planning and real guiding. The difficulty is that while we are attempting to correct mistakes already made we are making the same foolish mistakes all over again." Among the mistakes she cited was the failure to require subdivision developers to donate large enough portions of land for parks. She also lamented the lack of trained planning staff on the city planning board.[42]

Manley channeled her interest in planning into the promotion of social welfare, specifically into slum improvement. Between 1948 and 1949 she was appointed to the Coconut Grove Slum Clearance Committee for rezoning, joining a panel of distinguished local architects including Alfred Browning Parker and Robert Law Weed, as well as Robert Fitch Smith, former chairman of the Dade County Planning Board. While the Grove's black neighborhood had been zoned for business and multiple housing, more than 80 percent of the land was occupied by single family, wooden vernacular structures. The owners of these houses had no zoning protection, and more importantly, the Federal Housing Administration ensured that loans could not be granted for single family dwellings in the neighborhood, since zoning for individual houses was not permitted.[43]

In their final report, the committee called for restricting business property to certain main streets and proposed that old and new multiple-unit housing bordering those streets be reinforced with duplex and single family zoning. The proposed change in the zoning ordinance was twice put before the city commission, which rejected it, before it was placed on the November 1949 election ballot. The citizens who met to consider the ordinance voted unanimously in favor of the zoning change, and the code was amended.[44]

Manley's involvement with the African American community of Coconut Grove went beyond her commitment to the rezoning committee. She donated her architectural services for the design of a building, the Saint Albans nursery school. Essentially a one-story masonry structure, it is barely distinguishable from the surrounding fabric. In fact, it is difficult to know how much of Manley's original design (if any) may have survived because no plans have been found. However, the fact that she donated a design for a nursery school to serve working mothers received some attention in the press during Manley's lifetime and suggests the strength of her social consciousness and her devotion to the underprivileged black community in her own neighborhood.

Between 1949 and 1953, Manley served as a member of the Board of Directors for the Greater Miami Urban League and as the chairman of the Committee on Civic Design for the South Florida Chapter of the American Institute of Architects, for which she once again tackled issues of slum clearance and neighborhood planning. Samuel Kruse, a Miami architect who served with Manley on the committee, recalled that she was "a force with which governmental agencies had to reckon. With Manley at the helm . . . problems were tackled." Kruse elaborated: "The test of her influence in civic matters occurred during the 1951 State Legislature when her committee, with the aid of the League of Women Voters, influenced the Dade County Commission to form a County Planning Board with a technically trained planner as the Director of a technical and lay staff."[45]

As head of the civic design committee, she, along with her four associates—Tom Madden, Frank Watson, Sam Kruse, and Joe Smith—set out to analyze an existing neighborhood in the city and to propose an alternative model for a new neighborhood plan. Their case study was a small sector of present-day Little Havana located along SW Eighth Street and Twenty-seventh Avenue. They sketched a diagram pointing out that single family houses in the area were surrounded on all sides by businesses and apartments and demonstrating that citizens were required to cross busy streets to get from their residences to public amenities such as schools, churches, and playgrounds. They noted that the area had no open space, and they blamed current zoning and a lack of planning for the residences' difficulties (figure 142).

In sharp contrast to this existing condition, Manley and her colleagues presented a diagram of their ideal neighborhood at a public meeting to discuss the ways Miami could accommodate its fast-growing population. Emphasizing the importance of the "neighborhood unit," Manley spoke on behalf of the group: "Public planning should move upward from the neighborhood unit. There is where people spend from one-half to two-thirds of their time. It is a prime factor in human living since the home and neighborhood environment contribute so much to the comfort or discomfort of a person."[46]

Manley's group designed a neighborhood of ninety acres to accommodate approximately 368 families. Essentially conceived as a large superblock, it was to be bounded by an arterial road to the west from which a series of smaller, dead-end streets diverged, providing access to the neighborhood. The group believed that such infrastructure would increase green space and provide a buffer from traffic. The proposed neighborhood would be composed of single family residences and apartment buildings organized loosely along the smaller cul-de-sacs. Public amenities such as a school, community center, and church were situated toward the center of the plan, easily accessible from the arterial road. A shopping center anchored the plan at the intersection of the main arterial roads (figure 143).

The plan was never executed, but neighborhoods based on similar planning concepts were built throughout the country in the 1960s and 1970s. Unfortunately, in Miami, as in many other places, these new planning ideals proved in time to be highly detrimental to the development of the city. Miami's fledgling downtown, with its ring of inner city suburbs, was abandoned in favor of countless single family suburban neighborhoods interconnected by a system of large arterial roads. Public amenities such as churches and community centers were excluded from these neighborhoods, and most public buildings were placed along the large arterial roads—rendering them inaccessible to pedestrians. Despite the good intentions of Manley and her colleagues, these planning principles produced a sprawling, disconnected city with a highly segregated zoning ordinance.

Overlapping her public service to the local civic design committee, Manley also served on many state and national boards; the National Committee on Urban Planning and Housing of the American Institute of Architects, on which she served between 1949 and 1953, was one of the most important. Her extensive service at the national level made her a formidable authority on matters of contemporary urban development. Thomas Creighton, editor of *Progressive Architecture*, complimented Manley's civic activities when he wrote: "I do not know of anyone whose interest in service to the public on the part of the architectural profession has been more constructive than hers. Her contributions to the fields of urban planning and urban redevelopment have been extremely important."[47]

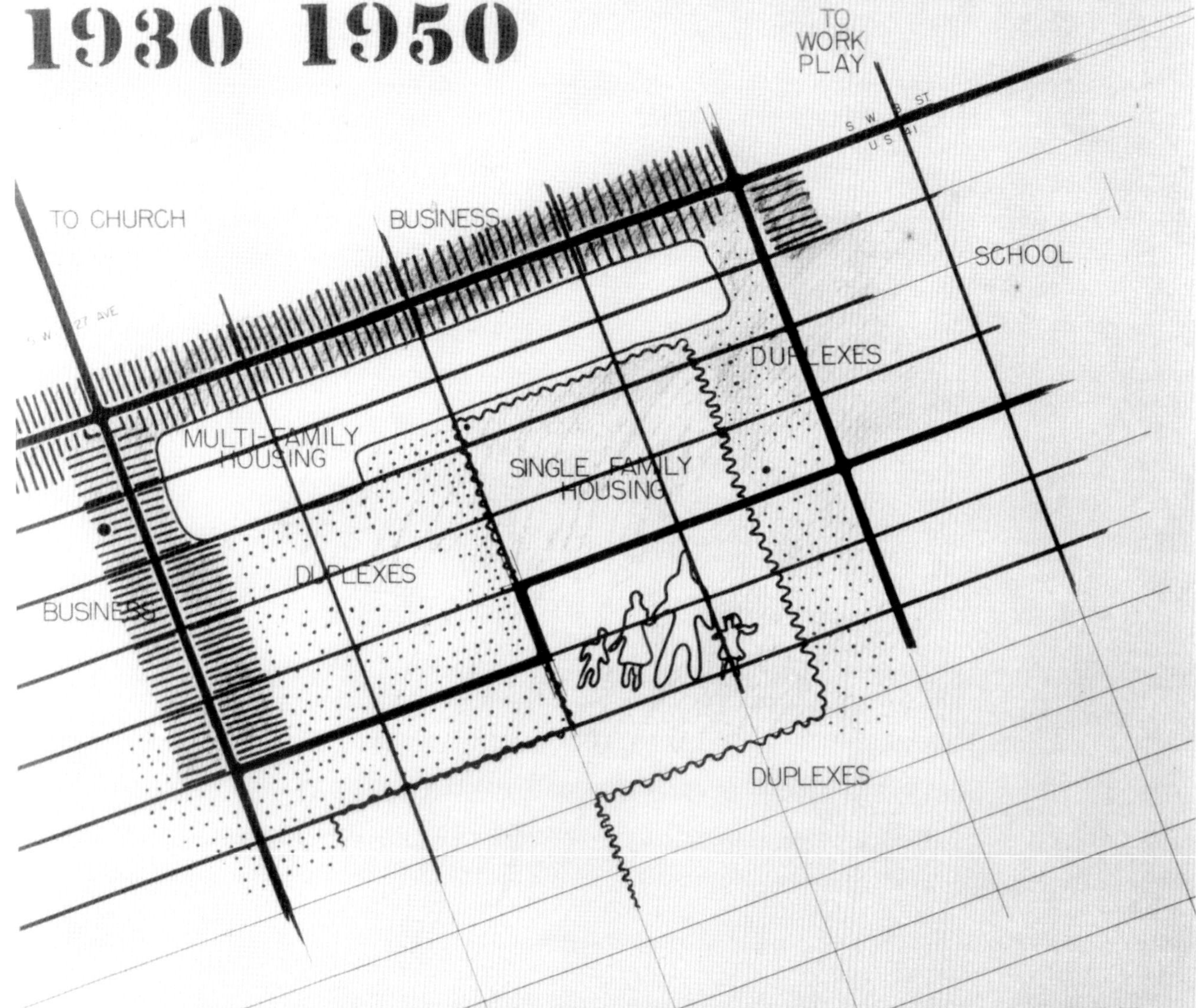

FIG. 142. Diagram of existing neighborhood plan. Courtesy of the Historical Museum of Southern Florida, Marion Manley Collection.

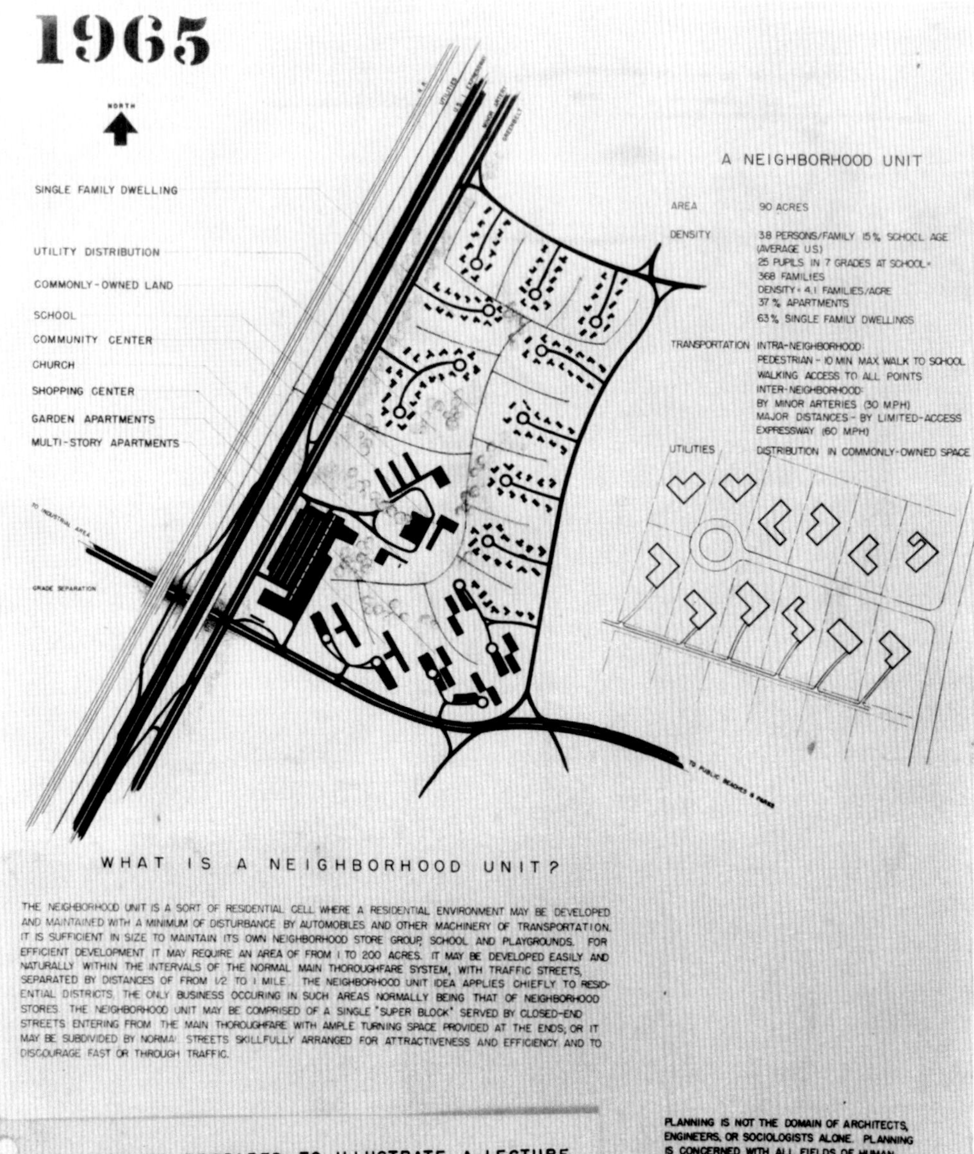

FIG. 143. Diagram of proposed "ideal" neighborhood unit. Courtesy of the Historical Museum of Southern Florida, Marion Manley Collection.

Manley was seventy years old in 1963 when she worked on her "ideal" neighborhood plan. She maintained an active practice and continued to design and build houses through the next decade. She was productive during her final years, maintaining a seemingly endless enthusiasm for and dedication to the discipline of architecture. In 1973 she was presented with a Gold Medal Award by the Florida Association of Architects for her leadership and service to the profession. This was followed in 1975 by the Silver Medal Award from the Florida South Chapter of the American Institute of Architects in recognition of the quality of her architectural work as well as her continued leadership. Douglas Haskell, editor of *Architectural Forum*, may have said it best when he wrote a letter supporting Manley's nomination to the American Institute of Architects' College of Fellows: "The fact that an architect who shines in good works also shines in good work is not to be overlooked—it seems to be a combination that is not universal."[48]

Marion Isadore Manley died on February 18, 1984, at the age of ninety. For more than six decades, she challenged herself to evolve with the times, and this kept her at the forefront of Miami's architectural scene (figure 144). From one-room bungalows to university campuses to large-scale neighborhood plans, the breadth, versatility, and longevity of her career are noteworthy. But it is perhaps her small-scale projects that are most compelling.

Following local stagnation during the Depression and the preoccupation with the war effort during most of the 1940s, the influx of new residents after World War II brought a building boom, and Miami flourished. Today many of the modest and compact buildings built in the two decades following the end of World War II, including many of Manley's domestic buildings, have been demolished and largely replaced by new, overscaled, Mediterranean revival structures that bear little or no resemblance to the original Mediterranean buildings of the 1920s and 1930s. Most significantly, local developers have cleared South

FIG. 144. Marion Manley. Courtesy of the Historical Museum of Southern Florida, Marion Manley Collection.

Florida's lush landscape in order to construct these new houses, and in so doing they have dramatically altered the original character of the city.

Manley was an advocate of sustainable architecture long before it was fashionable, and much of her work attests to a keen understanding of local materials and methods of construction, as well as to a respect for the native Florida landscape she strove to preserve. Her sensibility would serve us well today.

—CP

CATALOG OF WORKS

1924–25 Hunt House
3447 Sheridan Avenue
Miami Beach, Florida

1925 Quinn House
477 NE Ninety-second Street
Miami Shores, Florida

1925–26 Scott House
598 NE Fifty-sixth Street
Morningside, Florida

1928 Rosshart and Newman House
145 NE Ninety-fourth Street
Miami Shores, Florida

1929 Bogert House
601 Grand Concourse
Miami Shores, Florida

Dooly House
1291 NE Ninety-sixth Street
Miami Shores, Florida

1933 U.S. Post Office
300 NE First Avenue
Miami, Florida
Paist and Steward Architects

1935 Terletzky House
Lot 7, Ye Little Wood
Coconut Grove, Florida

1936 Grimes House
1206 Castile
Coral Gables, Florida

Ostlund House
900 Alhambra Circle
Coral Gables, Florida

Ward House (No. 1)
300 Cadima
Coral Gables, Florida

Ward House (No. 2)
230 Aledo
Coral Gables, Florida

Ward House (No. 3)
1216 Castile
Coral Gables, Florida

1937 Gardener Royce Cottage
4094 Park Avenue
Dade County, Florida

Jamieson House
Cutler Road
Miami, Florida

1938 Davenport House
De Lido Island
Miami Beach, Florida

Fink House
760 Anastasia Avenue
Coral Gables, Florida

Von Paulson House
Coconut Grove, Florida

Head House
Coconut Grove, Florida

1939 Marks House
Key West, Florida

Glessner House
Fort Lauderdale, Florida

1940 Store Building for H. Bert Albury
Lots 18 and 19, Commodore Plaza
Coconut Grove, Florida

Music Auditorium
University of Miami
Coral Gables, Florida
(unbuilt)

Rosensteil Lab of Marine and Atmospheric Science
University of Miami
Virgina Key, Florida
(unbuilt)

Shopfront
Commodore Plaza
Coconut Grove, Florida

1942–57 Woodlawn Cemetery
Service building, sundial, paved walkways, and fountain
Miami, Florida
In collaboration with the sculptor Edgar L. Sutton

1944 Aquarium
University of Miami
Virginia Key, Florida
(unbuilt)

1945–46 Master Plan
University of Miami
Coral Gables, Florida
In collaboration with Robert Law Weed

1946 Memorial Classroom Building
University of Miami
Coral Gables, Florida
In collaboration with Robert Law Weed

1947 American Legion Community Building
South Miami, Florida

Student Recreation Center
University of Miami
Coral Gables, Florida
In collaboration with Robert Law Weed

Temporary Wooden Buildings
University of Miami
Coral Gables, Florida

1948 Men's Dormitories
Florida State University
Tallahassee, Florida
In collaboration with Guy Chandler Fulton
(unbuilt)

Sarepta B. Terletzky House
Douglas Road
Miami, Florida

Veterans Housing Project
University of Miami
Coral Gables, Florida
In collaboration with Robert Law Weed

1949 Baptist Student Center
University of Miami
Coral Gables, Florida

Town Shores Housing Project
Miami, Florida
In collaboration with William Green
(unbuilt)

1950 Gaines Wilson House, addition
3853 Little Avenue
Coconut Grove, Florida

1951 St. Bede's Episcopal Church
University of Miami
Coral Gables, Florida

Wylie House
NE 1/4, Section 31-54-41, Erwin Road
South Miami, Florida
(demolished)

Cantebury House
University of Miami
Coral Gables, Florida

Koubek Center, University of Miami
2705 SW Third Street
Miami, Florida

Rinehart House
Lot 4, Palm Vista Subdivision
South Miami, Florida

Ring Theater
University of Miami
Coral Gables, Florida
In collaboration with Robert Little

1951–52 Bell House
The Moorings
Coconut Grove, Florida
(demolished)

1952 Olson House
Galleons Beach, Manasota Key
Sarasota, Florida

1953 Cracker-style Cottage, for Peyton Wilson
Homestead, Florida

1954 John Ringling Museum, addition
Sarasota, Florida
In collaboration with Guy Chandler Fulton

1955 Manley House
4070 Battersea Road
Coconut Grove, Florida

1956 Anderson House
4050 Battersea Road
Coconut Grove, Florida

Springview Elementary School
Miami Springs, Florida

Sullivan House
Old Cutler Road at SW 129th Terrace
Miami, Florida

1957 Thayer House
Saint Gaudens Road
Coconut Grove, Florida

Hector House
SW Forty-seventh Avenue, Erwin Road
Coconut Grove, Florida

1958 Moultrop House
4161 Battersea
Coconut Grove, Florida

1959 House
8375 SW Fifty-second Avenue
Miami, Florida

1960 Quaker Meetinghouse
Sunset Drive
South Miami, Florida

1961 Mr. and Mrs. Stanley Rinehart Jr. House, addition
5401 SW Ninety-eighth Terrace
Miami, Florida

Johnson, Lane, Space and Co. Brokerage Firm
Le Jeune Road
Coral Gables, Florida

1962–63 Mrs. Forbes-Hawks House, addition
4030 Poinciana Avenue
Coconut Grove, Florida

Sadler Cottage
981 NE Seventy-eighth Terrace
Miami, Florida

Sengra Graham Office Building
Miami Lakes, Florida
In collaboration with Robert Little

1963 Brown House
Lot 20, Pennsylvania Key Club
Islamorada, Florida

Chapman Cottages
SW Eightieth Street
Dade County, Florida

Miami Lakes Houses for the Sengra Development Corporation
Prototypes L, M, N, and O
Miami Lakes, Florida
In collaboration with Robert Little

Retail Shops for Lake Patricia Shopping Center
Miami Lakes, Florida
In collaboration with Robert Little

Quatrefoil Company Cottages
Jackson Avenue
Coconut Grove, Florida

1964 Altmayer House
SW 80th Avenue and 144th Street
Dade County, Florida

Gables Secretarial Services, office interior
2419–21 Le Jeune Road
Coral Gables, Florida

Professional Building for Patricia Lake Shopping Center
Miami Lakes, Florida
In collaboration with Robert Little

Smith House
Miami, Florida

Zim House
Plantation Key
Tavernier, Florida
(unbuilt)

1966 Graves Cottage
Lot 13, Section 2
Key Heights Subdivision
Plantation Key, Florida

Mactye House, renovations
4985 Lakeview Drive
Miami Beach, Florida

1967 Ford House, addition
5845 SW Ninety-seventh Street
Miami, Florida

Scott House
17010 SW Seventy-seventh Avenue
Miami, Florida

Zim Shore House
Plantation Key, Florida

1968 Altemus House, addition
3820 Crawford Avenue
Coconut Grove, Florida

Barker House
Lot 8, Block 6
Key Heights Subdivision
Plantation Key, Florida

1970 Grosvenor House, renovation
3995 Douglas Road
Coconut Grove, Florida

Shoemaker House
Lake Placid, Florida

1971 Branning House
North Rolling Hill Road
Plantation Key, Florida

1972 John and Susan Rothchild House
417 Riverside Drive
Everglades City, Florida
(unbuilt)

Year Unknown Sullivan House
Old Cutler Road at SW 129th Terrace
Miami, Florida

House for J. Wilson Smith and Laurence Cardwell
Northwest corner of Bauer Drive and Kingman Road
Dade County, Florida

House
8020 SW 142nd Terrace
Miami, Florida

TIMELINE

1893 Is born April 29 near Junction City, Kansas, Cherrycroft Homestead (youngest of nine children)

1911 Graduates from Junction City High School

1911–14 Attends University of Kansas

1914 Transfers to University of Illinois at Urbana (Architecture Department)

1917 Graduates from University of Illinois with a bachelor of science degree in architecture; attends summer school at University of Michigan, with concentration on design; is hired as junior draftsman, Walter De Garmo's office; converts Key West convent into military barracks; moves to Philadelphia to design ships for the Emergency Fleet Corp. of the U.S. Shipping Board

1918 Is hired as designer, Martin L. Hampton's office; is licensed in the State of Florida (September 6, certificate no. 105)

1919–20 Works as architect, Gordon E. Mayer's office

1920 Is elected treasurer of the Florida Business and Professional Women's Club

1921 Becomes a partner, firm of Mayer and Manley

1922–23 Is senior draftsman, James J. Baldwin's office, Anderson, South Carolina

Circa 1924 Returns to Miami and establishes independent architectural office

1925–27 Is a member of American Institute of Architects (AIA), Florida chapter

1929 Closes architectural office as a result of the Depression

1929–33 Works as senior draftsman/associate architect, Phineas Paist's office

Circa 1934 Reestablishes independent architectural practice

1937 Is reinstated as member of AIA, Florida chapter

1938 Serves as secretary, Florida South Chapter, AIA

1938–45 Becomes a member of Coral Gables Board of Supervising Architects

1939–42 Works on editorial staff, *Florida Architecture and Allied Arts*

1940 Is hired by President Bowman Ashe to work on architectural drawings for the University of Miami (March)

1940–45 Is a delegate to national AIA conventions

1941–42 Serves as president, Florida South Chapter, AIA

1942 Enrolls in summer city planning course at MIT

1942–45 Serves on City of Miami's planning board

May 16, 1943 Attends National Conference on Planning in New York City

May 26, 1943 Attends annual meeting of the AIA in Cincinnati, Ohio

1943–45 Is V-12 navy program mechanical drawing instructor, University of Miami

1943 Relocates her independent architectural office onto University of Miami campus

1945 Represents Florida AIA chapters in Atlantic City; hired in October, along with Robert Law Weed, to design the new University of Miami master plan

1945–46 Serves as vice president, Florida Association of Architects (two terms), and chairman of Unification Committee for Florida Association of Architects from inception of program to final completion

1947 Is chairman of Florida Association of Architects committee to revise and amend their by-laws and AIA representative at Pan American Congress of Architects, Lima, Peru; attends University of Miami

1947–49 Serves as delegate to national AIA conventions

1948–49 Is a member of Coconut Grove Slum Clearance Rezoning Committee

1949 Becomes chairman of Committee to Revise and Amend By-Laws, South Florida Chapter, AIA; is unsuccessful candidate for vice president of national chapter, AIA

1949–52 Serves on Committee of International Relations, National Chapter, AIA

1949–53 Is a member of Board of Directors, Greater Miami Urban League; is chairman of Committee on Civic Design, South Florida Chapter, AIA; is a member of Committee on Urban Planning and Housing, National Chapter, AIA

1950 Is AIA representative at Pan American Congress of Architects, Havana, Cuba

1951 Is a member of Advisory Committee to Planning and Development Branch for Slum Clearance and Urban Redevelopment (Feiss Committee)

1951–52 Serves as president, Coconut Grove Civic Association, and member of AIA Joint Committee with AIA–National Association of Housing Officials and Public Housing Authority (Wurster Committee)

1951–53 Is delegate to national AIA Convention

1952 Is national AIA representative at Pan American Congress of Architects, Mexico City, Mexico; president, Coconut Grove Civic Club

1952–53 Is a member of Executive Committee, Florida South Chapter, AIA

1953 Serves as cochairman of Printed Program Committee, AIA 1953 Regional Conference of South Atlantic District

1954 Is hired by the Florida State Board of Control to design addition to the John Ringling Museum in Sarasota, Florida

1956 Is nominated for AIA College of Fellows Election (March 15)

1957 Receives Bertha Foster Award of Chi Omega Alumnae Association

1968 Relocates office from Old Post Office building in Coconut Grove to Commodore Plaza in Coconut Grove

1973 Receives gold medal award, Florida Association of Architects

1975 Receives silver medal, Florida South Chapter of the AIA

1984 Dies February 18 in Miami

NOTES

ABBREVIATIONS

AIA American Institute of Architects
BFA Bowman Foster Ashe, President, University of Miami
MIM Marion Isadore Manley
RLW Robert Law Weed
UM The University of Miami

INTRODUCTION

1 While very few women architects were as successful as Manley in establishing independent practices, there were notable exceptions, including Julia Morgan and Mary Colter, whose brilliant work has been celebrated in monographs.

2 Judith Paine, "Pioneer Women Architects," in *Women in American Architecture: A Historic and Contemporary Perspective*, ed. Susana Torre (New York: Whitney Library of Design, 1977), 54. As Clare Lorenz has noted, only in the Nordic countries was there a "long tradition" of women architects, estimated at 20 percent of the profession. Clare Lorenz, *Women in Architecture: A Contemporary Perspective* (London: Trefoil Publications, 1990).

3 "A Thousand Women in Architecture, Part 1," *Architectural Record* 103, no. 3 (March 1948): 105.

4 Molly Sinclair, "Miami: An Unplanned Disaster?" *Miami Herald*, January 28, 1973, E24.

5 Marion Manley, taped interview by Emily Perry Dieterich, May 7, 1974.

6 Lester Manley, "Lester's Recollections," Joan Manley Altmayer collection.

7 Sinclair, "Miami: An Unplanned Disaster?" E24.

8 Emily Newell Blair, as quoted in Barbara J. Harris, *Beyond Her Sphere: Women and the Professions in America* (Westport, Conn.: Greenwood Press, 1978), 127.

9 The other four schools where architectural education was available to women before 1875 were the Cooper Union, co-educational from the time of its founding in 1859; the Massachusetts Institute of Technology; and Cornell and Syracuse Universities. Paine, "Pioneer Women Architects," 55.

10 University of Illinois Annual Register, 1917–18, 514.

11 As quoted in Joan Draper, "The Ecole des Beaux-Arts and the Architectural Profession in the United States," in *The Architect: Chapters in the History of the Profession*, ed. Spiro Kostof (New York: Oxford University Press, 1977), 217.

12 For a history of the Cambridge School of Architecture and Landscape Architecture, see Dorothy May Anderson, *Women, Design, and the Cambridge School* (West Lafayette, Ind.: PDA Publishing, 1980).

13 Manley did share office space with another woman architect, Dorothy McKenna, from 1959 until her death in 1984, although she all but retired from active practice in about 1973.

14 *American Architect and Building News* 1 (September 30, 1876): 313, quoted in Paine, "Pioneer Women Architects," 60.

15 Gwen Harrison, "Architect Spells Profession, Nickname, for Marion Manley; It's Her Hobby, Too," *Miami Herald*, May 11, 1952, 14E.

16 F. H. Bosworth Jr. and Roy Childs Jones, *A Study of Architectural Schools* (New York: C. Scribner's Sons, 1932), 96.

17 William Houser, "Exponent of Personality: Close Supervision of Work Has Earned Her Reputation for Being Rugged on Job," *Miami Herald*, "Florida Living," January 25, 1953, 3.

18 Harrison, "Architect Spells Profession, Nickname, for Marion Manley," 14E; Beatrice Washburn, "A Woman of Architecture Who Can Wield a Shovel," *Miami Herald*, September 23, 1956, G2.

19 Sinclair, "Miami: An Unplanned Disaster?" E24.

20 Darwina L. Neal, in the introduction to Anderson's *Women, Design, and the Cambridge School*, records that "the three major objections to hiring women which Mr. Frost encountered in his peers were that women would disrupt morale in an office of men, could not supervise construction, and would take jobs to which men were entitled" (xv).

21 Sinclair, "Miami: An Unplanned Disaster?" E24.

22 "Incidentally," *Junction City [Kans.] Union*, January 22, 1957, 2; Trip Russell, taped interview by Emily Perry Dieterich and Jose Rodriguez, January 10, 1990.

23 Terry Johnson King, "She's Got a Blueprint for Old Age," *Miami Herald*, May 9, 1974.

24 Jan Hochstim, interview by authors, March 2006.

25 Marjory Stoneman Douglas, interview by Emily Perry Dieterich, November 29, 1989.

26 Marjory Stoneman Douglas, with John Rothchild, *Voice of the River: An Autobiography* (Englewood, Fla.: Pineapple Press, 1987), 174–201; Russell interview, by Dietrich and Rodriguez, January 10, 1990; Nancy F. Cott, *The Bonds of Womanhood: "Woman's Sphere" in New England, 1780–1835* (New Haven: Yale University Press, 1977).

27 Douglas, *Voice of the River*, 174. Douglas's chronological sequence is confusing in this passage. Elizabeth Virrick did not come to Miami until the late 1940s, but this suggests that Manley was living at the Gullivers' during that period and, vaguely, that only then did she become "one of my [Douglas's] best friends." But Douglas has elsewhere said that she and Manley shared a house during the Great Depression.

28 Michael Grunwald, *The Swamp: The Everglades, Florida, and the Politics of Paradise* (New York: Simon and Schuster, 2006), 204.

29 Mary Morrison, "Rose Fleming, Architect," *Hearth and Home* 6, no. 6 (February 7, 1874): 82.

30 Editorial, *American Architect and Building News* 1 (September 30, 1876): 313.

31 Temple Hoyne Buell, October 29, 1953, letter, supporting Manley's election to fellowship in the AIA, AIA Archives, Washington, D.C. Buell became a highly successful architect in Denver with "the largest architectural firm in the Rocky Mountain area" according to the Web site of the charitable foundation founded in 1962 that bears his name, a foundation best known in architectural circles today for establishing in 1982 the Buell Center for the Study of American Architecture at Columbia University, www.buellfoundation.org/.

32 Sinclair, "Miami: An Unplanned Disaster?" E24.

33 Marion Manley, "Synopsis of Marion I. Manley, from the Latest Edition of Who's Who in America," undated typescript, in Historical Museum of Southern Florida, Marion Manley Collection.

34 Emily Adams Perry, "Marion Isadore Manley: Pioneer Woman Architect," in *Florida Pathfinders*, ed. Lewis N. Wynne and James J. Horgan (Saint Leo, Fla.: Saint Leo College Press, 1994).

35 Nathan Clifford Ricker, whom the University of Illinois claims as the first graduate—in 1873—of an architecture program in the United States, and who studied briefly at the Bauakademie in Berlin, became dean of the College of Engineering at Illinois and taught history of architecture classes until he retired in 1916. "From its beginning, Ricker had guided the department [of architecture] and had been almost entirely responsible for its success. . . . The University of Illinois library now [1932] contains fifty bound volumes of his translations of needed foreign works on architecture. Much of this work has never been published, so that it has only been available at Illinois." Bosworth and Jones, *A Study of Architectural Schools*, 94–95.

36 See Gwyndolyn Wright, "On the Fringe of the Profession: Women in American Architecture," in *The Architect: Chapters in the History of the Profession*, ed. Spiro Kostof (New York: Oxford University Press, 1977), 292, and Anderson, *Women, Design, and the Cambridge School.*

PRACTICING FROM THE OUTPOST

1 Lester Manley, "Lester's Recollections," and "Reminiscences of Things Past," both in Joan Manley Altmayer Collection. We are indebted to Emily Perry Dieterich for finding and transcribing these interviews.

2 Seth H. Bramson, *Speedway to Sunshine: The Story of the Florida East Coast Railway* (Canada: Boston Mills Press, 2002).

3 Ibid.

4 Lester Manley, "Lester's Recollections," in Joan Manley Altmayer Collection. Born in 1883, Lester graduated from Kansas University with a law degree and was admitted to the Kansas Bar in 1908. He subsequently held a variety of jobs and in 1910 began working for his older brother, Rufus, traveling around the southern states promoting the use of creosoted wood block paving. In the 1920s, he worked in construction and real estate. With partner Arthur Ward, he developed and sold 1,500 Shenandoah properties.

5 "Explains Adaptation of New Architecture," undated clipping, H. George Fink Scrapbook, ca. 1925, courtesy of Arva Moore Parks from her private collection.

6 Arva Moore Parks, *George Merrick's Coral Gables, "Where Your 'Castles in Spain' Are Made Real"* (Miami: Centennial Press, 2006), 38–40.

7 Bosworth and Jones, *A Study of Architectural Schools*, 94–96; the quote is from Rexford Newcomb, *Mediterranean Domestic Architecture in the United States* (Cleveland, Ohio: J. H. Hansen, 1928).

8 The Villa Vizcaya has been the subject of numerous publications, including *Vizcaya: An American Villa and Its Makers.* (Philadelphia: University of Pennsylvania Press, 2007). It is the only house in Miami consistently mentioned in standard histories of American architecture.

9 Ellen Caroline Buckley, "Revisiting the Architecture of Walter De Garmo: Lessons for the Future of Speculative Housing in Florida" (master's thesis, University of Miami, 2003).

10 Elizabeth Guyton, "Biographies," in *Coral Gables: An American Garden City*, ed. Roberto M. Behar and Maurice G. Culot (Paris: Norma Editions, 1997), 202.

11 Sinclair, "Miami: An Unplanned Disaster?" E24.

12 Manley became the second woman architect licensed in the state; the first was Agnes Ballard. A complete list of licensed women architects has been compiled by Nancy Hadley, archivist and records manager for the AIA Knowledge Resources.

13 Chas. F. Kieder, "Modern Architects Give Many Services to Client in Addition to Designing," *Miami Daily News and Metropolis*, July 19, 1924, 14.

14 Marion Manley, interview by historian Arva Moore Parks, Miami, 1977.

15 Perry, "Marion Isadore Manley," 24.

16 Arva Moore Parks, *George Merrick's Coral Gables: "Where Your 'Castles in Spain' Are Made Real"* (Miami: Centennial Press, 2006), 5.

17 Maurice G. Culot, introduction to *Coral Gables: An American Garden City*, ed. Roberto M. Behar and Maurice G. Culot (Paris: Norma Editions, 1997), 15–30.

18 Parks, *George Merrick's Coral Gables*, 8–22.

19 Morningside Historic Designation Report, National Register of Historic Places, 9.

20 Typescript, Spear/Harris Papers [circa 1980s], Brockway Memorial Library Collection, Miami Shores, Florida.

21 Maria Temkin, Miami Shores Thematic Group Nomination Proposal, National Register of Historic Places, Brockway Memorial Library Collection, Miami Shores Florida, November 30, 1987, 5.

22 "Sales Totals of Large Project Unprecedented," *Miami Daily News and Metropolis*, December 4, 1925, 1–8.

23 Maria Temkin, Miami Shores Thematic Group Nomination Proposal, National Register of Historic Places, Brockway Memorial Library Collection, Miami Shores, Florida, November 30, 1987.

24 Douglas, *Voice of the River*, 175.

25 Ibid., 42, 77–78, 86, 89.

26 Marjory Stoneman Douglas, *Florida: The Long Frontier* (New York: Harper and Row, 1967), 9–10.

27 Pamphlet compiled by Mrs. S. J. Kent and Mrs. David R. Thurman, "The First Sixty Years of the Housekeeper's Club" (Coconut Grove: Housekeeper's Club, 1951), 7, Miami Public Library, Florida Collection.

28 *History of the Miami Woman's Club, 1900–1955* (Miami: Miami Woman's Club, 1955), 11–12.

29 Pamphlet compiled by Mrs. S. J. Kent and Mrs. David R. Thurman, "The First Sixty Years of the Housekeeper's Club" (Coconut Grove: Housekeeper's Club, 1951), 7, Miami Public Library, Florida Collection.

30 "Business Women's Club to Be Formed Thursday Night Is [the] Plan Discussed," *Miami Daily News and Metropolis*, February 9, 1916.

31 Marion Manley, "Synopsis of Marion I. Manley, from the Latest Edition of Who's Who in America," undated typescript, Historical Museum of Southern Florida, Marion Manley Collection.

32 Up until 1920 only five women had membership in the American Institute of Architects. They were Louise Blanchard Bethune (1888, New York), Lois L. Howe (1901, Boston area), Henrietta Dozier (1905, Florida), Marica Mead (1918, New York), and Theodate Pope Riddle (1918, Connecticut). The list was compiled by George E. Pettingill and Nancy Hadley, librarians for the AIA Archives in Washington, D.C. We are indebted to Nancy Hadley, AIA archivist and records manager, for this list.

33 Marjory Stoneman Douglas, *Coral Gables, America's Finest Suburb* (Coral Gables, Fla.: Parker Art Print Assn., [circa 1920s]), 19–20.

34 Perry, "Marion Isadore Manley," 25.

35 Guyton, "Biographies," 202, 205.

36 "The Miami Post Office, Paist and Stewart Architects," *Southern Architect and Building News* 27 (1931): 28, 36.

37 Ibid.

38 "Letter to Engineer, U.S. Post Office from Alfred Browning Parker, F.A.I.A.," September 11, 1973, Historical Museum of Southern Florida, Marion Manley Collection.

39 The other set of surviving working drawings from the period is the Terletzky residence, Historical Museum of Southern Florida, Marion Manley Collection.

40 Guyton, "Biographies," 201.

41 Randolph Williams Sexton, *Spanish Influence on American Architecture and Decoration* (New York: Brentano's, 1927), 10.

42 Jo Werne, "Coral Rock Homes, They're Cool," *Miami Herald*, November 23, 1975, IL.

43 Denman Fink, "Castles in Spain Made Real" in *The Story of Coral Gables* (Coral Gables, Fla.: G. E. Merrick, ca. 1926), 15.

44 Dorothy McKenna, at her Coconut Grove home, interview by the authors, March 2003.

45 Ibid.

46 Ellen Uguccioni, Report of the City of Coral Gables Historic Preservation Department to the Historic Preservation Board on the Designation of the Residence at 760 Anastasia Avenue as an Historic Landmark, May 17, 1994, 2–4.

47 *Florida Architecture and Allied Arts* (1938): 30.

48 Ibid., 23.

49 Marion Manley. "Tunisian Architecture Liked by Owners, Modified in Relation to Florida Climatic Conditions," *Miami Herald*, May 6, 1937, 14.

50 Marion Manley, "Synopsis of Marion I. Manley, from the Latest Edition of Who's Who in America," undated typescript, Historical Museum of Southern Florida, Marion Manley Collection.

MANLEY AND THE UNIVERSITY OF MIAMI

1 "University of Miami at Coral Gables to be Part of Luxurious Riviera Development," *Coral Gables Bulletin* 3 (June 1925): 1.

2 William H. Nicholas, "Miami's Expanding Horizons," *National Geographic* 98, no. 5 (November 1950): 562; UM Archives, President's Record, UM Libraries, Coral Gables, hereinafter cited as UM Pres. Record.

3 MIM to "Father" [Charles Haines Manley], September 29, 1926, photocopy in the archives of UM, the gift of Pam Admire.

4 Harold H. Martin, "They Love it at Sun-tan U," *Saturday Evening Post* (November 19, 1949): 146.

5 Houser, "Exponent of Personality," 3; records MIM's "very deep affection for Dr. Ashe, for he used his great gift of encouragement throughout the job."

6 Martin, "They Love It at Sun-tan U," 144.

7 The fee may well have been for a published map/plan for the "Future Campus of University," *[Coral Gables] Riviera*, June 14, 1940. See Figure 56.

8 BFA to "Mr. Hiss, Bus. Mgr.," Memorandum, May 14, 1940, UM Pres. Record.

9 *[Coral Gables] Riviera*, ibid. On this plan, proposed buildings south and west of intersection of Le Jeune Road and University Drive include an auditorium on a triangular plot bounded by University Drive, Segovia, and Escobar.

Charlton W. Tebeau, *The University of Miami: A Golden Anniversary History, 1926–1976* (Coral Gables Fla.: University of Miami Press, 1976), 115, notes that implementation of this published plan "would have meant the demolition of a considerable amount of residential property."

10 Harrison, "Architect Spells Profession, Nickname, for Marion Manley," 14E.

11 An English translation of Le Corbusier's *Vers Une Architecture* of 1921 was published as *Towards a New Architecture* in 1927.

12 Marion Manley, "Synopsis of Marion I. Manley, from the Latest Edition of Who's Who in America," undated typescript, Historical Museum of Southern Florida, Marion Manley Collection: "Coral Gables Bd. of Architects is a Board of Review. After 7½ years I resigned because there were too many rules left over from the Pseudo-Spanish era. No chance for anyone to produce a distinguished piece of Architecture."

13 That MIM may not have valued this early work is supported by the fact that plans for the music auditorium did not survive among her papers given to the Historical Museum of Southern Florida in 1987 by Dorothy McKenna, who had shared office space with MIM from the 1960s through the later part of her life.

14 Arva Moore Parks, *The Pathway to Greatness: Building the University of Miami, 1926–2001* (Coral Gables, Fla.: University of Miami, 2001), 35, 40, 41.

15 Tebeau, *University of Miami*, 107–11. In the fall of 1943, Melvin Edward Whitmire, the first of thousands of veterans who would follow him at the war's end, registered for classes (Tebeau, *University of Miami*, 118).

16 Clarence Stein was not at MIT in the summer of 1942, a period when he was ill. We have not yet determined whether MIM met Stein before his coming to lecture at UM January 15, 1945, though they might well have met at national planning conferences she attended before that date. Stein's acquaintance with MIM is clear after his Miami visit, as documented in Hermann H. Field, Architects Committee of the National Council of American-Soviet Friendship, Inc., to MIM, February 16, 1945, Historical Museum of Southern Florida, Marion Manley Collection: "Clarence Stein has suggested my getting in touch with you in connection with a group of four Soviet engineers plus interpreter . . . [about] a visit in Florida to study recent housing projects. . . . Clarence Stein felt that rather than suggesting various projects or people for them to visit that it would be preferable for them to come directly to you and discuss their problems with you."

17 Memorandum, W. J. Hester, Secretary, to Mr. Maynard, Treasurer, February 8, 1943. UM Pres. Record.

18 MIM to BFA, February 10, 1943, and BFA to MIM, February 13, 1943, both in UM Pres. Record. George A. Brockway, an industrialist from Cortland, New York, wintered in Miami Beach. Though never a member of UM's board, he was an effective campaigner for its financial support and a major donor. William Marina and Charlton W. Tebeau, *Rendezvous with Greatness: The University of Miami at the "Edge" of the Twenty-first Century* (Coral Gables, Fla.: University of Miami Press, 2001), 89, 106.

19 MIM to BFA, February 10, 1943. UM Pres. Record. During the First World War for the Emergency Fleet Corporation of the U.S. Shipping Board, in Philadelphia, MIM designed ships.

20 MIM to BFA, April 15, 1943, and BFA to MIM, April 19, 1943, both in UM Pres. Record: "I had suggested to you that we pay you $200.00 per month. I now suggest that we pay you $250.00 for twelve months, because we should like to have you do some sketching in connection with building proposals, such as you have done in the past and probably with the same results about the final buildings."

21 *Bulletin of the University of Miami*, vol. 17 (1943), vol. 18 (1944): "Marion I Manley, B.S. in Architecture–Mechanical Drawing"; replaced, vol. 19 (February 1, 1945) by "Warren B. Longenecker, Professor of Mathematics–Math. and Mechanical Drawing," vol. 19: "The school moved to a trimester plan to meet Navy requirements."

22 MIM to BFA, Director, War Manpower Commission, Grand Theater Building, Atlanta, Georgia, April 15, 1943. UM Pres. Record.

23 It is unclear whether this large classroom building was ever built. No working drawings for it have come to light.

24 Correspondence of 1947 between Edward Ball and J. H. Walton Smith suggests that the St. Joe Paper Company of Jacksonville was on the verge of financing construction of MIM's aquarium design. Archive of the Rosenstiel School of Marine and Atmospheric Science, in the Rosenstiel School of Marine and Atmospheric Science Library, Virginia Key, Miami, Florida, hereinafter cited as Rosenstiel Archive.

25 Robert Moses lectured at UM's Winter Institute, March 1946. F. G. Walton Smith invited him and Earl M. Rader, Dade County Engineer, to lunch to discuss aquariums (FGWS to EMR, February 25, 1946), Rosenstiel Archive.

26 MIM to Dr. F. G. Walton Smith, November 17, 1948, Rosenstiel Archive.

27 I. D. MacVicar, "Proceedings of the Gulf and Caribbean Fisheries Institute," UM, November 1949: "A Dade County Aquarium and Marine Lab is not by any means a dead issue. It is true that our first financial plan was not successful, as the private interests withdrew after forfeiting $50,000 to the county. This money has been deposited in a special aquarium fund, and the Board of the County Commissioners is now working on a plan that we have every reason to believe will be successful. Under this plan the County will own and operate the Aquarium instead of leaving it to private interests. It is our intention to construct a Marine Laboratory for the University of Miami, at no cost to the University, and it is our hope that the staff of the Marine Laboratory will, in turn help us with the technical operation of the Aquarium."

28 John L. Skinner, B.A., University of Toronto; M. Arch., Harvard; Fellow, American Academy in Rome; had headed the Department of Architecture, Georgia Institute of Technology, before coming to the University of Miami as instructor in Architecture in 1927

and becoming professor in 1928 in an architectural program that ended in the early 1930s.

29 Tebeau, *University of Miami*, 115.

30 "Campus Farewell for Miss Manley," *Miami Herald*, August 29, 1948, 2-C. The two men besides Ashe were Julian Eaton, a local banker and a board member since 1942 who would become its president in 1945; and William Hester, secretary of the university. Tebeau, *University of Miami*, 117.

31 Tebeau, *University of Miami*, 117–18. Memorandum, October 27, 1943, Office of the Secretary to MIM, documents that she was informed of University's land purchases.

32 Typescript copy of the citation, UM Pres. Record.

33 RLW to BFA, August 16, 1944, UM Pres. Record. See Douglas, *Voice of the River*, 175, for Douglas's comments about Manley not receiving due credit.

34 "Campus Farewell for Miss Manley."

35 As quoted in nomination form, National Register of Historic Places, for Beverly Shores Century of Progress Architectural District, Beverly Shores, Indiana, Item 7, p. 4.

36 RLW to BFA, April 23, 1945, and reply of the same day; RLW to BFA, August 23, 1945, all in UM Pres. Record.

37 Under the GI Bill, the federal government obligated itself to subsidize tuition, fees, books, and educational materials for veterans and contribute to living expenses incurred while attending college. It permitted veterans free choice of educational institutions and stipulated that colleges were free to admit those veterans who met their admissions requirements.

38 RLW to BFA, September 14, 1945, UM Pres. Record.

39 RLW office archive, publicity release, January 16, 1947, records RLW's release "from service in the Army as Deputy Chief of Air Installations for the Air Transport Command, Army Air Forces, when he served in Headquarters in India, Burma, and China, South America and on the Pacific Coast."

40 Memorandum, BFA to Mr. Maynard, Treasurer, November 13, 1945, specifies monthly fee, noting: "Miss Manley is not now (after November 1, 1945) an employee of the University. The payment authorized to her in this memorandum is not salary but architectural fees; therefore, no deductions of any kind are to be made."

41 Clarence Stein Papers, no. 3600, Archives, Cornell University, Box 6, Folder 89, Division of Rare and Manuscript Collections, Cornell University Library, http://rmc.library.cornell.edu/EAD/htmldocs/RMM03600.html.

42 RLW to BFA, September 14, 1945, "The work is well underway on the G.I. housing." The plan to build traditional dormitories was abandoned when funding for apartments was promised. UM Pres. Record. *Ibis* (Spring 1946): 153.

43 Le Corbusier, *The City of To-morrow*, translated from *Urbanisme*, Frederick Etchells, 8th ed. (Cambridge, Mass.: MIT Press, 1971; translation copyrighted 1929), 189, 215–17.

44 Martin, "They Love It at Sun-tan U," 146.

45 "Miami University Adds Two More Building Groups to Its Brand-New and Growing Campus," *Architectural Forum* 90 (June 1949): 71.

46 Tebeau, *University of Miami*, 119. "All science laboratory changes were made between the close of the spring semester of 1946 and the opening of the first summer session. During the summer, library space was expanded, and equipment was procured for the new laboratories. In June actual work began on the construction of the new classroom building. Because of delays in obtaining

Government permission to secure the temporary buildings, orders were placed July 10 for lumber. During August and September, 28 of these temporary buildings were constructed on the Main Campus to provide the additional space needed." Jay F. Pearson, "The Story of Expansion," *Ibis* (1947): 202–3. Pearson was UM vice president.

47 MIM to RLW, August 30, 1946, UM Archives, UM Libraries, Coral Gables, box 21, Robert Law Weed, 1944–60.

48 RLW to BFA, Memorandum, August 12, 1945. UM Archives, UM Libraries, Coral Gables, box 21, Robert Law Weed, 1944–60: "Miss Manley, we understand, investigated and found that certain layouts had been established . . . and . . . expressed the opinion that some record drawing be made of this work at this time. Apparently the contractor had been informed verbally as to where to locate the building[s] and just how to build them. We expressed concern to Miss Manley regarding the placing of a number of temporary buildings without our first having the opportunity to check and determine if these buildings would interfere with the planning and the progress of the permanent work now going on at the site." RLW reports that MIM had drawings made and found that a building had been put directly in the path of a drive and asked "to correct the condition," but that Dr. Pearson "expressed the feeling" that the building "should remain in the location. . . . In a case of this kind where the permanent construction and our immediate development Is affected, we feel that we should be given the opportunity to express an opinion."

49 We are indebted to Malinda Cleary for finding and transcribing minutes of the Commission of the City of Coral Gables for March 18, 1947, as well as resolution no. 2798, which basically confirms zoning exception in residential zone permitting the buildings made by Zoning Board of Appeals, March 10, 1947, "subject, however, to the following conditions: (a) That this exception shall be in effect only for a period of one year from this date, but shall be subject to renewal upon application at that time (b) [setbacks specified] . . . (c) That the space between the property line and the buildings be landscaped so as to screen such buildings; and (d) That the University agree, in writing, to conform to the conditions imposed herein." "Old Army Housing Made New U. of M. Buildings," *Miami Herald*, September 11, 1947, 2B.

50 Jay F. Pearson, "The Story of Expansion," 202–3.

51 "Miss Manley Has Had Charge of the Temporary Buildings' Designs." "$6,000,000 University Job Rushed," undated newspaper clipping, ca. Autumn 1947.

52 Aerial views and campus maps of 1950s show additional buildings near these two laboratories, whose origins and fates remain murky to this author. Perhaps they too were war-surplus structures, the "greenhouse with adjoining greenhouse seeding plots to be used for research in horticulture" mentioned by Pearson in "The Story of Expansion," as "expected to be built," in a paragraph about "immediate plans for the year of 1947–48."

53 *Miami Daily News*, September 10, 1947.

54 Douglas, *Voice of the River*, 175; Perry, "Marion Isadore Manley," 30n37.

55 "Memorial Classroom Building, University of Miami, Coral Gables, Florida," RLW office archive, typescript press release identified by notation "A 47-114 # 1021." Carie Penabad found typescripts of press releases in RLW office archive, including the above and "University of Miami Expansion Program," 12/6/46; "533 Veteran Housing Units for University of Miami Revolutionary Design Made $4,969,000 Loan Possible," 1/24/47; "Re-establishment of

Veterans in Civilian Life, Veterans Housing University of Miami," January 16, 1947.

56 "University of Miami Moves Back to Boom-Bought Campus," *Architectural Forum* 89 (July 1948): 79.

57 "Memorial Classroom Building," RLW office press release.

58 "University of Miami Moves Back to Boom-Bought Campus," I82.

59 Tebeau, *University of Miami*, 121.

60 RLW press release,"533 Veterans Housing Units."

61 Phillips to MIM, October 25, 1946; MIM to Phillips, October 31, 1946, William Lyman Phillips papers, Historical Museum of Southern Florida. We are indebted to Joanna Lombard for these references.

62 Phillips to Leon H. Zack, July 13, 1947, Phillips Papers. We are indebted to Rocco Ceo for this reference.

63 See n56 above.

64 Major publications of UM campus in American architectural journals include "University of Miami Moves Back to Boom-Bought Campus," *Architectural Forum* 89 (July 1948): 76–82; "Miami University Adds Two More Building Groups to its Brand-New and Growing Campus," *Architectural Forum* 90 (June 1949): 70–75; "At Miami University, Remodeling," *Architectural Forum* 98 (June 1953): 128–32; "Ring Theater, Miami, Fla.," *Progressive Architecture* 34 (August 1953), 114–17.

65 *Saturday Evening Post* (November 19, 1949). "Modern College: Miami's New Buildings Set New Campus Style," *Life* (December 27, 1948): 72–73. Martin, "They Love It at Sun-tan U," 26–27, 144, 146, 148–50. Nicholas, "Miami's Expanding Horizons," *National Geographic* 98, no. 5 (November 1950): 561–94.

66 *Ibis* (1947), back matter among unnumbered advertising pages headed "Freshman Appeal."

67 John J. Koubek gave his former home at 2705 Southwest Third Street to UM in 1942 as a memorial to his wife, Roe Garibaldi Koubek. MIM's work on the house is documented in her signed blueprints dated 9/4/51. For more than 35 years, following renovations subsequent to MIM's work, it has been an educational and cultural center in the heart of Little Havana.

68 Robert M. Little to Miss Florence H. Gervais, Secretary to the Jury of Fellows, the American Institute of Architects, December 30, 1955. AIA Archives, Washington, D.C.

69 "Ring Theater, Miami, Fla.," *Progressive Architecture* 34 (August 1953): 114–17.

DESIGNING POST-WORLD WAR II SOUTH FLORIDA

1 Jan Hocstim, *Florida Modern* (New York: Rizzoli, 2004), 26. Alfred Browning Parker's houses received widespread coverage in the *House Beautiful* "Pace Setters" program, placing him among the top national leaders of residential modernism.

2 Philip Wylie (1902–71) was a writer. His work includes hundreds of short stories, articles, serials, syndicated news columns, novels, and works of social criticism. He served on the Dade County Florida Defense Council and was director of the Lerner Marine Laboratory. "Textbook House Shows How to Beat the Florida Climate," *Architectural Forum* 94 (February 1951): 132–33.

3 Jean Taylor, *The Villages of South Dade* (Saint Petersburg, Fla.: B. Kennedy, 1986). In 1897 W. A. Larkins moved to South Dade with his family and settled at the southernmost end of present-

day Ingraham Highway. In 1906, prompted by the completion of the Miami-Homestead extension of the Florida East Coast Railway, he purchased a twenty-acre parcel of land south of present-day Sunset Drive and opened a store and packing house on the property. The community, slowly developed by Larkins, was incorporated in 1927 and later renamed South Miami.

4 "Trees Design a House," *Florida Architecture and Allied Arts* (1953): 41.

5 Ibid., 42.

6 Beatrice Washburn, "A Woman of Architecture Who Can Wield a Shovel," *Miami Herald,* Septeber 23, 1956, G2.

7 Ibid.

8 "Built in USA since 1932," in *Built in USA, 1932–1944*, ed. Elizabeth Mock (New York: Museum of Modern Art, 1944), 20.

9 Ronald W. Haase, *Classic Cracker Florida's Wood-frame Vernacular Architecture* (Sarasota, Fla.: Pineapple Press, 1992), 10. Originating in southern Georgia, the term "cracker" came into use to describe many nineteenth-century Florida pioneers who cracked their corn to make meal–a staple in their diet. By extension, the lightweight wooden architecture that they produced throughout Florida was labeled cracker vernacular.

10 Taylor, *The Villages of South Dade*, 157.

11 "Cracker Style Cottage," *Miami Herald*, "Florida Living," August 23, 1953, 3.

12 Arva Moore Parks, "The History of Coconut Grove, Florida, 1821–1925" (master's thesis, University of Miami, 1971), 7.

13 Arva Moore Parks and Donna Knowles Born, "A History of 'Snug Harbor,' the Property and Residence" (1990), 1–38, 43–46, typescript, Arva Moore Parks Collection.

14 "Second Story on Stilts," *House and Home*, August 1953, 86–91.

15 Ibid.

16 Marjory Stoneman Douglas, *The Joys of Bird Watching in Florida* (Miami: Hurricane House, 1969), 2.

17 We are indebted to Pam Admire of Miami, Florida, who donated this notebook to UM School of Architecture Library.

18 Additional houses designed and built during this period include a cottage for Mr. and Mrs. Horace Brown (1959), rental cottages for Mr. and Mrs. Edward Chapman (1963), and a cottage for Mr. and Mrs. Harold Graves (1966).

19 Katherine Graham, *Personal History* (New York: Alfred A. Knopf, 1997), 113.

20 John Ormsbee Simonds Collection, University of Florida Smathers Libraries, Special Area and Studies Collection, January 2006.

21 "There's Always [a] Way to Do It Better," *Miami Herald*, July 22, 1962, 4F.

22 "Miami Lakes Opens Today," *Miami Herald*, House and Home Section, July 22, 1962.

23 Typescript of poem, ca. 1965, Historical Museum of Southern Florida, Marion Manley Collection.

24 Eugene and Gwladys Scott at their residence, interview by Carie Penabad, April 2008.

25 Georgia Tasker, "Keepers of the Land," *Miami Herald*, Home and Design, May 15, 2005, 12–13H.

26 Eugene and Gwladys Scott at their residence, interview by Carie Penabad, April 2008.

27 Ibid.

28 Ibid.

29 Ibid.

30 Georgia Tasker, "Open to Nature: Two Houses Designed in the '60s Are Models for Green Living," *Miami Herald*, Home and Design, September 2, 2007, 3–4H.

31 "Sarasota Spectacle: Theater Brought from Venice Opens with Opera," *Life* (February 17, 1958).

32 David Weeks, "The Dream Realized: The Building of the Museum," in *John Ringling, Dreamer, Builder, Collector: Legacy of the Circus King* (Sarasota, Fla.: John and Mable Ringling Museum of Art, 1996), 10, 15.

33 Patricia Ringling Buck, *The John and Mable Ringling Museum of Art* (Sarasota, Fla.: John and Mable Ringling Museum, 1988), 11.

34 Ibid., 12.

35 Arthur Everett Austin Jr. and Marian Murray, *The Asolo Theater in Sarasota at the John and Mable Ringling Museum of Art* (Sarasota, Fla.: St. Petersburg Printing, 1952) 3–5.

36 Creighton Gilbert, *The Asolo Theater* (Sarasota, Fla.: John and Mable Ringling Museum, 1959).

37 Ibid.

38 *The House John and Mable Ringling Built* (Sarasota, Fla.: State of Florida, 1980), 4. In 1952 the Florida State Board of Control commissioned F. B. Stresau, landscape architect of Fort Lauderdale, to design a new master plan for the estate.

39 Minutes of special meeting of city commission, May 14 and 21, 1946.

40 Marion Manley, "Synopsis of Marion I. Manley, from the Latest Edition of Who's Who in America," undated typescript, in Historical Museum of Southern Florida, Marion Manley Collection.

41 Ibid.

42 Sinclair, "Miami: An Unplanned Disaster?" E24.

43 Marjory Stoneman Douglas, "Communities Face Their Slums . . . in Coconut Grove, Florida," *Ladies Home Journal* (October 1950). This committee was the outcome of years of protest that culminated in a meeting of two hundred Coconut Grove citizens who gathered at the American Community Legion Hall on August 30, 1948. Those in attendance voted to incorporate a nonprofit organization called "the Coconut Grove Citizens Committee for Slum Clearance." The group elected a board of directors to oversee four committees: a Survey Committee, a Rezoning Committee, a Sanitation Committee, and a Committee for the Study of Rents.

44 Ibid.

45 Letter to the Jury of Fellows from H. Samuel Kruse, November 13, 1953, Marion Manley Collection, AIA Archive of Women in Architecture, Washington, D.C.

46 "A Fresh Idea for Planners: Scientific Planning Is Necessary for Comfortable Living [in] Dade County," *Miami Herald*, October 7, 1951, 1G.

47 Letter to Jury of Fellows from T. H. Creighton, November 11, 1953, Marion Manley Collection, AIA Archive of Women in Architecture, Washington, D.C.

48 Letter to the Jury of Fellows from Douglas Haskell, n.d., Marion Manley Collection, AIA Archive of Women in Architecture, Washington, D.C.

SELECTED BIBLIOGRAPHY

ARCHIVAL SOURCES

Altmayer, Joan Manley. Private collection. "Lester's Recollections." Typescript by Lester Manley, 1956.

———. "Reminiscences of Things Past." Transcript of group interview with Marion Manley and others, 1973.

Architectural Drawings for and Photographs of Buildings of the University of Miami. University Archives, University of Miami Libraries, Coral Gables, Fla.

Manley, Marion. Collection. Historical Museum of Southern Florida, Miami.

SECONDARY SOURCES

Anderson, Dorothy May. *Women, Design, and the Cambridge School.* West Lafayette, Ind.: PDA Publishers, 1980.

"At Miami University, Remodeling." *Architectural Forum* 98 (June 1953): 128–32.

Austin, Arthur Everett Jr., and Marian Murray. *The Asolo Theater in Sarasota at the John and Mable Ringling Museum of Art.* Sarasota, Fla.: St. Petersburg Printing, 1952.

Bayer, William. "Miss Manley Charges 'Gross Mishandling': Architect Sees 'Politics' Blocking Plans for Ideal Miami Homesites." *Miami Herald*, October 7, 1951.

Behar, Roberto M., and Maurice G. Culot, eds. *Coral Gables: An American Garden City.* Paris: Norma Editions, 1997.

Bosworth, F. H., Jr., and Roy Childs Jones. *A Study of Architectural Schools.* New York: C. Scribner's Sons, 1932.

"Campus Farewell for Miss Manley." *Miami Herald*, August 29, 1948, 2C.

"Cracker Style Cottage." *Miami Herald*, "Florida Living," August 23, 1953, 3.

Culot, Maurice, and Jean-Francois Lejeune, eds. *Miami: Architecture of the Tropics.* Miami: Center of for the Fine Arts; Brussels: Archives d'Architecture Moderne, 1993.

Douglas, Marjory Stoneman. "Coral Gables: America's Finest Suburb, Miami, Florida." Coral Gables: Parker Art Printers, ca. 1923.

———. *Florida: The Long Frontier*. New York: Harper and Row, 1967.

———. *The Joys of Birdwatching in Florida*. Miami: Hurricane House, 1969.

Douglas, Marjory Stoneman. With John Rothchild. *Voice of the River: An Autobiography*. Englewood, Fla.: Pineapple Press, 1987.

Dunlop, Beth. *Miami: Mediterranean Splendor and Deco Dreams*. New York: Rizzoli, 2007.

Fink, Denman. "Castles in Spain Made Real." In *The Story of Coral Gables*. Coral Gables, Fla.: G. E. Merrick, ca. 1926.

Florida Architecture and Allied Arts. Annual publication, 1935–48.

"A Fresh Idea for Planners: Scientific Planning Is Necessary for Comfortable Living [in] Dade County." *Miami Herald*, October 7, 1951, 1G.

From Wilderness to Metropolis: The History and Architecture of Dade County, 1825–1940. 2d ed. Miami: Metropolitan Dade County (Fla.), Office of Community Development, Historic Preservation Division, 1992.

A Guide to the Architecture of Miami. Miami: Florida South Chapter, American Institute of Architects, 1963.

Grunwald, Michael. *The Swamp: The Everglades, Florida, and the Politics of Paradise*. New York: Simon and Schuster, 2006.

Haase, Ronald W. *Classic Cracker: Florida's Wood-frame Vernacular Architecture*. Sarasota, Fla.: Pineapple Press, 1992.

Harris, Barbara J. *Beyond Her Sphere: Women and the Professions in American History*. Westport, Conn.: Greenwood Press, 1978.

Harrison, Gwen. "Architect Spells Profession, Nickname, for Marion Manley; It's Her Hobby, Too." *Miami Herald*, May 11, 1952, E14.

Harwood, Kathryn Chapman. *The Lives of Vizcaya: Annals of a Great House*. Miami, Fla.: Banyan Books, 1985.

Hochstim, Jan. *Florida Modern: Residential Architecture, 1945–1970*. New York: Rizzoli, 2004.

Hollingsworth, Tracy. *History of Dade County, Florida*, s.v. "Marion I. Manley." Coral Gables: Parker Art Printing, 1949.

Houser, William. "Exponent of Personality: Close Supervision of Work Has Earned Her Reputation for Being Rugged on Job." *Miami Herald*, "Florida Living," January 25, 1953, 3–5.

King, Terry Johnson. "She's Got a Blueprint for Old Age." *Miami Herald*, May 9, 1974.

Lorenz, Clare. *Women in Architecture: A Contemporary Perspective*. London: Trefoil Publications, 1990.

Manley, Marion. "Tunisian Architecture Liked by Owners, Modified in Relation to Florida Climatic Conditions." *Miami Herald*, May 6, 1937, 14.

Marina, William, and Charlton W. Tebeau. *Rendezvous with Greatness: The University of Miami at the "Edge" of the Twenty-first Century*. Coral Gables: University of Miami Press, 2001.

Martin, Harold H. "They Love It at Sun-tan U." *Saturday Evening Post* (November 19, 1949).

"Miami University Adds Two More Building Groups to Its Brand-new and Growing Campus." *Architectural Forum* 90 (June 1949): 70–75.

Millas, Aristides J., and Ellen J. Uguccioni. *Coral Gables, Miami Riviera: An Architectural Guide*. Miami: Dade Heritage Trust, 2003.

Mock, Elizabeth, ed. *Built in USA, 1932–1944*. New York: Museum of Modern Art, 1944.

"Modern College: Miami's New Buildings Set New Campus Style." *Life* (December 27, 1948): 72–73.

Newcomb, Rexford. *Mediterranean Domestic Architecture in the United States*. Cleveland: J. H. Hansen, 1928.

Parks, Arva Moore. *George Merrick's Coral Gables: "Where Your 'Castles in Spain' Are Made Real."* Miami: Centennial Press, 2006.

———. *Miami, the American Crossroad: A Centennial Journey, 1896–1996.* [Needham Heights, Mass.]: Simon and Schuster Custom Pub., 1996.

———. *Miami, the Magic City.* [Tulsa, Okla.]: Continental Heritage Press, [1981].

———. *The Pathway to Greatness: Building the University of Miami, 1926–2001.* Coral Gables: University of Miami, 2001.

Perry, Emily Adams. "Marion Isadore Manley: Pioneer Woman Architect." In *Florida Pathfinders*, ed. Lewis N. Wynne and James J. Horgan. Saint Leo, Fla.: Saint Leo College Press, 1994.

"Ring Theater." *Progressive Architecture* 34 (August 1953).

Rybczynski, Witold, and Laurie Olin. *Vizcaya: An American Villa and Its Makers.* Philadelphia: University of Pennsylvania Press, 2007.

"Second Story on Stilts." *House and Home* 4, no. 2 (August 1953): 86–91.

Sexton, Randolph Williams. *Spanish Influence on American Architecture and Decoration.* New York: Brentano's, 1927.

Sinclair, Molly. "Miami: An Unplanned Disaster? 'Yes,' says Marion Manley, the Pioneer Architect Who Watched It Happen." *Miami Herald*, January 28, 1973, E1, 24.

Tebeau, Charlton W. *The University of Miami: A Golden Anniversary History, 1926–1976.* Coral Gables: University of Miami Press, 1976.

"Textbook House Shows How to Beat the Florida Climate." *Architectural Forum* 94 (February 1951): 132–33.

Torre, Susana, ed. *Women in American Architecture: A Historic and Contemporary Perspective.* New York: Whitney Library of Design, 1977.

"Trees Design a House." *Florida Architecture and Allied Arts* (1953).

"University of Miami Moves Back to Boom-Bought Campus and into First Unit of All-Modern Educational Plant." *Architectural Forum* 89, no. 1 (July 1948): 76–82.

Washburn, Beatrice. "A Woman of Architecture Who Can Wield a Shovel." *Miami Herald*, September 23, 1956, G2.

Weed, Robert Law. *Robert Law Weed, A.I.A., Architect.* New York: Architectural Catalog, 1937.

Werne, Jo. "Coral Rock Homes, They're Cool." *Miami Herald*, November 23, 1975, L1.

Wright, Gwendolyn. "On the Fringe of the Profession: Women in American Architecture." In *The Architect: Chapters in the History of the Profession*, ed. Spiro Kostof, 280–308. New York: Oxford University Press, 1977.

INDEX

References to Marion I. Manley are abbreviated MIM. References to captions and illustrations are italicized.